Southern & Eastern England

Hidden Places, Great Adventures
and the Good Life

Daniel Start, Lucy Grewcock & Elsa Har

D1335814

522 568 86 9

WILD
guide

Contents

Regional Overview

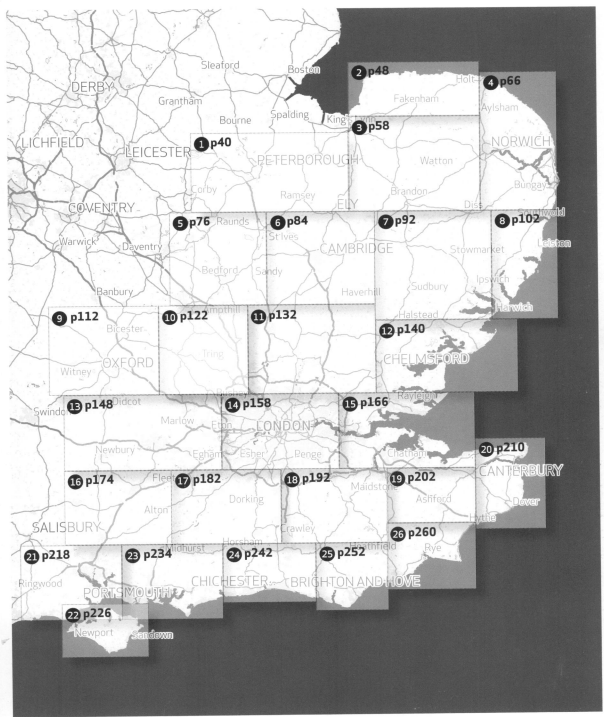

1 p40
2 p48
3 p58
4 p66
5 p76
6 p84
7 p92
8 p102
9 p112
10 p122
11 p132
12 p140
13 p148
14 p158
15 p166
16 p174
17 p182
18 p192
19 p202
20 p210
21 p218
22 p226
23 p234
24 p242
25 p252
26 p260

Introduction

Explore ancient forests and lost ruins, swim in secret coves and find smugglers' sea caves. Buy local produce and picnic in a meadow of orchids and rare butterflies. Watch the sunset from an Iron Age hillfort, search for nightjars at dusk, then wild camp as the sky turns indigo and fills with stars.

The *Wild Guide* is a celebration of the most beautiful places that lie hidden, just off the beaten path. It's your guide to a lifetime of joyful exploration and simple pleasures. And these special places are on your very doorstep – if you know where to look.

Great adventures

In our modern digital world, much is made of our new-found freedoms – to work remotely, be contactable anywhere and always be online. Yet these 'freedoms' keep us tethered to our technology, disconnected from our surroundings and busier than ever.

Our children spend more time indoors and in front of screens than ever before. Deprived of beneficial wild experiences, they can develop 'nature-deficit disorder' that can lead to attention problems, obesity, anxiety, and depression.

Our remedy is a big dose of simple adventures of the most natural kind. Exploring the wilder places that lie on the edge of everyday life and throwing yourself into new experiences makes us happier and healthier. There are rivers for swimming or canoeing in, moors and meadows to camp in, ancient pathways for night-time walks, woods and ruins to explore and subterranean worlds to discover. Straying out of your comfort zone is not without risk, but new adventures can bring an enormous sense of freedom and satisfaction.

Hidden places

Think of the South East and urban sprawl and gridlock on the M25 may come to mind. Yet once you know where to look you'll find a region of extraordinary history, peace and beauty. Its many great rivers beckon you to enter their cool waters; its varied coastline changes dramatically from great chalk cliffs to sweeping sandy dunes; its ancient woodland and parkland are filled with 1,000-year-old trees, ruined churches and strange follies.

Our formula for getting away from the crowds is based on the magic of some of these key places:

Wild coast: The intertidal zone is perhaps the greatest wild area in the UK today – a no-man's land continually covered and then revealed by the great ocean. Secret coves and caves await the adventurous, while precipitous cliffs and rugged coastal paths offer a challenge that rewards and invigorates in equal measure.

Rivers and lakes: The beautiful, natural waterways that shape our verdant landscape offer wonderful wild corridors that are ideal for swimming, canoeing, fishing and embracing a slower pace of life.

Sunset hillforts: To watch the sunset is to squeeze the very last juice from the day. It's a unique opportunity to feel the subtle changes around you as birds roost, dusk settles, and nocturnal creatures begin to stir. Hilltops provide an ideal vantage point and many are also rich in Iron and Bronze Age history.

Ancient woods: These rich fragments of once great forests are places to wander in peace and awe. They invite you to camp out, build dens, climb trees and forage for wild food.

Lost ruins and sacred places: There are so many relics of Britain's history to inspire us, from stone circles to lost villages, strange follies to wartime forts. Ruins offer adventure and romance, and transport us to another world and time.

Meadows and wildlife: To be surrounded by wild, unspoilt beauty, from carpets of divinely scented bluebells in May to the uplifting sight of a falcon swooping overhead, is to be reminded of the power of nature. It can help to reconnect us and reawaken our sense of wonder.

The good life

For a truly wholesome feel, travel to the locations in this guide by walking, canoeing, cycling, swimming or horse riding, and then eat hearty local food of known provenance, created with care. A bit of light foraging can be satisfying too, especially for the most abundant treats, including wild garlic, mussels and maybe a line-caught mackerel, all cooked up on a little driftwood fire. After some stargazing, camp on a beach or by a stream – perfect for a quick dip in the morning.

We chose to write our second Wild Guide about southern and eastern England because we wanted to show how many simple and amazing adventures can be found close to the big cities. The South East is a place we know, love and grew up in, so the idea of an intimate local guide, filled with secret destinations and special places, appealed. Along the way we have met many people living simpler, richer lives, such as artisan producers making traditional foods and smallholders who tend to their pigs and chickens alongside guests.

The end result is a compendium of wonderful adventures and wild places. It is packed full with memories of wild campsites, night-walks, foraging missions, sunset hilltop hikes, canoe trips at dawn and countless dips into chalky streams and still lakes. And all without flying, or queuing, or paying much at all. We hope this book inspires many more wild and wonderful escapades – do write and tell us how you get on.

Dan, Elsa and Lucy

adventure@wildthingspublishing.com

Finding your way

Each wild place can be located using the overview maps and the directions, but to be sure of finding your way you will need to use the latitude and longitude provided. This is given in decimal degrees (WGS84) and can be entered straight into any web-based mapping program, such as Google, Bing or Streetmap. The latter two will also provide Ordnance Survey mapping. Print out the map before you go - or save a 'screen grab' - in case there is no mobile reception. You can also enter the co-ordinates into your GPS, car Sat Nav (enable decimal degrees) or your PDA / telephone, if it has GPS enabled (try the ViewRanger app). If you have paper maps, look up the equivalent national grid reference in the conversion table at the back of the book. Approximate walk-in times are given for one way only, and abbreviations in the directions refer to left and right (L, R) and north, east, south, west (N, E, S, W).

Wild, safe & responsible

1. Only use designated areas for fire (or the area below the high water mark on beaches).
2. Fasten all gates and if you must climb them, use the hinged side.
3. Keep your dogs under close control, especially around livestock.
4. Keep to public paths unless you are on Access Land.
5. Take your litter home, and gain good karma by collecting other people's.
6. If you wash in streams or rivers, only use biodegradable soap, or none at all.
7. Take special care on country roads and park considerately.
8. Take map, compass, whistle and waterproof clothing when venturing into remote or high areas.
9. Always tell someone where you are going, and do not rely on your mobile phone.
10. If you do wild camp, use sites at least 20 minutes walk from any road. Arrive late and leave early.

Best for
Secret beaches

Although highly developed, the region has some fantastic coast, including sea caves on the Isle of Wight, dunes along Chichester Harbour and Camber Sands, and wild under-cliff beach where the Sussex Downs meet the sea. The secret smugglers' coves of Kent give way to Essex creeks, islands and 'secret waters' famous in *Swallows and Amazons* almost a century ago. The Suffolk shore is one long stretch of sand, while Norfolk boasts seals and England's only desert island.

The long stretches of inter-tidal foreshore beneath cliffs or beyond the creeks are without doubt this region's wildest places. Before setting off, check the tide times carefully. Remember that both high and low tides are much more extreme during the full and new moon 'springs' that occur every fortnight. Sea kayaks are an amazing way to explore, and they allow access to truly remote beaches where you can cook your supper on a fire and wild camp until dawn.

Gun Hill, Burnham Overy Staithe (North Norfolk 4)

Stiffkey, Garborough Creek (North Norfolk 6)

Horsey Gap (Norfolk Broads 1)

Dunwich Heath, Minsmere (Suffolk Coast, 1)

Beaumont Quay (Essex Coast & Creeks 2)

Botany Bay, Broadstairs (East Kent 5)

Lydden Spout, Dover (East Kent, 2)

Rocken End, St Catherine's (Isle of Wight 4)

East Head, West Wittering (West Sussex 1)

Atherington Beach, Climping (Mid Sussex Downs 2)

Cuckmere Haven, Seaford (East Sussex 2)

Falling Sands, Beachy Head (East Sussex 4)

Fairlight Glen, Coverhurst (Romney Marsh 3)

Best for
Swimming &
canoe adventures

The South East is blessed with many grand rivers, most of which are excellent for swimming and canoeing. With inland water quality the best in living memory, more and more people are taking to the waters.

Many of the region's rivers have been turned into 'navigations' with locks and weirs. This means they are always deep enough to swim or boat in, and you have good rights of access. We have swum at all the places listed in the 'rivers & lakes' sections, though for non-navigations and most lakes (and all places marked ❓) you will need to use your discretion, especially if people are fishing or watching wildlife. If asked to leave, do so. A word of warning: water quality can be affected after very heavy rain, or during droughts — if concerned swim breaststroke and keep your mouth above the water.

For those who would like to canoe there are many new and affordable types of boat. Plastic 'sit-on-tops' are unsinkable while stand up paddle boards and inflatable canoes are much easier to transport — make sure you buy one with multiple chambers and don't use inflatables if you plan to venture out to sea.

Wadenhoe, R Nene (Fens & Nene Valley 3)

Scolt Head Island (North Norfolk 3)

Outney Common, R Waveney (Norfolk Broads 8)

Coltishall, R Bure (Norfolk Broads 13)

Felmersham, R Great Ouse (Bedford & Great Ouse 7)

Nayland, R Stour (Inland Suffolk 4)

Buscot weir, R Thames (Oxford & Cotswolds 8)

Newark Priory, R Wey (Surrey Hills 7)

Ensfield Bridge, R Medway (High Weald 3)

Anchor Inn, R Ouse (Mid Sussex Downs 4)

Best for
Ancient forest &
noble trees

Our ancient forests are remnants of the primordial wild woods that once covered the land. While much of England's woodland was being cleared for agriculture before the Iron Age, large tracts in southern England – such as those in the New Forest and Epping – survived thanks to draconian Norman hunting laws. Today, Surrey, Hampshire and Sussex are the most wooded counties in England, and Kent wins the prize for the most ancient trees.

Trees are some of our oldest living organisms – some churchyard yews even pre-date Christianity. Look for ancient beeches and oaks that have been pollarded – a practice that allowed medieval commoners to legally gather poles - now leaving extraordinary twisted shapes. Build a den, set up a rope swing or hide in a hollow trunk. Practice your climbing and set up lookouts across the forest, or buy a hammock tent and sleep out in the canopy.

Best for
Ruins & follies

Once-grand abbeys sit lonely by riverbanks; serene church towers are shrouded in ivy; crumbling castles sit in isolation, surrounded by marsh. There are over a hundred ruined churches in Norfolk alone, and almost as many lost villages. At Dunwich in Suffolk an entire town was swallowed by the sea.

Throughout the South East the shells of medieval castles and abbeys have returned to nature, such as that at Old Bayham, overgrown with great tree roots. There are decaying follies from the 18th century – strange towers, grottoes, facades and pyramids – built by the eccentric and romantic. More recent are the remnants of war, from Napoleonic Martello towers, to great 1940s gun towers in the sea.

The atmosphere of a ruin can alter with the sunlight and seasons. Wildflower-filled graveyards can be glorious on summer days and welcoming ruins can turn eerie after dark. Many lie just off the footpath and are cared for by local volunteers; others are managed by English Heritage but are free to enter 'at any reasonable hour between dawn and dusk'. Tread gently as you explore.

Lilford Park Folly, Achurch (Fens & Nene Valley 11)

St Benet's Abbey, River Bure (Norfolk Broads 20)

St Andrew's Church, Covehithe (Suffolk Coast 11)

Houghton House, Nr Ampthill (Bedford & Great Ouse 14)

Martello Tower 19 (East Kent 11)

Camber Castle (Romney Marsh 11)

St Dunstan in the East (London 14)

Bayham Old Abbey (High Weald 13)

Maunsell Forts (Thames Estuary 9)

Mad Jack Fuller's Tower (East Sussex 13)

Best for
Sacred & ancient

Humans first inhabited the South East over three quarters of a million years ago – a time when mammoths and sabre-toothed tigers roamed the land. Waves of colonisation since then have left their imprint – and the marks of many faiths – in sacred stones, barrows, burial cairns and pathways. To experience these places is to stand in awe of our most ancient history.

Retrace one of our many ancient pathways, from Roman roads to drovers' tracks, tidal causeways and pilgrim routes. Marvel at the enormous motifs etched into the chalk hillsides of the Downs, many of them still mysteries. Explore a pagan labrynth 'mizmaze' or discover the earliest work of the saints and missionaries. Some of the local Christian shrines date back almost 1,500 years, such as the remote St Peter on the Wall – one of the oldest Christian buildings in Britain – while the Greensted Church is thought to be the oldest wooden church in the world.

Best for
Sunset hillforts & wild highs

The South East might be short of mountains, but there are still plenty of high tops and ancient hillforts from which to survey the surrounding land, as our forefathers would have done. The great chalk escarpments of the North and South Downs cross the landscape, peppered with lookouts, earthworks and burial cairns. To the west the ancient Ridgeway strikes up across the Thames Valley, rising first on the Hampshire Downs and then the North Chilterns.

Climb up above the rest of the world — it's a true escape from the everyday and as the world shrinks below, so we regain new perspectives on life. Fly a kite, play rolly pollies and stay out to watch the sunset. As dusk falls go for a night-walk then lie back and count the galaxies for an hour or two. Bring a torch for your return or bivvy out until dawn.

Ivinghoe Beacon (North Chilterns 17)

Dunstable Downs Ridge (North Chilterns 19)

Deacon Hill, Pegsdon Hills (Herts & Lea Valley 14)

Beacon Hill, Burghclere (Hampshire Downs 17)

Uffington White Horse (Berkshire & Thames 20)

Old Winchester Hill (West Sussex 16)

Cissbury Ring, Findon (Mid Sussex Downs 15)

Mount Caburn, Glynde (Mid Sussex Downs 16)

Black Down, Haslemere (Surrey Hills 14)

The Pulpit, Perry Wood, Selling (Kent Downs 8)

Firle Beacon (East Sussex 16)

Hampstead Heath Tumulus (London 16)

Best for Spring

Spring is a time of new beginnings: snowdrops rise from bare earth, then crocuses carpet the ground, daffodils burst into bloom, and bluebells turn ancient woodlands into a shimmering sea of colour and scent. From April, rare oxlips and wood anemones can be found on forest floors, and the aroma of wild garlic is everywhere. This is the season to see rare snake's head fritillaries transform Suffolk's meadows, while native orchids emerge as the weather warms.

As May takes hold, the first oak leaves unfurl and forests turn verdant. Hawthorn, hedgerows and orchards bloom in the lengthening days. This is a fantastic time for walking ancient paths and tiny lanes. Pack a backpack, take a bivvy bag and make like a pilgrim for a few days; in these months before summer you'll have wild England all to yourself.

Best for
Summer

Summer is a time to make the most of wild swimming, camping and dusk walks. This is glow-worm season, with warm evenings giving the best chance of sightings. Pack a flask of hot chocolate, let the kids stay up late, and go for a long night-walk to look for their green glow. With wildflowers now in full force, butterflies are abundant, and seasonal campsites and eateries are open. Cool off in reed-fringed rivers, picnic in meadows and canoe-camp along remote waterways.

Head to the beach to swim, rockpool, fish and explore sea caves. As the day draws to a close, build a driftwood fire and cook your supper over its flames. For the best ending to the day, skinny dip under the full moon.

Holkham Beach (North Norfolk, 5)

Pamber Forest butterflies (Hampshire Downs 20)

Ridley Wood holloway (New Forest 14)

The Devil's Jumps, Treyford (West Sussex 15)

Chanctonbury Ring, South Downs (Mid Sussex Downs 14)

Stow Maries glow-worms (Essex Coast & Creeks 24)

Westleton Heath glow-worms (Suffolk Coast 18)

Cavenham Heath nightjars (Inland Suffolk, 10)

Piddington Wood butterflies (Oxford & Cotswolds 24)

Sharpenhoe Clappers butterflies (Herts & Lea Valley 15)

Canoe 'champing', All Saints Church (Fens & Nene Valley 31)

River Bure/Ant canoeing (North Broads 4, 5)

Botany Bay (East Kent, 5)

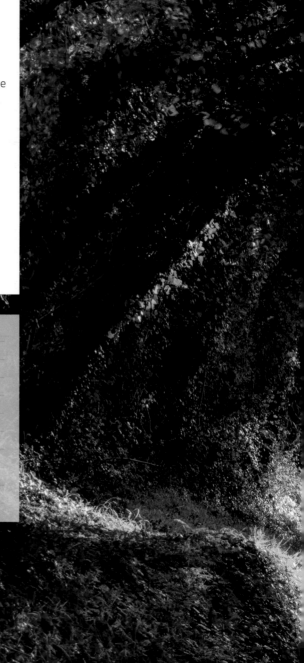

Best for
Autumn

The low light is at its most beautiful in autumn. Make the most of shorter days and climb a hill to watch the dawn. Morning mists are perfect for visiting atmospheric ruins, and blue skies make a wonderful backdrop to autumnal leaves – especially fine in southern England's many beech forests.

This is the time of rutting stags locking antlers in woodland clearings. It is the season of mellow fruitfulness so gather sloes for your gin, apples and blackberries for your pies. It is also mushroom season, and a trusted guidebook or a trip with a professional forager is a worthwhile investment. And never ever eat anything you are not 100 per cent sure of.

Best for
Winter

Frosty mornings mean wrapping up warm in hats and scarves and stepping out into a silent world with the crunch of glittering white grass underfoot. Perhaps the greatest natural wonders at this time of year are the birds: murmurations of starlings at dusk, the screeching of roosting rooks or the honking of pink-footed geese.

In winter it is even more important to venture outside into daylight, and an hour a day will do wonders to keep 'seasonal affective disorder' at bay. The brave swim every day of the year, and research has shown this boosts the immune system and reduces the incidence of cold and flu – build up to it with lots of summer training first. And after all your exertions, pubs with real fires offer cosy respite…

Best for
Wild camping

When the working day ends jump on a train, take to the hills, cook your supper with the sunset and sleep out under the stars, lulled by hooting owls. There is no greater adventure than wild camping – but you will need to be discreet, as technically it is only legal with the permission of the landowner.

Camp at least a 20-minute walk from the nearest car park, road or building. (We've marked such spots with the 'stargazing' symbol ⊡ to give you some inspiration.) Pitch your tent late and take it down very early. For the ultimate lightweight experience, invest in an adventure 'tarp' or a 'bivvy bag' which allows you to see the stars and is less likely to offend the early morning farmer. Most importantly, leave no trace. If you plan to sleep higher up – atop hills and downs – make sure you have enough layers, including a hat and a thermal mat to insulate you from the cold ground.

Ermine Street, Broxbourne Woods (Hertfs & Lea Valley 12)

Ivinghoe Beacon area (North Chilterns 17)

Methersgate Quay, Deben Estuary (Suffolk Coast 5)

Sea Wall, Dengie Marsh (Essex Coast & Creeks 16)

Pegsdon Hills (Herts & Lea Valley 14)

Chapel Bank old graveyard (Romney Marsh 12)

Northeye lost village (East Sussex 12)

The Long Stone at Mottistone (Isle of Wight 12)

Walland Marsh dark skies (Romney Marsh 17)

Beacon Hill, East Harting (West Sussex 14)

Best for
Food and foraging

Free of food miles, local produce can be a highlight of any trip, and it reveals fascinating insights into an area's cultural and natural history. Across the South East, gamekeepers, fishermen, cider-makers and microbreweries keep the larders and bars of atmospheric eateries well-stocked, while kitchen gardens add authentic local colour and flavour.

Search for samphire on the Norfolk marshes, pick young nettles for soup, gather wild garlic for pesto or seek out elderflower for homemade Champagne. Indulge in soft fruit at a pick-your-own or gather your picnic supplies from one of the many farm stores or pop-up roadside stalls selling homegrown produce. Or for a really new experience join a local expert forager and learn how to identify, harvest and prepare a truly local feast.

Shellfish & samphire (North Norfolk 25)

Wild Food courses at Assington Mill (Inland Suffolk 34)

Mersea and Blackwater oysters (Essex Coast & Creeks 31)

Strawberries and fruit, Cammas Hall (Herts & Lea Valley 33)

Saturday market at Wyken Vineyard (Inland Suffolk 23)

The Pheasant, home-grown grub (Inland Suffolk 31)

The Pot Kiln deer stalking (Berkshire & Thames 37)

Gunton Arms, venison (Norfolk Broads 35)

The Pig, Brockenhurst (New Forest 27)

The Woolpack Inn, Totford (Hampshire Downs 29)

The Horse Guards Inn, Tillington (West Sussex 26)

The Wild Mushroom, Westfield (Romney Marsh 24)

Crab Sheds, Steephill Cove (Isle of Wight 20)

Southwold Harbour fish huts (Suffolk Coast, 20)

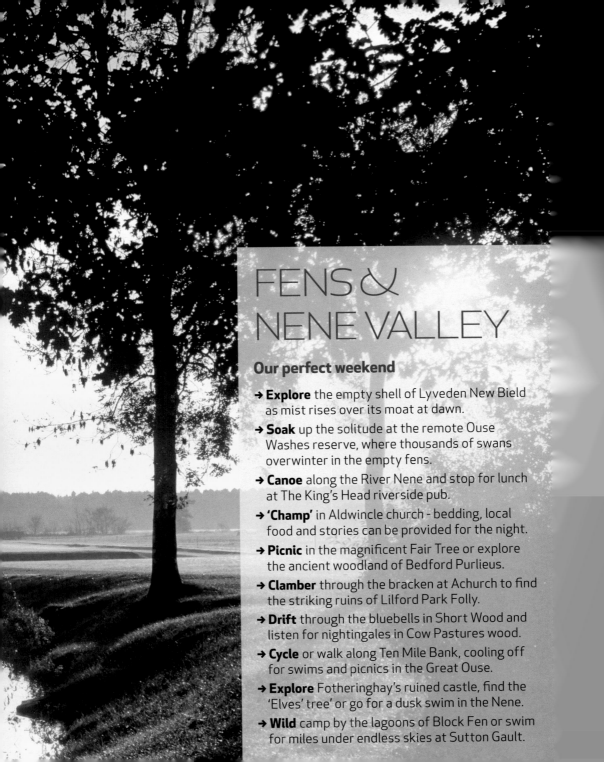

FENS &
NENE VALLEY

Our perfect weekend

→ **Explore** the empty shell of Lyveden New Bield as mist rises over its moat at dawn.

→ **Soak** up the solitude at the remote Ouse Washes reserve, where thousands of swans overwinter in the empty fens.

→ **Canoe** along the River Nene and stop for lunch at The King's Head riverside pub.

→ **'Champ'** in Aldwincle church - bedding, local food and stories can be provided for the night.

→ **Picnic** in the magnificent Fair Tree or explore the ancient woodland of Bedford Purlieus.

→ **Clamber** through the bracken at Achurch to find the striking ruins of Lilford Park Folly.

→ **Drift** through the bluebells in Short Wood and listen for nightingales in Cow Pastures wood.

→ **Cycle** or walk along Ten Mile Bank, cooling off for swims and picnics in the Great Ouse.

→ **Explore** Fotheringhay's ruined castle, find the 'Elves' tree' or go for a dusk swim in the Nene.

→ **Wild** camp by the lagoons of Block Fen or swim for miles under endless skies at Sutton Gault.

Stagnant and shrouded in mists, the pre-drained fens were once feared. This desolate marsh of reed-beds, pools and mires, interspersed by inland waterways was navigable only in shallow, punt-like boats.

Against violent protests from locals, 40,000 acres of peat-rich fens were gradually drained and enclosed in the 17th century, causing the neighbouring farmland to sink by up to 20 feet. Few areas of fenland survived, and those pockets that did include the rare landscapes at Woodwalton and Holme fens, where England's lowest point is almost ten feet below sea level.

Today, these cut wetlands form a mosaic of flat farmland and protected landscapes, filled with birdlife. Seasonally flooded, the Ouse Washes nature reserve is the UK's largest area of washland and is visited by thousands of winter swans and wildfowl.

During harder winters you can also skate, as locals have done for centuries: the earliest travellers strapped flattened animal bones to their feet, while Victorian metal workers introduced steel blades and wooden soles, creating 'Fen Runners.'

But for the best swimming and canoeing, head west of the fens to the friendlier landscapes of the upper Nene Valley. Here, a chain of wildlife-rich wetlands splash the floodplains, and watery meadows fringe the riverbanks. The razed riverside castle at Fotheringhay is where Mary Queen of Scots was beheaded and, today, the lonely mound that remains is a good place for a picnic. Moated and roofless, the nearby ruins of Lyveden New Bield are a must-see, while an ancient manor lies beneath the turf in Helpston village and, hidden in bracken behind the church at Achurch, a striking folly is all that remains of a lost village.

Nearby, at the reedy lakes near Thrapston, the hinged windows of bird hides open onto heron nests and, in summer, the empty grass trails that weave between these wetlands feel delightfully soft beneath bare feet. Further north, towards Peterborough, are patches of ancient woodland flooded with bluebells and dotted with veteran trees, like the magnificent Fair Tree near Kings Cliffe, which is big enough for a family picnic inside – if you're good enough to climb it.

3

LAKES & FENS

1 BLOCK FEN, MEPAL

Very wild, abandoned former sand and gravel pits, now a network of five lakes used for angling, swimming and occasional jet-skiing.

→ From Mepal take the A142 W, pass the outdoor centre (CB6 2AZ) on L and at roundabout take road signed Block Fen, which turns L to become a dirt road with lake to R and many more beyond. Also the wild New Bedford River at Sutton Gault (The Anchor Inn, CB6 2BD, 01353 778537).

2 mins, 52.4349, 0.1034 🏖🏊🚻⛲

2 TEN MILE BANK, DOWNHAM MARKET

A quiet, broad stretch of Great Ouse river with pontoons and grassy banks N to Denver Sluice and S to Brandon Creek. A little lane, perfect for cycling, follows on one side and the Fen River Way footpath on the other. Remote, beautiful fenland.

→ From the bridge at Ten Mile Bank (PE38 0HB, off A10 3½ miles S of Downham Market roundabout) explore along the riverbank lane 3 miles N or S. Train at Downham Market and Littleport.

2 mins, 52.5525, 0.3586 🚴🏊🏊⛲

3 WADENHOE, R NENE

A lovely riverside pub and footpath, and pretty church, make this a wonderful place for messing about in the water.

→ Park at the pub (Kings Head, PE8 5ST, 01832 720024) and follow the river path towards the church and then upstream, for up to ½ mile.

3 mins, 52.4390, -0.5156 🏖🚻⛪🚶⛲

4 WATER NEWTON, R NENE

Pretty circular river walk with weir and swimming, near station and Peterborough.

→ From Water Newton off A1 W of Peterborough, cross at the mill lock (PE8 6LY), walk upstream to the weir and then return via the lower river section and footbridge. Also reached from Castor across the railway line, or via Ferry Meadows cycle route. Or walk 1½ miles down Nene Way from Wansford station.

15 mins, 52.5640, -0.3706 🚻🚴🚶⛲

5 FEN SKATING

The shallow, flooded fens are ideal for ice-skating, and races became popular in the 19th century, though warmer winters mean they are rare now. Beware of deep water and ask for local advice.

→ Good spots include Welney Wash (between the 2 rivers), and Whittlesea Wash (N of Whittlesea off the B1040). Further S in Cambridgeshire, St Ives flooded Meadow nr the Dolphin Hotel (P27 5EP); Bury Fen (between Earith and Bluntisham villages) or Mere Fen (between Swavesey and Over) are also good.

5 mins, 52.5292, 0.2728 ⛰▼

6 SYKES LANE, RUTLAND WATER

One of the newest official lake beaches in the UK. Hambleton peninsula is also lovely to explore, with views of the submerged church.

→ At Sykes Lane tourist centre (LE15 8PX, 01780 686800 but entrance 400 W of this). Signed off A606, E of Oakham.

2 mins, 52.6625, -0.6174 🏖

ANCIENT & RUINED

7 FOTHERINGHAY CASTLE, R NENE

On the banks of the Nene, this was the site of Mary Queen of Scots' execution and King Richard III's birth. Perfect spot for a river swim. From here, a footpath leads SE to Warmington, passing a magical tree with a tiny 'elf door' in the trunk.

→ Signed 400m SE of The Falcon, Fotheringhay (PE8 5HZ, 01832 226254, good food).
2 mins, 52.5243, -0.4363 🖼️🏛️⛵

8 ALL SAINTS CHURCH RUIN, DENTON

A shell since the early 1960s, some sections date to the 12th century. The original bells hang in St Mary's (Stilton) and John Clare's wife is said to be buried here. Carol services are still sometimes held.

→ Exit Caldecote dir Denton. In Denton, pass red phonebox on L and take first L immediately after semi-detached house (PE7 3SD). Continue for 50m – ruin visible on R opposite farmhouse and barns.
1 min, 52.4766, -0.3083 ✝️

9 LYVEDEN NEW BIELD

This roofless, moated Elizabethan lodge was never completed. Started by Sir Thomas Tresham, Lyveden remains virtually unaltered since work stopped at his death in 1605. Visit at dawn or dusk to see the ruin loom over the misty moat.

→ NT car park off Harley Way (PE8 5AT), between Oundle and Brigstock. Signed from A6116 nr Brigstock, or A427 nr Oundle. Or take footpath from Wadenhoe (PE8 5ST, 1½ miles SE).
10 mins, 52.4568, -0.5532 🖼️

10 TORPEL MANOR FIELD

Noted by John Clare, a Norman manor house once stood on this rare neutral grassland, and traces of its earthworks and defensive walls can still be seen. Nearby is Clare's cottage in Helpston (12 Woodgate, PE6 7ED).

→ At junction of B1443 and Langley Bush Rd, Helpston, just W of Helpston Garden Centre (PE6 7DU). Access through gate with info board.
5 mins, 52.6351, -0.3578 🖼️

11 LILFORD PARK FOLLY

A beautiful folly arch, built from rubble after the local landowner demolished the village and St Peter's Church.

→ At Achurch (PE8 5SL) take dead end road by the large cross to St John The Baptist church. Walk into the scrub where the far graveyard wall crumbles completely. Clamber 50m to the folly nr the river.
2 mins, 52.4378, -0.4991 🖼️🖼️

ANCIENT WOODLAND

12 OLD SULEHAY, NR WANSFORD

Mixed woodland full of wildlife wonders. Visit in winter for spurge laurel and stinking hellebore; spring for nesting birds, primroses and bluebells; summer for bellflowers,

lizards and grass snakes; or autumn for berries and crab apples.

➜ From main crossroads in Yarwell at stone bus shelter (PE8 6PN), take Wansford Rd N (dir Wansford) for ½ mile to find footpath on L through gate.

1 min, 52.5746, -0.4340 📍🚶

13 CASTOR HANGLANDS, WILD GARLIC

A good place to forage for wild garlic, this secluded mosaic of woodland, grassland, scrub and wetland has abundant wild flowers and orchids. Walk to the Granary Tea Room from here.

➜ From Granary Tea Room at Willow Brook Farm (PE6 7EL) turn L, dir Barnack. At first crossroads, turn L and follow ¾ mile to large layby at Southey Wood entrance on R. Cross road and follow footpath 750m E along field edge to reserve sign.

5 mins, 52.6008, -0.3517 📍

14 AVERSLEY WOOD BLUEBELLS

This wood has star-shaped 'armed' ponds, manmade for easy cattle watering. Bullock Road, an ancient track, runs along the SW edge, where 200,000 cattle were once driven each year. Half a mile SE, Archer's Wood was once a haunt of highwaymen.

➜ From The Greystones pub in Sawtry (PE28 5ST), exit village W on Gidding Rd, dir Hamerton. Continue 2¼ miles and at sharp R bend find byway sign to wood ahead on L, after approx 700m. Limited parking. Slightly shorter footpath access from carpark on St Judith's Lane, Sawtry, PE28 5XE.

10 mins, 52.4235, -0.2932 📍🚶

15 SHORT WOOD, BLUEBELLS

Spring bluebells and leafy dog's mercury carpet this fragment of the medieval Rockingham Forest. Other wildflowers (primrose, wood speedwell, wood melick) are abundant. Adjacent (SW), Glapthorn Cow Pasture wood has nuthatches, warblers and nightingales.

➜ From Main St, Southwick (PE8 5BL), turn R (S) just before the church, dir Oundle. After ½ mile, just past a water tower and broad verge on R, a footpath leads R across fields to Short Wood and continues to Cow Pastures.

3 mins, 52.5101, -0.5048 📍

16 BEDFORD PURLIEUS, WILDFLOWERS

England's most flower-rich wood is dominated by oak and ash, with small-leaved lime, hazel, wych elm and field maple.

➜ Footpath entrance opposite Yaxley and Old Sulehay turnoff, 1¼ miles W of Wansford on road to Kings Cliffe. Tricky parking.

1 min, 52.5785, -0.4477 📍

17 KINGS CLIFFE HOLLOW 'FAIR TREE'

Hide in the hollow trunk or climb up into the the central branches.

➜ In Kings Cliffe take Willow Ln (PE8 6XT), signed Millennium Wood, past the school, follow for about a mile. Tree on L on woodland edge.

20 mins, 52.5771, -0.5222 📍 V

18

18

17

31

WILDLIFE WONDERS

18 OUSE WASHES, BEWICK'S SWANS

The UK's largest area of 'washland', or seasonally flooded grazing pasture, has thousands of ducks and swans in winter, with lapwings and redshank in spring. The shallow Dec–March flood levels offer the best bird watching. A true fenland experience.

→ RSPB Ouse Washes reserve, Counter Wash, Chatteris, PE15 0NF. From SW end of Manea village (PE15 0LS), take L signed to Welches Dam and follow 2 miles to car park at end.

2 mins, 52.4515, 0.1632

19 WOODWALTON FEN, MARSH HARRIERS

Rare and isolated fenland, home to marsh harriers. The most westerly of the East Anglican fens, and one of the few that survived 17th- and 19th-century drainage.

→ In Ramsey Heights (approx 2 miles S of B1040/B660 junction in Ramsey St Mary's) head W down Chapel Rd dead end (PE26 2RS) and straight on track after 1 mile between fields to bridge and fen.

10 mins, 52.4478, -0.1851

20 HOLME FEN BIRCH WOODLAND

Believed to be the lowest point in Britain (2.75m below sea level), this wetland is rich in dragonflies and has England's largest area of pure birch woodland.

→ From Holme turn L after The Admiral Wells (PE7 3PH) on B660 onto unnamed rd. After ½ mile find footpath access on R across the ditch. Several other access points on reserve edges.

5 mins, 52.4881, -0.2303

21 HERONRY LAKE, TITCHMARSH

This network of lakes is rich in herons and wildfowl, with butterflies in the nettlebeds and damselflies on floating reed islands. In summer the soft grass paths around the lakes are perfect for barefoot runs.

→ Park on Meadow Ln, Thrapston nr Sailing Club (NN14 4QL). Heronry Lake is on the far side of the sailing lake - follow the footpath around the lake edge to reach it. Explore more of the lakes network for more grassy paths.

20 mins, 52.4106 -0.5203

SLOW FOOD

22 DOVECOTE FARM, GEDDINGTON

Farm shop, PYO, restaurant and tea rooms. Outdoor seating surrounded by countryside.

→ Newton Rd, NN14 1BW, 01536 742227. 52.4439, -0.7026

23 THE OLD BARN, WADENHOE

Home-made grub in a rustic barn conversion with patio garden. Lovely Nene Valley walks. Kings Head pub two mins walk away.

→ Mill Lane, PE8 5XD, 01832 721129. 52.4394, -0.5108

24 GRANARY TEA ROOM

17th-century grain store turned tea room in the heart of John Clare countryside. Home-cooked breakfasts and hearty lunches. Farm shop adjacent. From here, footpaths lead to Castor Hanglands Nature Reserve.

→ Willow Brook Farm, Stamford Road, Helpston Heath, PE6 7EL, 01780 749483. 52.6131, -0.3501

25 CHEQUERED SKIPPER, ASHTON

Thatched country pub with large grassy garden that doubles as the village green. Food is sourced from local Oundle suppliers and the Ashton Estate.

→ The Green, Ashton, PE8 5LD, 01832 273494. 52.4822, -0.4462

26 THE KINGS HEAD, WADENHOE

Home-cooked food and locally sourced meats served in a riverside meadow. Try the beef from Woodward's Farm, sourced a few miles across the fields.

→ Church Street, Wadenhoe, PE8 5ST, 01832 720024. 52.4389, -0.5142

27 OUNDLE MARKET

Oundle's regular Thursday market features local producers, with the farmers' market held second Saturday of the month, 9am–2pm.

→ Oundle Market Place, PE8 4BA. 52.4808, -0.4671

28 SHIP INN, BRANDON CREEK

Superb riverside setting at the confluence of the Little Ouse and Great Ouse. Lovely garden, cosy interior, decent local food.

→ Brandon Creek, PE38 0PP, 01353 676228. 52.5008, 0.3666

29 HILL FARM PYO & FARM SHOP

Good range of seasonal soft fruits to pick or buy, with sweetcorn and pumpkins in September/October. Other produce sold, plus coffee and home-made cake.

→ Chesterton, PE7 3UA, 01733 233270. 52.5347, -0.3370

30 ACWELLSYKE B&B

Two-room B&B with extensive gardens and quiet spots by the stream. Tranquil setting, half a mile from the nearest road.

→ Keeper's Lodge, off Grafton Rd, Brigstock, 01536 373121.
52.4378, -0.6132

31 'CHAMPING', ALL SAINTS CHURCH

Book a canoe trip along the River Nene and sleep inside Aldwincle village church. Local meals, bedding and storytelling can be provided.

→ All Saints Church, Aldwincle, 01604 832115, see 'champing' on Canoe2.co.uk
52.4254, -0.5218

32 THE ARC CABIN, ELTON

Rustic cabin with weathered furniture, thumbed novels and crocheted rugs. Wood-burning stove for winter and a riverside veranda for summer. Village setting with Black Horse pub nearby (PE8 6RU, 01832 281222).

→ The Island House, Duck Street, Elton, PE8 6RJ, 07747 011701.
52.5346, -0.3994

33 LILFORD LODGE FARM

300-acre mixed farm with fishing rights on the River Nene. Simple rooms in the converted 19th-century farmhouse give a taste of Nene Valley farm life.

→ Barnwell, Nr Oundle, PE8 5SA, 01832. 272230.
52.4516, -0.4708

34 FOURWINDS LEISURE, MARCH

Campsite backs onto the Old River Nene, with fishing, archery and canoe hire. Surrounded by open farmland.

→ 113 Whittlesey Road, March, PE15 0AH, 01354 658737.
52.5547, 0.0561

35 THE SECRET GARDEN TOURING PARK

Eleven-acre, summer-only camping site with 25 pitches. Choice of plot types, with play areas, picnic spots, on-site brewery, shop and bushcraft courses.

→ Mile Tree Lane, Wisbech, PE13 4TR, 01945 585044.
52.6541, 0.1322

36 FENLAND CAMPING AND CARAVAN

Quiet and secluded site with 10 grass pitches for tents and 10 hard standings for caravans. Outdoor chess and games for children.

→ 50A March Road, Wimblington, PE15 0RW, 01354 740354.
52.5196, 0.0820

37 INDIGO CAMPING

Yurt, tipis and bell tents on a smallholding with pigs, chickens and sheep. Good for wildlife watching and stargazing. Fire pits and BBQ provided.

→ Hills and Hollows, Barnwell Road, PE8 5PB, 01832 272585.
52.4651, -0.4693

38 NENE VALLEY COTTAGES

Three self-catering cottages, surrounded by open fields and set down a secluded track. Modern interiors and uninterrupted rural views. Nearest pub a 30-min walk across fields.

→ Hall Farm, Wigsthorpe, PE8 5SE, 01832 733125.
52.4238, -0.4516

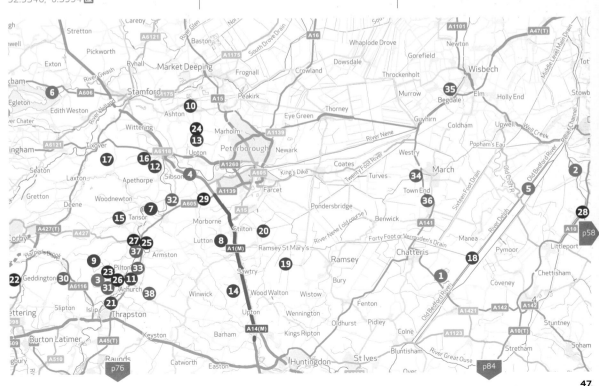

NORTH NORFOLK

Our perfect weekend

→ **Land** like Robinson Crusoe at Scolt Head – Britain's only desert island – or bivvy out under the stars at Gun Hill.

→ **Skip** around the grassy ramparts of Warham Camp, then retreat to the Three Horseshoes for rabbit pie by the fireside.

→ **Spook** yourself at dusk in the lost villages and ruined churches of Egmere and Appleton.

→ **Forage** for mussels, clams and cockles at Stiffkey Marsh then cook them up at High Sand Creek campsite.

→ **Walk** out across the cockle beds to swim with seals at Blakeney Point – but know your tides.

→ **Discover** the secret Brickyard Campsite or hide out in the woods at Dreamy Hollow.

→ **Gasp** at the Snettisham Spectacular, where tens of thousands of waders swarm the skies.

→ **Taste** spiced rum at the Lord Nelson, whiskey-infused salmon at Cley Smokehouse or freshly baked bread from Bircham Windmill.

Emerald-green samphire tickles the saltmarshes, glistening channels weave through the mudflats, and marram grasses anchor the dunes beneath brilliant blue skies and dark starry nights.

A world like no other, the north Norfolk coastline cedes to the sea each day, nurturing fragile habitats and wildlife so astounding they can seem almost alien to England: 10,000 waders flood the skies at high tide in Snettisham reserve, pink-footed geese swarm the winter marshes at Holkham, and liquid-eyed seals loll all year on the sand and shingle ridge at Blakeney Point.

Reliably popular with summer crowds, swathes of yellow sand lick along the coast. But just as Norfolk's tides come and go, the beaches empty when the schools return, leaving tranquil spaces of sanctuary and solitude. A wealth of local produce blesses this shoreline, making a bold mark on Britain's culinary map. Cley smoked fish and sweet Cromer crab have been delicacies for decades and can be ordered from any true Norfolk menu, while everything from fresh mussels to blue cockles can be gathered from the shoreline or bought by the bag from unmanned roadside stalls.

Understanding the transient nature of Norfolk's tides opens up the world between land and sea, where submerged shipwrecks like the SS Vina at Brancaster are exposed at low water. A whaleback of white sand and dune hills, Scolt Head is Britain's very own desert island, accessible only by sailing or swimming. The island's north shore lays open to the sea, while the south-east forms a network of pools and snaking sandy channels which, with low tides and a little local knowledge, you can navigate by walking along the cockle path, wading through the shallows and squelching across the mud in bare feet.

Between these wild spaces, the flint and pebble cottages of former sea ports cluster along the coast. One of the prettiest is Burnham Overy Staithe, where Admiral Lord Nelson learned to swim and sail. Nearby, in his home village of Burnham Thorpe, you can can still find Nelson's favourite seat in his refreshingly rustic local. A pub with no bar, The Lord Nelson serves blended rums and local ales to a room of crooked timbers and crackling log fires.

6

WILD BEACHES

1 HOLME DUNES, THORNHAM

Remote, wild beach and dunes with lakes and wetlands birds.

→ 2 miles W of Brancaster on the A149 (PE36 6LT), turn R into Staithe Lane and continue ½ mile to park at end. Bear L then R along marshes to dunes and lake. Good swimming at all tides with deeper tidal channel on R. Lifeboat Inn (PE36 6LT, 01485 512236) has rooms.
20 mins, 52.9763, 0.557 🏖️🚗📷🐚

2 BRANCASTER BEACH

Wonderful long beach with views to Scolt Head west and wreck of SS Vina (see below). Deep channel at E end of beach makes a great swimming pool at low tide.

→ Signed from the church in Brancaster, just W of The Ship (PE31 8AP, 01485 210333). After 1 mile park at golf club (PE31 8AX). The Jolly Sailors (PE31 8BP, 01485 210314) and the White Horse (PE31 8BY, 01485 210262) in Brancaster Staithe are good food pubs.
2 mins, 52.9755, 0.6362 🍴📷🅿️

3 SCOLT HEAD ISLAND EAST

Remote swimming and sailing spot on this desert island nature reserve.

→ At low/falling tide the 'cockle path' from Burnham Overy Staithe offers an adventurous approach: wade across harbour channel N, follow muddy path ¾ mile N, crossing bridge then a deep wade to Scolt Head beach. Or catch the boat trip (07776 302413) from Burnham Overy Staithe.
20 mins, 52.9779, 0.7502 🏖️🚶📷🛶🐚

4 GUN HILL, BURNHAM OVERY STAITHE

One of the best beaches and dunes in Britain. Panoramic views and rare summer butterflies.

→ From Burnham Overy Staithe harbour (PE31 8JE) follow coast path E for 1½ miles. Where path turns sharp R (E), bear L (W) across the sand to the high point. Some swim to Scolt Head.
40 mins, 52.9765, 0.7519 📷🚶🐚

5 HOLKHAM BEACH, WELLS

A huge, well-known expanse of forest-backed sand and dune. Good swimming only at high tide.

→ At crossroads 1½ miles W of Wells (A149) with The Victoria L (NR23 1RG), turn R through gates and park in Lady Ann's Drive (NR23 1RJ) opp. Cross dunes through forest. Bear L for naturist section and Gun Hill after 2 miles (see above), R for forested stretch to Wells. Local food at The Victoria (NR23 1RG, 01328)
10 mins, 52.9758, 0.8032 🛶🚶🅿️

6 STIFFKEY, GARBOROUGH CREEK

Popular LT swimming hole in the tidal creeks of Stiffkey marshes and flats. Mud slides and jumps in the vast expanse of the flats.

→ Leave Stiffkey W, dir Wells, and turn R after Red Lion (NR23 1AJ, 01328 830552) into The Greenway. Pass High Sand Creek campsite (NR23 1QF, 01328 830235) and park at bottom of track (500m). Bear R (E) along woods 500m, joining Garborough Patch Pit Creek, then follow path to L, crossing 6 mini footbridges, to arrive at sand flats. Follow creek (L) 200m to find sharp bend and pool to the R. Mud on L side, sand on R.
15 mins, 52.9634, 0.9366 🔺⛺🏕️

7 BLAKENEY POINT POOL

Dramatic low-tide walk across the cockle beds and salt marshes to sand banks and pool at Blakeney Point. Many seals.

→ Know your tides! Set off 2 hrs before LT. From Morston harbour (NR25 7BJ) follow path along creek N, crossing two tributary footbridges (500m), then bear L along edge of salt marshes for ¾ mile with Blakeney

11

9

13

Channel on your R. Once well past the old lifeboat station on opp (N) bank, bear off path R towards Blakeney Point, across cockles, mud, sands and shallow water for ¾ mile. At the point, continue on to find a place to swim in the deep pool as the channel turns N out to sea. Never approach seals on foot: allow them to come to you in the water. Or take a boat trip.
40 mins, 52.9696, 0.9583 ▼▲◐

8 SALTHOUSE MARSHES, CLEY
Quiet shingle sand beach, deeply shelved for swimming. Nature reserve.
→ 300m E on A149 from the popular Dun Cow pub (NR25 7XA, 01263 740467) find beach footpath opp tiny Grouts Ln, through nature reserve. Also Cley beach with parking (NR25 7RY). Good camping at Foxhills on Weybourne Rd (NR25 7EH, 01263 588253).
5 mins, 52.957, 1.0921 ⬆▲◐

ANCIENT & SACRED

9 ST MARY, APPLETON RUINED CHURCH
This round-towered ruin is all that remains of the Saxon village of Appleton, standing above the raised earthworks of the old streets and houses.

→ From the Folkes Arms (PE31 6BJ, 01485 600210 – log fires, local food), head W on on A148, dir Kings Lynn. Turn R onto B1440, dir Sandringham. Take second R towards Appleton Farm. Ruin looms ahead.
3 mins, 52.8163, 0.5292 ▣

10 ST EDMUNDS, EGMERE
This ruined church stands dramatically on a mound in the remains of old Egmere village.
→ From A149 Wells-next-the-Sea, head S on B1105 dir Fakenham. After approx 6 miles, turn R (clearly signed Creake Rd), opposite Walsingham turnoff. Continue ½ mile to cattle grid, estate entrance and obvious ruin. On private land, but clearly visible from the road. Little Walsingham farm shop and cafe nearby (NR22 6BU, 01328 821877).
1 min, 52.9004, 0.8186 ✝

11 BACONSTHORPE CASTLE
This 15th-century manor house was once the moated and fortified home of the ambitious Heydon family. Built, enlarged and abandoned over two centuries, it's now an evocative and remote English Heritage ruin.
→ Signed N from The Street, Baconsthorpe (NR25 6LL). Free entry.
2 mins, 52.8991, 1.1530 ▣

12 WARHAM CAMP

One of Norfolk's most impressive hillforts, found at the end of a tiny track. Probably built by the Iceni in the second century BC and occupied until the tribe was wiped out by the Romans after Boudicca's uprising.

➜ In Warham, take single-track road S for Wighton, opposite the Three Horseshoes (NR23 1NL, 01328 710 547). After approx ½ mile, trackway leads R past metal gate. No car parking at trackway, best walk from Warham, or cycle.
15 mins, 52.9302, 0.8904 🚫 📷

13 SS VINA, BRANCASTER

This former merchant-navy vessel became stranded on a sandbank in 1944. Visible at low tide and submerged at high. Fast tides make this a dangerous site, and crossing to the wreck/Scolt Head Island West is possible only with extreme care.

➜ Shallowest ford is at far E end of Brancaster beach (1 mile from clubhouse, PE31 8AX) on cockle beds, beyond wreck and between transmitter and church tower landmarks. Depart 1–2 hours before LT and ford the channel while water is still flowing seaward. Mark the best crossing point in sand to assist your return.
40 mins, 52.9852, 0.6543 ⚠ 🔽 📷

WOODLAND & MEADOWS

14 THURSFORD WOOD

25 acres of woodland, pasture and ponds with around 70 ancient pollarded oaks – some of England's oldest – as well as bluebells and a mass of ferns, fungi, mosses and lichens.

➜ Off A148 on R, a mile W of Thursford (NR21 0BJ). Or it's a nice walk from the footpath behind Thursford church – 300m W then S to the wood.
5 min, 52.8613, 0.9396 🚶

15 RINGSTEAD DOWNS

A dry glacial valley, home to brown argus butterflies, warblers and rare wild flowers. The Woodland Garden has tree swings.

➜ From The Gin Trap inn, Ringstead (PE36 5JU), head S for Sedgeford. After 400m, take unsigned track R to rough parking area on reserve edge. Buy supplies from Walsingham Farm Shop branch at Norfolk Lavender (PE31 7JE, 01485 570384).
2 mins, 52.9318, 0.5166 🚶

16 WIVETON DOWNS & BLAKENEY ESKER

Left behind by retreating glaciers, this gravel ridge is covered in heather and gorse and has sweeping views of the coast and surrounding farmland.

17

18

19

→ From the Wiveton Bell pub, Wiveton (NR25 7TL) follow bend S, dir Holt, then take first R opposite Cley turnoff, past grass parking area. Follow for less than a mile to signed reserve car park on L.
2 mins, 52.9392, 1.0213

WILDLIFE WONDERS

17 SNETTISHAM SPECTACULAR
Tens of thousands of waders swarm the skies when exceptionally high tides force them off the mud flats. Autumn/winter brings the greatest numbers.

→ Signed along Beach Rd off A149 near Snettisham. RSPB parking (PE31 7PS) approx 1½ miles up Beach Rd on L. Follow footpaths to the 'Loop Trail' at the reserve's southern tip – the hides here give some of the best views. Timetables available from the RSPB (01485 542689).
30 mins, 52.8745, 0.4708

18 SEALS, BLAKENEY POINT
Up to 800 common and grey seals live year-round on this shingle and sand dune ridge, where they've been protected since 1976. Access restricted during breeding seasons.

→ Boats leave from The Quay, Blakeney, NR25

7NF. Try 01263 740038, Beansboattrips. co.uk. Or book at The Anchor in Morston (NR25 7AA, 01263 741392). Short crossing plus viewing time, with optional landing on Blakeney Point where allowed. (1–2 hours).
5 mins, 52.9560, 1.0169

19 GOOSE MIGRATIONS, HOLKHAM
100,000 pink-footed geese overwinter on the marshes near Holkham Beach and Scolt Head Island. They take to the skies at dawn, flying inland to the sugar-beet fields, and return to the marshes at dusk, a sound and sight that is truly awe-inspiring.

→ Stake-out in a Holkham Estate hide (Lady Ann's Drive, Holkham Hall Estate, NR23 1RG). Washington Hide is a good spot – turn L at the bottom of Lady Ann's Drive following track for one mile, keeping the pinewoods on your R. Or look to the skies if you're anywhere within a few miles.
20 mins, 52.9665, 0.8143

SLOW FOOD

20 THE SALTHOUSE DUN COW
Modernised yet rustic foody pub with great views over bird-filled saltmarshes from the garden. Self-catering accommodation.

→ A149 Coast Rd, Salthouse, NR25 7XA,
01263 740467.
52.9522, 1.0856 🍴

21 BACK TO THE GARDEN, LETHERINGSETT
Large farm shop and café selling full range of
foods, plus home-made meals to take away.
Everything grown/made on site or produced
locally. PYO at Sharrington Strawberries 1¼
miles dir Thursford (NR242PH).
→ Letheringsett, Holt, NR25 7JJ,
01263 715996.
52.9036, 1.0427 🍴

22 BIRCHAM WINDMILL
Buy bread or bake your own in the original
coal-fired oven, then climb to fifth floor
to see the sails in action. Tea room sells
own produce.
→ Bircham Windmill, Great Bircham, PE31 6SJ,
01485 578393.
52.8629, 0.6134 🍴

23 THE LORD NELSON, BURNHAM THORPE
Nelson was a regular at this 17th-century
pub, and his favourite seat is still in the
snug. Good food, beer and locally blended
rum served from the tap room. Village has a

lovely remote feel. Many excellent beaches
nearby.
→ Walsingham Road, Burnham Thorpe, PE31
8HN, 01328 738241.
52.9386, 0.7548 🍺

24 CLEY SMOKEHOUSE
Duck and seafood smoked on site. Also
whiskey & ginger salmon, Norfolk bloater
(herring smoked whole) and freshly landed
Cromer crabs.
→ High Street, Cley, NR25 7RF, 01263 740282.
52.9523, 1.0431 🍴

25 SHELLFISH & SAMPHIRE
The intertidal zone is ideal for mussels,
blue clams, cockles and occasional oysters.
Check there's an R in the month and only
harvest shellfish when mature. There's local
samphire to sample from June to September
(only pick the tip of the plant) as well as
mackerel to spin for and fishing trips to join.
→ Anywhere along the coast, including
Old Hunstanton, Wells-next-the-Sea and
Brancaster Staithe. Find samphire in muddy
marshes – wear wellies, avoid nature reserves.
For fishing trips try Norfolkfishingtrips.co.uk
in Docking, PE31 8BW, 01485 517610.

29

GURNEYS FISH SHOP.

29

Traleblazer Case

26

LOCAL
SAMPHIRE
2.95

25

26 THE REAL ALE SHOP, WELLS

Rustic ale shop on a classic Norfolk barley farm. Stocks bottled beers from more than 13 Norfolk breweries. Also farm cottage accommodation.
→ Branthill Farm, Wells-next-the-sea, NR23 1SB, 01328 710810.
52.9290, 0.8270

27 BYFORDS, HOLT

A local institution, selling everything from bread, cheese and chutney to take-away pizzas and hearty meals. Filled picnic hampers available. Cafe and accommodation on site.
→ 1–3 Shirehall Plain, Holt, NR25 6BG, 01263 714816 (shop) 01263 711400 (café).
52.9062, 1.0884

28 WIVETON HALL CAFÉ, HOLT

Colourful café and shop with goods sourced from estate's own farm and garden. Estate walks and PYO also here.
→ Holt, NR25 7TE, 01263 740515.
52.9540, 1.0322

29 GURNEY'S FISH SHOP, BURNHAM

This nostalgic village has excellent independent shops, with Gurneys the place to buy everything from wet fish to soups, pies and pâtés. Humble Pie deli (01328 738581) nearby is good for bread, cheese and meats.
→ Market Place, Burnham Market, PE31 8HF, 01328 738967.
52.9455, 0.7259

30 WALSINGHAM FARM SHOP

Sells Walsingham meats, eggs and veg, plus handmade cheeses and Norfolk ham. Their restaurant, The Norfolk Riddle, is nearby. Shop has a larger branch at Norfolk Lavender (NR22 6DJ, 01328 821903).
→ Guild Street, Little Walsingham, NR22 6BU, 01328 821877.
52.8955, 0.8746

31 THE THREE HORSESHOES

Traditional pub with local cider and microbrewery beers, home-made lemonade, and pies often on the menu.
→ The Street, Warham, NR23 1NL, 01328 710547.
52.9374, 0.8975

32 THE ANCHOR INN, MORSTON

Book a seal-watching trip at this nautical themed pub, which specialises in seafood caught minutes away. Walks and birdwatching nearby.
→ The Street, Morston, NR25 7AA, 01263 741392.
52.9547, 0.9873

33 BEACH HUT 61, OLD HUNSTANTON

Traditional beach hut with hob, crockery and beach kit. Rent by the day or week. Cook freshly caught or bought fish on the beach.
→ Old Hunstanton Beach. Contact 01485 211022, norfolkhideaways.co.uk
52.9553, 0.5036

CAMP & SLEEP

34 THE BRICKYARD CAMPSITE

Secretive campsite, which only reveals its exact location on booking. Secluded spots by woodland, grasses and brickworks ruins. Compost loo and bucket shower.
→ Three miles west of Wells-next-the-Sea. Norfolkbrickyard.co.uk, 01328 730663.
52.9610, 0.7765

35 DREAMY HOLLOW CAMPSITE, STANHOE

Small site in undulating woodland with WWI trench network. Large clearings for groups, secret spots for single tents. BBQ areas and 'jungle showers'.
→ Fakenham Road, Stanhoe, PE31 8PX (misleading), 07564 226780.
52.8788, 0.6702

36 BAGTHORPE TREEHOUSE, BURNHAM

Sleep in a four-poster among old oaks in the grounds of Bagthorpe Hall. Copper bathtub and large veranda for wildlife watching.
→ Bagthorpe Hall, Burnham Market, PE31 6QY, 0117 204 7830 through Canopyandstars.co.uk
52.9608, 0.6184

37 TOWER WINDMILL

Six-storey windmill rising over salt marshes. Built in 1816, and last used as a corn mill in 1914, run by NT. Sleeps up to 19.

46

→ Burnham Overy Staithe. Off the A149 coast road between Brancaster and Wells. PE31 8JB, 01263 740241. 52.9595, 0.7349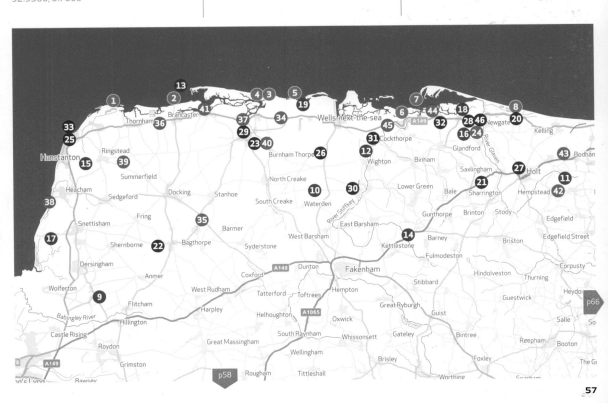

38 THE WILD DUCK, HEACHAM

A converted boat built in 1878, this three-bed hideaway nestles in the dunes, overlooking Snettisham reserve. Kids' room in the hull. BBQ and sun/viewing deck.

→ Heacham, PE31 7LH, 01359 270345. 52.9010, 0.4683

39 COURTYARD FARM BUNKHOUSE

Basic and remote self-catering barn with two bunk-rooms (sleeping four and eight). Horses accommodated, some tents accepted (call ahead).

→ Ringstead, PE36 5LQ, 01485 525251. 52.9299, 0.5696

40 WHITEHALL FARM, BURNHAM MARKET

Year-round campsite, two miles from The Lord Nelson pub and Burnham Market village. Glamping pod available.

→ Burnham Thorpe, PE31 8HN, 01328 738416. 52.9366, 0.7605

41 DEEPDALE BACKPACKERS

A working arable farm with several awards for its eco-credentials. Offers camping, glamping or bunkhouse accommodation. Village of Burnham Deepdale has everything you need for a car-free escape.

→ Burnham Deepdale, PE31 8DD, 01485 210256. 52.9655, 0.6845

42 BACONSTHORPE MEADOWS

Five-acre campsite on a working family farm with poppy fields. On-site shop, family vibe, quiet after 10pm.

→ Pitt Farm, Baconsthorpe, NR25 6LF, 01263 713395. 52.8903, 1.1440

43 BRECK FARM CAMPSITE, HOLT

Family site that's been running for 50 years. Set on a working farm, with free-range eggs and other produce sometimes sold.

→ Holt, Norfolk, NR25 6QL, 01263 588236. 52.9246, 1.1500

44 SCALDBECK COTTAGE CAMPSITE

Norfolk flint cottage and tiny camping field with upturned rowing boats and access to the marshes. Pre-booked cooked breakfasts offered. B&B available.

→ Stiffkey Rd, Morston, NR25 7BJ, 01263 740188. 52.9558, 0.9818

45 HIGH SAND CREEK, STIFFKEY

Simple camping beside marsh sands, with the sea on your doorstep. Popular with families.

→ Vale Farm, The Greenway, Stiffkey, NR23 1QP, 01328 830235. 52.9530, 0.9244

46 CLEY WINDMILL, CLEY-NEXT-THE-SEA

Unique rooms in a 19th-century windmill. Antique furniture, open fires, sea and marsh views. Meals served in the beamed dining room.

→ Cley-next-the-Sea, Holt, NR25 7RP, 01263 740209. 52.9547, 1.0428

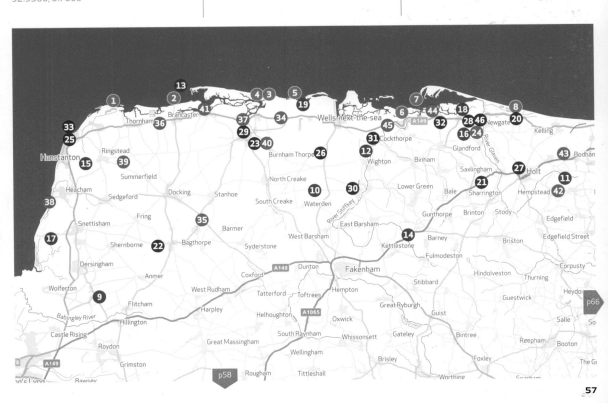

BRECKLAND & MID NORFOLK

Our perfect weekend

→ **Stand** alone at Blood Hill barrow or explore the ruins of Warren Lodge in Thetford Forest.

→ **Enter** the ice house at the ruins of Weeting Castle near St Mary's church.

→ **Splash** and swim in the River Wensum at Swanton Morley, or by the green at Ringland.

→ **Find** rare bird cherry blossom and bluebells in Wayland Wood, setting for the *Babes in the Wood* legend.

→ **Camp** in the long grasses and tranquil fields at Gorsey Meadow and Spring Farm.

→ **Dine** on Breckland rabbit and Norfolk asparagus, washed down with whisky distilled the traditional way at the Stratton Hotel.

→ **Plunge** into pure waters at Botany Bay or Ickburgh, in the headwaters of the Wissey.

→ **Spot** the haunting yellow eyes of stone curlew at Weeting Heath and listen for the laughter of green woodpeckers.

→ **Canoe** past the hidden church in the woods at Santon Downham.

Sheltered from the windswept north and distanced from the bustle of the Broads, inland Norfolk has a quiet beauty and distinct local character that sets it apart from the coastal fringe.

As you journey towards the interior, driving deep into East Anglia, proud Corsican pines line the roads, standing to attention while smaller saplings peer out between them. Scots pines wave you in with outstretched branches, while others slouch and twist like giant bonsai, their hips cocked forward or their backs slumped and bent.

This is Breckland. Dry and infertile, it owes its name to its sandy soils – 'breck' meaning 'land that is quickly exhausted'. With the country's lowest rainfall, some of the highest summer temperatures and hardest winter frosts, it's the closest Britain comes to desert.

But wind the clock back a hundred years and Breckland was a treeless heathland. For centuries, rabbits nibbled furiously at the ground, farmed for their meat and fur. Evidence of this thousand-year-old practice can be seen at Thetford Warren Lodge, and rabbit pie still features on the traditional menus at The Leaping Hare, the Stratton Hotel and Elveden Estate, while East Wrentham and Weeting are home to surviving sections of the original heath.

The planting of Thetford Forest began after WWI, anchoring the loose soils while developing a strategic timber reserve. The 20,000 acres that were planted here created Britain's largest low-lying pine forest, now an atmospheric and fragrant place to bike, hike and horseride.

Between and beneath these pine rows are ancient flint mines and prehistoric trackways, such as Grime's Graves and Harling Drove. England's most prosperous region in the Middle Ages, Norfolk's rich history also lives on through its ruined castles – such as the striking remains at Castle Acre, Weeting and New Buckenham – and it medieval churches, including St John's at Beachemwell and St James' near Bawsey. Of the thousand or more Saxon and Norman churches that once peppered Norfolk's flats, 659 survive – more than in the rest of England put together.

Today, central Norfolk is one of the most sparsely populated areas in Britain – an extraordinary turnaround from its heyday. As the Industrial Revolution took hold elsewhere in England, it seemed to largely pass Norfolk by, leaving it almost untouched – a lapse which, I'm sure you'll agree, has in fact been a great blessing.

1

RIVERS & LAKES

1 SANTON DOWNHAM, LITTLE OUSE
Pretty chalk stream running through Thetford Forest. Chalky riverbed, up to 2m deep.

→ Signed from Brandon (A1065). You can swim below bridge and village hall in the village here, and downstream on the river path, or continue and turn R before level crossing (signed St Helen's) and go ¾ mile to parking and footbridge (IP27 0TT) near Santon church. Or it's a 2½ mile riverside walk from Brandon station.

2 mins, 52.4530, 0.6863 🏊🚶‍♂️🏞️

2 ICKBURGH, R WISSEY
Enchanting shallow woodland pool with lakes downstream.

→ Turn R off A1065 at Ickburgh, a mile N of Mundford, and continue a mile, bearing R, to find bridge and pool by road. From here walk downstream to the Lynford lakes.

1 min, 52.5225, 0.6979 🚶‍♂️🏞️

3 LYNFORD LAKES
Wonderful series of sandy bays and lakes in forest. Lynford Arboretum opposite.

→ N of Mundford (A1065) turn R down Lynford Road a mile, past hotel, to find car park on L.

5 mins, 52.5191, 0.6835 🅿️❓

4 RIVER WENSUM, SWANTON MORLEY
Family friendly river beach and paddling, weir and rope swing.

→ Head N out of village, past church, until road swings round to R after ¾ mile to find bridge and gate on L. Further weir 300m upstream.

5 mins, 52.7268, 0.9909 ❓🚶‍♂️🍴

5 RINGLAND, RIVER WENSUM
A small village green area by the pub leads down to the paddling in the river by road bridge. Deeper downstream.

→ By the Swan Inn (NR8 6AB, 01603 868214).

1 min, 52.6781, 1.1649 🚶‍♂️🍴🏞️

6 BAWSEY COUNTRY PARK, KING'S LYNN
Fabulous blue lakes with abundant sand beaches, birch-covered hill and heathland, and popular swimming close to King's Lynn.

→ N on A149 King's Lynn bypass. At hopsital take B1145 signed Gayton to find rough entrance on R after 2 miles.

5 mins, 52.74691, 0.48382 ❓

7 BOTANY BAY, LAKENHEATH FEN
Remote, wild and wonderful lakes and river swimming in the Little Ouse. Large nature reserve, restoring traditional fenland habitat.

→ Take a beautiful riverside walk 2–3 miles downstream from Lakenheath station through the nature reserve. Or by road, turn L ½ mile N of station (Cowle's Drove public byway, opp Moor Drove). Continue 2–3 miles on track beyond King Cobb industrial units. Good place for stargazing.

5 mins, 52.44542, 0.46746 🏊⛺🏕️🏞️

ANCIENT RUINS & WAYS

8 CASTLE ACRE PRIORY AND CASTLE
Sheep graze the water meadows around this romantic ruined priory. Dating back to 1090, it's one of England's largest monastic sites but has a fee. The Norman castle keep in the lovely village is free to enter.

→ Follow brown English Heritage signs through Castle Acre (PE32 2XD). The castle is back in the village down Pye Lane. Several eating options. The Ostrich (PE32 2AE, 01760 755398) is good for a pint or bite.

1 min, 52.7011, 0.6825 🏛️🍴✝️

9 ST JAMES' CHURCH

Hilltop ruin including a Norman archway. A recently excavated skeleton is thought to have died from swordfight wounds during a raid by Viking Norsemen.

→ From A149, Kings Lynn, head E on B1145 dir Bawsey. Entering Bawsey, take farm track on L after Bawsey sign and park (PE32 1EU). Follow track for ½ mile to the ruin.

10 mins, 52.7587, 0.4627

10 WEETING CASTLE

Ruined medieval moated house with a three-storey tower and ice-house, behind beautiful St Mary's church.

→ Weeting is signed from the A1065. Follow All Saints road to the church on the E side of village (IP27 0QZ). Walk through gate to ruin. Ice house is in NW corner behind trees. 2 miles SW is the traditional rabbit-grazed heathland of Weeting Heath (52.4620, 0.5859).

1 min, 52.4710, 0.6163

11 NEW BUCKENHAM CASTLE KEEP

New Buckenham Castle was demolished in 1649, and this stone keep is all that remains.

→ 100m W of New Buckenham (B1113) find footpath on R at bend (stone/redbrick barn conversion). 2 miles W, the remains of Old Buckenham Castle lie NE of Old Buckenham village, a mile up Abbey Rd on L. Private but visible from road (52.4917, 1.0504).

8 mins, 52.4716, 1.0677

12 BLOOD HILL, THETFORD FOREST

For years this round barrow was concealed by forest. Now revealed, it is protected by a low fence and sits in a silent and lesser-visited section of forest. No one knows the origins of its name, but a holy well can be found to the S.

→ Down the wide 'ride' on the W side of the A134, between Two Mile Bottom picnic site and Harling Drove. Continue straight for 700m. The holy well of St Helen and the remains of her church (St Helen's Oratory) are 200m S, with the river Little Ouse beyond. Can also be reached from Santon Downham.

10 mins, 52.4557, 0.7076

13 GODWICK ABANDONED VILLAGE

One of Britain's best examples of a deserted medieval village, which functioned until the 17th century. Perhaps abandoned due to poor harvests and weather. A church ruin rises above the earthworks of the village buildings.

20

→ From St Mary's Church (Church Ln, Tittleshall, PE32 2QD), head N with church on R. Where road bends L before junction, find footpath on R. Follow for approx ½ mile to church tower.

12 mins, 52.7619, 0.8173 🖼️ ✝️

14 ST JOHN'S, BEACHAMWELL

Falling into disrepair when Catholic England came to an end, only the dramatic 14th-century tower of this ancient parish church still remains.

→ From Barton Bendish village centre (PE33 9GF) exit E for Beachamwell. Continue for 1¾ miles to sharp L-hand turn. Follow footpath over high ridge on R. After ½ mile, take L turn where path splits. Continue to ruin at St John's farm.

20 mins, 52.6217, 0.5739 🚶

15 THETFORD WARREN LODGE

A two-storey, 15th-century ruined gamekeepers lodge, in forest just off the main road. Built for defence against armed poachers, later used by local warreners. Explore the surrounding woodland rides of Thetford Warren, where they bred their rabbits. Fantastic fungi in autumn.

→ A mile W on the B1107 (Brandon Rd) from the A11 (Thetford). 200m past the golf club (IP24 3NE) find car park on left and lodge is obvious, 200m W.

2 mins, 52.4239, 0.7069 🏞️

16 HARLING DROVE

Used for centuries to herd sheep from fenland pastures to market, this prehistoric trackway (also called Hereward Way) is lovely and sandy and cuts through Thetford Forest from east to west.

→ From A11 N of Thetford, take A1075 signed Dereham/Wattam. After approx 2 miles, find pull-in and byway entrance on L (IP24 1RU). From here, track leads W to Wyrley's Belt or E to Roundham Heath (both around 1½ miles). Continue on main road another 100m for Wretham Heath nature reserve car park.

1 min, 52.4609, 0.7905 🚶

WOODLAND & WILDLIFE

17 WAYLAND WOOD, WATTON

As old as the last ice age and listed in the Domesday Book, this ancient wood was the setting for the nursery tale *Babes in the Wood*. In spring, you'll find bluebells, orchids and bird cherry blossom.

→ Parking area (IP25 6HN) is on A1075 a mile S of Watton.

1 min, 52.5601, 0.8348 📍

18 FOXLEY WOOD, FOXLEY

Norfolk's largest remaining tract of ancient woodland is a butterfly hot-spot with more than 350 types of flowering plants. Discover banks of spring primroses, followed by bluebells and orchids.

→ Car park (NR20 4QR) is on lane between Themelthorpe and Foxley (A1067).

1 min, 52.7652, 1.0358 📍

19 EAST WRETHAM HEATH

Splendid for its sheer diversity, this is the Brecks' oldest reserve and largest area of open heathland. Find gnarled old Scots pine trees, nightjars and stone curlews, with their haunting yellow eyes. Also stoats, roe deer and thousands of rabbits.

→ As for Harling Drove listing.

1 min, 52.4620, 0.8142 🏞️

20 ROYDON COMMON, KING'S LYNN

Grazed by sheep and ponies, this lonely tract of Norfolk is abundant with flowering heather in late summer. Visit on a summer eve for twinkling glow-worms and rattling nightjars, or by day for up to 15 species of dragonflies and 30 of butterfly.

→ Car park is 500m W of Roydon on the Lynn Rd (250m W of Chapel Rd turn off).
1 min, 52.7767, 0.5154 🚶

SLOW FOOD

21 DENVER WINDMILL

Listed mill, grinding local wheat. Tearoom and shop sells the mill's own bread and biscuits. Should be open again soon, following refurbishment.

→ Sluice Rd Denver, PE38 0EG. Check opening here: denver-windmill.co.uk
52.5850, 0.3676 🍴

22 ASHILL FRUIT FARM

Family fruit farm with over 40 varieties of apples, pears, plums and soft fruits. Buy fruits, preserves, cakes and cloudy apple juice.

→ Swaffham Road, Ashill, IP25 7DB, 01760 440050.
52.5983, 0.7827 🍴

23 NORFOLK ASPARAGUS

Norfolk produces England's tastiest asparagus, and this farm is said to grow the best. Steam for 7 mins, eat with butter. Shop open April–June.

→ Roudham Farm, NR16 2RJ, 01953 717126. Follow signs for Norfolk County Asparagus.
52.4468, 0.8744 🍴

24 ENGLISH WHISKY

Norfolk farmer James Nelstrop uses local barley and water from the Brecks aquifer to make his whiskey. Tours from 10–5.30pm.

→ Harling Road, Roudham, NR16 2QW, 01953 717939.
52.4506, 0.9145 🍴

25 ICENI BREWERY

Own ales, lagers and stouts to try and buy on site, or call ahead to watch the brewing process.

→ Foulden Road, IP26 5HB, 01842 878922.
52.5194, 0.6628 🍴

26 FRANSHAM MANOR FARM SHOP

Family-run farm shop selling veg/fruit, cakes and home-made meals. Open daily.

→ The Manor, Little Fransham, NR19 2JW, 01362 687603.
52.6697, 0.8091 🍴

27 THE DABBLING DUCK

Award-winning foodie pub with homespun interior and themed dining areas. Village setting by the green and duck ponds.

→ 11 Abbey Road, Great Massingham, PE32 2HN, 01485 520827.
52.7737, 0.6637 🍴

28 TWENTY CHURCHWARDENS

Quirky, converted schoolhouse with a proper English-pub vibe. Has beamed rooms and an open fire. Good value grub includes home-made pies.

→ Cockley Cley, Swaffham PE37 8AW, 01760 721439.
52.6061, 0.6454 🍺

29 THE OSTRICH, CASTLE ACRE

Atmospheric 400-year-old coaching inn with original features and fireplaces. Good food, gardens with kids' sandpit and beach hut.

→ Stocks Green, Castle Acre, PE32 2AE, 01760 755398.
52.7034, 0.6871 🍺

30 BEDINGFIELD ARMS

18th-century coach house serving lamb and venison from the owners' family farm, fish from King Lynn and veg from the pub garden. Opposite the moated NT property, Oxburgh Hall.

→ The Green, Oxborough, PE33 9PS, 01366 328300.
52.5828, 0.5733 🍴

STAY

31 GAMEKEEPER'S HUT, WESTFIELD FARM

Boutique heritage hut decorated with fishing tackle and decoy ducks. Bookable with the adjacent shepherd's hut. Space for tents. Stargaze at night, spot barn owls or stroll to the local pub.

→ 0117 204 7830 Canopyandstars.co.uk. Foulsham NR20 5RH, 01362 683333. (Royal Oak is NR20 5AH, 01362 680221).
52.7737, 1.0050 🏕

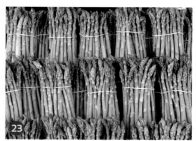

32 GORSEY MEADOW

Pitch your tent in the long grass meadow at Hockering House or stay in a furnished bell tent. Ageing oaks, barn owls and deer nearby. Compost loos and eco-showers.

➔ Heath Road, Hockering, NR20 3JB, 07909 510192.
52.6864, 1.0777 🔥

33 WOODSTOCK FARM

Small camping and caravan site with woodland trails. Shepherd's hut also available. Open year-round.

➔ Woodstock Touring Park, Gibbet Lane Wereham, PE33 9BE, 01366 500559.
52.5969, 0.4769 🌲

34 WEST LEXHAM BARN

Magnificent exposed-beam heritage barn for big gatherings (max 22). Stunning rural estate with rowing lake. Treehouse and glamping.

➔ West Lexham, Breckland, PE32 2QN, 01760 755602.
52.7205, 0.7277 🌲

35 YAXHAM WATERS

10-acre site with fishing lakes and café. Yurts, tipis and log cabins available.

➔ Dereham Road, Yaxham, NR19 1RF, 01362 696750.
52.6555, 0.9605 🔥 🎣

36 PARK FARM CAMPING

Year-round, no-frills camping in a secluded meadow with tree swing and fishing in the River Wensum. Pub & village shops nearby.

➔ Swanton Morley, Dereham, NR20 4JU, 01362 637950.
52.7091, 0.9984 🎣 ⛺

37 RECTORY FARM CAMPSITE

Simple, adults-only site on a Breckland farm that allows caravans and tents. Fishing lakes and holiday cottages available.

➔ Watton Rd, Hingham, NR9 4PP, 07919 530982.
52.5813, 0.9667

38 SPRING FARM CAMPSITE

Simple site with muntjac, barn owls, hares and more. Bring your rod to fish in the pond. Pub, shop and cafe in Shipdham village.

➔ Little Hale, Shipdham, IP25 7PL, 01362 822109.
52.6230, 0.8712 ⛺

39 THE FIRE PIT CAMP

Quirky, eco-friendly site with retro double-decker bus, fire pit and hand-built hazel tent. Individual pitches July-August, whole-site bookings in other months.

➔ The Firs, Wendling, NR19 2LT, 07717 315199.
52.6742, 0.8621 🔥

40 STRATTONS HOTEL

One of England's 'greenest' hotels in a listed building with award-winning restaurant serving Breckland produce, including rabbit!

➔ Ash Close, Swaffham, PE37 7NH, 01760 723845. Arrive by public transport for 10 per cent discount.
52.6489, 0.6869 🌲 🍴

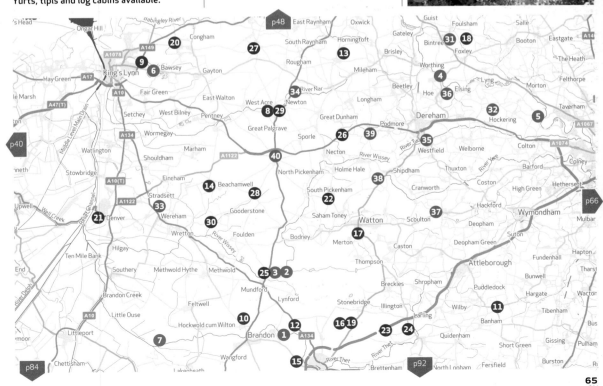

NORFOLK BROADS

Our perfect weekend

→ **Paddle** down the Ant to the isolated and ruined abbey of St Benet's.

→ **Climb** the tower of St Helen's church at Ranworth for spectacular Norfolk panoramas.

→ **Cower** as tens of thousands of Domesday rooks blacken the skies at Buckenham Carrs.

→ **Cycle** along the remote river Waveney between Mendham and Homersfield, dipping as you go.

→ **Swim** with seals at Horsey Corner and refuel with tea and cake at Waxham, one of England's oldest barns.

→ **Sleep** in the meadow at Deer's Glade, stay in the Lazy Shaman woodland retreat or camp on the clifftop at Overstrand.

→ **Forage** samphire, mussels and Cromer crabs, or buy by the bag from roadside stalls.

→ **Hug** the Grandparent Oak, then get lost deep in Bacton Woods.

→ **Splash** and paddle in the Broads at Salhouse, or take a longer swim at Thurne or Coltishall.

A silvery web of shallow, lock-free waterways, linked by the Rivers Bure, Yare and Waveney, this low-lying network of lakes is a secret world that's difficult to discover from the road and best explored by water.

The lakes of the Norfolk Broads were long thought to be natural, and it was not until the 1950s that botanist Joyce Lambert proved otherwise, revealing that their steep sides were hand-dug by our medieval ancestors, who quarried the land for peat fuel.

The UK's largest protected wetland, these prehistoric peat bogs are flanked by reed beds and fringed by marshland, which support fragile habitats, home to 'booming' bitterns and swallowtail butterflies. Here, you can pad along boardwalks to the lonely bird hides at Hickling or Barton, or pedal along tiny lanes to explore ecclesiastical remains like those of St Benet's Abbey, which crumble beside the River Bure.

East Norfolk is rich in ruined churches, many of the medieval remains lovingly cared for by locals. The church of St Martin's in Shotesham was recently stripped of its damaging ivy blanket by volunteers and, at Surlingham, the cherished remains of St Saviour's stand high above the River Yare, watching over the grave of local Norfolk naturalist Ted Ellis.

In the height of summer the Broads can become congested with boats, so explore the quieter upper reaches by canoe from Ant Bridge or Coltishall, where motor craft cannot go. The best river swimming is also from a canoe, with access to the Broads at Salhouse, How Hill and Thurne.

The most southerly Broad, where Norfolk eases into Suffolk, was the local river of the late Roger Deakin, the modern father of wild swimming. With easy riverside access for more than a mile, Outney Common is one of the best places to swim here, and is where Deakin paddled his canoe as part of a Radio Four documentary, detailing the natural history of Broadland and savouring the beauty of life in the slow lane.

13

WILD BEACHES

1 HORSEY GAP AND WINDMILL

Remote NT beach, with four miles of dunes and heath, between Winterton and Waxham. This vast expanse of dune and sand nurtures the Broads' only community of seals.

→ ½ mile N of Horsey (NR29 4AD) turn R at sharp L bend down unmarked track to car park. Camping at Walnut Farm (NR12 0EG, 01692 598217) or beach-side Waxham Sands (NR29 4EJ, 01692 598325) just beyond. Climb Horsey Windpump (NR29 4EF, £3.00 entry) for great views.

5 mins, 52.7593, 1.6534

2 NORTH GAP, ECCLES

Dunes, bays and sandy tombolos that reach out to artificial rock islands in the sea.

→ From Lessingham (NR12 0DJ) take road on bend signed Eccles, then after 1 mile take third L, signed North Gap (very limited parking at end). Often jet-skis at Sea Palling further S.

2 mins, 52.8037, 1.5786

3 WAXHAM AND SEA PALLING

Historic Great Barn with excellent café. Pretty sandy lane leads through dunes to the beach.

→ 3 miles N of Horsey NR12 0DZ (visit Great Barn, NR12 0EE, 01692 598824 on the way). Adjacent Sea Palling is much busier (jet-skis) with offshore rock reefs and artificial coves for swimming.

5 mins, 52.7801, 1.6203

CANOEING

4 RIVER BURE CANOEING

Several drop-off points on the Bure, including Buxton, Coltishall, Wroxham, Horning, S Walsham.

→ Norwich Rd, Wroxham, NR12 8RX, 0845 4969177 or 01603 783777. Thecanoeman.com

52.7115, 1.4074

5 RIVER ANT CANOEING, WAYFORD BR

A classic river, busy downstream to Barton Broad, but very quiet upstream.

→ Staithe Cottage, Wayford Bridge, NR12 9LN, 01692 582457. Bankboats.co.uk

52.77036, 1.47910

RIVERS & BROADS

6 MENDHAM, R WAVENEY

Rather wild and wonderful, meandering stretch of the mid-Waveney – warm and not too deep. Otters, kingfishers, and overhanging willows.

→ From Mendham road bridge (IP20 0NH) walk downstream on left bank (fishing path) for 200m to pool. Or upstream through meadows to wild, hidden reedy pools (bear L on footpath from church in Mendham and ½ mile to reach the river).

10 mins, 52.3934, 1.3307

7 HOMERSFIELD, R WAVENEY

Secluded river dip with swing.

→ 2 miles N of Mendham (IP20 0NH) on a tiny lane (Regional Cycle Route 40) find footpath on L after IP20 0NS, just before Valley Farm on R at fork.

2 mins, 52.4129, 1.3605

8 OUTNEY COMMON, R WAVENEY

Ancient common land, popular for canoeing and swimming.

→ Turn off A143 onto B1332 at the roundabout signed Ditchingham and find footpath/track immediately on L (parking at Duke of York, NR35 2JL, 01986 895558). Follow path through woods, then over bridge. Bear R along river bank to large pool with willows and sandy bottom, plus rope swing

(500m). Or keep exploring upstream. Canoe hire from Outney Meadow Caravan Park (NR35 1HG, 01986 892338).

10 mins, 52.466, 1.4325

9 BUNGAY, R WAVENEY

Lovely riverbanks and meadows in backwaters of this alternative little town. Many independent cafés and shops.

➔ From Outney Common (see above) cross roundabout onto Bridge Street, then first take R after bridge (Falcon Lane, NR35 2JG). Also try swimming at the Locks Inn riverside music pub downstream at remote Geldeston (NR34 0HS for satnav, 01508 518414).

5 mins, 52.4572, 1.4413

10 RIVER ANT, HOW HILL

Classic but busy Broads river with three windmills and a boarding point for Barton Broad electric boat trips. Tea rooms and gardens at How Hill.

➔ Signed How Hill from A1062 before Ludham from W. Find car park (NR29 5PG) and then follow footpath down to river. Swimmers head up or downstream a little way to avoid congestion at the boathouse.

5 mins, 52.7178, 1.5083

11 BLICKLING MILL, R BURE

Lovely clear pool and chute below mill, with paddling and a deeper section where the water rushes out from under the arches. Interesting pyramid mausoleum in nearby Blickling estate woods.

➔ On tiny lanes (NR11 6PX) between Itteringham and Ingworth, ½ mile N of NT car park on the NW edge of the Blickling estate, from which you can also follow woodland walk E to the mausoleum 52.8193, 1.2135.

20 mins, 52.8279, 1.2099

12 BUXTON MILL POOL, R BURE

A huge mill pool with a strong race, right by the road. More secluded upstream.

➔ Look for a large white mill building (NR10 5JE) just outside Buxton on the road to Lamas. Upstream footpath is on the river's R bank, accessed via front of mill. Also on the Bure Valley Railway from Wroxham.

5 mins, 52.7566, 1.3144

13 COLTISHALL/HORSTEAD, R BURE

This is a quiet and idyllic stretch of the Bure with fabulous river swimming, upstream of all the pleasure boats.

➔ Start at the river bridge in Coltishall (NR12

9

7AA) and explore upstream, up to 2 miles to the bridge at Little Hautbois (NR12 7JR). There's also a large mill pond and grassy area 200m downstream of Coltishall bridge (Horstead Mill, NR12 7AT). Look out for the ruins of St Theobald's (see listing) though not easily accessible from river path.

10 mins, 52.7313, 1.3478 🏛️✝️🚶🏊‍♂️

14 SALHOUSE BROAD, WOODBASTWICK

One of the few Broads lakes you can easily swim in, with beachy area and canoe hire.

→ Car park on N side of road ½ mile W of the Fur and Feathers (NR13 6HQ, 01603 720003) in Woodbastwick. Pretty walk from carpark and WC.

15 mins, 52.6893, 1.4288 🚣🏊‍♂️

15 ROCKLAND BROAD, R YARE

Broad and river swims on the less touristy Yare river. Watch out for boats.

→ From the New Inn (NR14 7HP, 01508 538211) near Rockland St Mary, walk on footpath NE to the broad. Footpath along the River Yare leads to the Beauchamp Arms (NR14 6DH, 01508 480247).

10 mins, 52.59209, 1.44606 🐄🏊‍♂️

16 WEAVER'S WAY, R THURNE

Swim from the reeds with windmills on the skyline at this wide, wild and iconic stretch of the Broads.

→ Thurne is signed off the B1152 about halfway between Acle and Martham/Potter Heigham. Head for The Staithe (NR29 3BU) opposite the Lion Inn (NR29 3AP, 01692 670796). Walk down to the main river then head upstream/N for 10 mins and enter the river through the reeds (watch for boats). Camping at Clippesby Hall (NR29 3BL, 01493 367800) and Bureside (NR29 3BW, 01493 369233).

10 mins, 52.6897, 1.5488 🏊‍♂️🚣🏕️

SACRED & RUINED

17 ST THEOBALD'S

Pilgrims once flocked to see the image of St Theobald at this rugged, round-towered, 11th-century church. Beautiful wild flowers.

→ From Coltishall (NR12 7AA) head N, signed 'Byway to Lt Hautbois'. After ½ mile, opposite fishpond on R, find kissing gate on L and follow track to the church. NB 100m before the church a track leads to the remains of a 13th-century castle with intricate moat remains.

2 mins, 52.7342, 1.3486 🏛️✝️

6

10

18 ST MARTIN'S RUIN

Set at a junction of sunken lanes, beside the newer church of St Mary's, this roofless ruin has recently been cleared of ivy and elder by volunteers.

→ From All Saints church in Shotesham (NR15 1YJ), follow Roger's Ln SW, dir Saxlingham. Take second R for Stoke Holy Cross (Hawes Green). Where road bends sharp R, find ruin in trees on the corner (NR15 1UW).

2 mins, 52.5401, 1.2992 ✝ ▣

19 ST SAVIOUR'S RUIN

Atmospheric, overgrown Norman church, set on a mound. Functioning for seven centuries and still used for burials. Naturalist Ted Ellis, who created Surlingham's world-class nature reserve a mile to the NE, lies here.

→ From St Mary's church in Surlingham (NR14 7DF), follow the footpath L round the church. Continue through woodland to the ruin. Nearby, The Ferry House (NR14 7AR, 01508 538659) is a friendly place for a drink by the R Yare.

5 mins, 52.6094, 1.4073 ▣ ✝ ⛰

20 ST BENET'S ABBEY, R BURE

Impressive riverside ruin on classic Broads stretch. Hidden away in the depths of Broadland, away from roads, towns and phone reception, this Anglo-Saxon monastery was abandoned in the 1530s.

→ Heading into Ludham, turn R off A1062 just after Ludham Bridge (Dog Inn, NR29 5NY, 01692 630321). Then turn R after ½ mile down track, to road end and parking.

5 mins, 52.6863, 1.5251 ▣✝🚶⛵⛰

21 BURGH CASTLE ROMAN FORT

A spectacular and well-preserved ancient monument, once one of a chain of forts along the Saxon Shore. Stands elevated above the Broads with majestic views over the rivers Yare and Waveney.

→ Clearly signed from Church Ln, Burgh Castle (NR31 9QB). Or walk here from Gt Yarmouth along the Angles Way (4 miles).

3 mins, 52.5825, 1.6522 ▣🔍B

22 ST HELEN'S TOWER, RANWORTH

Climb 89 steps inside the 100ft church tower, ascend the two ladders and open the trap door to the roof for panoramic views.

→ Panxworth Church Rd, Ranworth, NR13 6HS. Approx 700m W of The Maltsters pub (NR13 6AB, 01603 270900).

5 mins, 52.6792, 1.4841 ✝

24

WOODLAND & WILDLIFE

23 GRANDPARENT OAK, BACTON WOOD

Sitting beside a path in mature woodland, this gnarled sessile oak is thought to be more than 200 years old. Bacton Wood has lots of smaller intriguing trails.

→ From Edingthorpe village (NR28 9TJ), follow sign for 'N Walsham via quiet lanes' ½ mile to crossroads, then straight on ½ mile for Bacton Wood Picnic Area (NR28 9UE). The red and yellow trail leads past the oak (oak is approx ½ mile from car park).

10 mins, 52.8240, 1.4292 ⛲

24 SISLAND CARR, BLUEBELLS

Visit this mixed woodland and wet meadow site in May for one of the UK's most magnificent bluebell displays.

→ From A146 at Loddon, turn on to Mundham Rd, signed for Mundham and Sisland. After 450m take single lane rd R to Sisland. Fork R at redbrick house 400m, and follow track 600m to the wood.

10 mins, 52.5400, 1.4571 ⛲🏕🚣

25 ROOK ROOST, BUCKENHAM CARRS

Coming in to roost just after sunset, up to 80,000 rooks blacken the skies in a dramatic swirl on wintery evenings (Oct–March). The phenomenon was noted in the Domesday Book. Clear skies and full moons give the best views, and the sound of the rooks can be heard for miles around across the River Yare.

→ From Buckenham station, walk N up Station Rd to the copse on the L with small brick shelter beneath ancient willows (NR13 4HW). This makes a good viewing spot, although you can see and hear the birds from anywhere nearby.

5 mins, 52.5995, 1.4717 🏠🚣

SLOW FOOD

26 TRULY LOCAL, STALHAM

Everything sourced from within a 35-mile radius, including veg, meats, smoked fish and hand-brewed beer.

→ 44 High Street, Stalham, NR12 9AS, 01692 582438.

52.7721, 1.5134 🍴

27 THE WALPOLE ARMS, ITTERINGHAM

Village pub with award-winning seasonal menu chalked-up daily. Cromer crabs, Morston mussels and Gunton Estate venison.

23

16

→ The Common, Itteringham, NR11 7AR, 01263 587258. Village also has a community shop and café (NR11 7AF).
52.8295, 1.1866 🍴

28 BARN CAFE, WAXHAM
Restored 1580s barn that's one of England's oldest. Marvel at the ancient flint walls, oak beams and thatch, while filling your face with cake or ploughman's. Open April–November.
→ Coast Road, Waxham, NR12 0EE, 01692 598824.
52.7779, 1.6150

29 PRETTY CORNER TEA GARDENS
Originally a 1920s woodland pavilion, this café and tea garden serves home-made lunches and cakes, displays local artwork and sells Norfolk produce. The adjacent woods have bats, bullfinches, buzzards and more.
→ Upper Sheringham, Norfolk NR26 8TW, 01263 822766.
52.9237, 1.2065 🍴

30 FORAGING WITH THE CANOE MAN
Collect mussels at low tide, catch Cromer crabs or go fungi foraging. Squelch across the mud to pluck a few fronds of samphire.
→ Norwich Rd, Wroxham, NR12 8RX, 0845 4969177 or 01603 783777. Thecanoeman.com
52.7116, 1.4072 🍴🛶

31 GELDESTON LOCKS INN
Isolated, traditional riverside pub overlooking marshland on banks of the Waveney. Simple, locally sourced menu, regular music nights.
→ Locks Ln, Geldeston, NR34 0HS for satnav, 01508 518414 Best reached by river (free overnight mooring) or bicycle (nr Route 30).
52.4638, 1.5168 🍴

32 DUKE'S HEAD, SOMERLEYTON
Redbrick pub with Waveney River views. Menu largely sourced from the Somerleyton Estate farm. Tranquil setting.
→ Slug's Lane, Somerleyton, NR32 5QR, 01502 730281.
52.5157, 1.6517 🍴

33 THE FUR & FEATHER, WOODBASTWICK
Thatched rural pub on village edge. Serves ale from Woodforde's brewery, next door (tours offered 01603 720353). Menu includes Norfolk seafood and ale-infused dishes.
→ Woodbastwick, NR13 6HQ, 01603 720003.
52.6828, 1.4425 🍴

34 SARACEN'S HEAD, WOLTERTON
Remote country inn, surrounded by fields. Log fires, B&B rooms and outside seating in old stable yard. Focus on fresh, seasonal and local. The magnificent Wolterton Hall with ruined church tower (NR11 7BB, 01263 584175) is nearby and open all year for walks.
→ Wolterton, Near Erpingham, NR11 7LZ, 01263 768909.
52.8442, 1.2222 🍴

35 GUNTON ARMS, THORPE MARKET
Grand, thousand-acre deer park with country pub and rustic restaurant. Own venison served, some meals cooked on an open fire, antlers on the wall in the Elk Room.
→ Cromer Road, Thorpe Market, NR11 8TZ, 01263 832010.
52.8582, 1.3329 🍴

CAMP & SLEEP

36 WHITLINGHAM BROAD CAMPSITE
Set on an 80-acre country park, with spacious pitches and one car-free field. Glamping and on-site shop.
→ Whitlingham Lane, NR14 8TR, 07794 401591.
52.6214, 1.3356 ⛺

37 OVERSTRAND CAMPSITE, OVERSTRAND
Small, tent-only site on a cliff-top, with easy beach access. Ten pre-erected tents and 45 unmarked pitches.
→ Beach Close, Overstrand, NR27 0PJ, 0333 4561221.
52.9201, 1.3400

38 WARDLEY HILL, KIRBY CANE
Simple, car-free site with long grasses, old oaks and streams creating a wilderness feel. Compost loos and campfires.
→ Wardley Hill Road, Kirby Cane, NR35 2PQ, 07733 306543.
52.4849, 1.4775 ⛺🏕

39 TOP FARM, MARSHAM
Isolated farm on an unmarked track, with elevated campsite near woodland. Shepherd's hut and eco bunkhouse also offered. BBQs and fire-pits supplied.
→ Kittles Lane, Marsham, NR10 5QF, 01263 733962.
52.7724, 1.2327 ⛺

40 MUNTJAC MEADOW AT DEER'S GLADE
Deer's Glade is open year-round and has a natural kids play area. The secluded, tent-

only Muntjac Meadow area hosts communal campfires most evenings and is open for a few weeks each summer only.

→ Whitepost Road, Hanworth, NR11 7HN, 01263 768633.
52.8549, 1.2916 🐕🔥

41 MANOR FARM, EAST RUNTON
Elevated and beautifully undulating site with woodland and sea views. Set on a working farm, accessed via a track.

→ Manor Farm, East Runton, NR27 9PR, 01263 512858.
52.9305, 1.2686 🐕

42 BURLINGHAM YURT
Set in Burlingham Hall's seven-acre garden, with 450-year-old sweet chestnuts. Wood burner, solar lighting, compost loo, shepherd's hut bathroom and stargazing hole.

→ Burlingham Hall, North Burlingham, NR13 4SZ, 01603 270455.
52.6434, 1.4919 🏡🎏

43 THE OLD VICARAGE CAMPSITE
Set on a working farm, this simple, tent-only site has no formal pitches in its car-free meadow. Wooden shower blocks, compost loos and free marshmallows for unique tents!

→ Moulton St Mary, NR13 3NH, 07775 871093.
52.6101, 1.5421

44 NORFOLK YURT HOLIDAY
Four-person yurts, set in a pretty paddock. Log burning stove, free logs, cooking facilities and BBQ.

→ Bridge House, Sea Palling Road, NR12 0TS. 01692 582463.
52.7828, 1.5740 🔥🍃

45 LAZY SHAMAN, BRISTON
Simple woodland retreat with six-person tipi. Opportunity to help out with forest management. BBQs, campfires and compost loos. Larger groups can bring additional tents.

→ Craymere Road, NR24 2LS, 01603 873290.
52.8375, 1.0564 🏔️🔥

46 HOW HILL WINDMILL
Converted grain mill set in How Hill National NR. Bring binoculars to spot barn owls and the ruins of St Benet's Abbey from the windows. Garden, BBQ, own mooring on River Ant.

→ How Hill, Ludham, NR29 5PG, 01692 678575.
52.7173, 1.5127 🍃

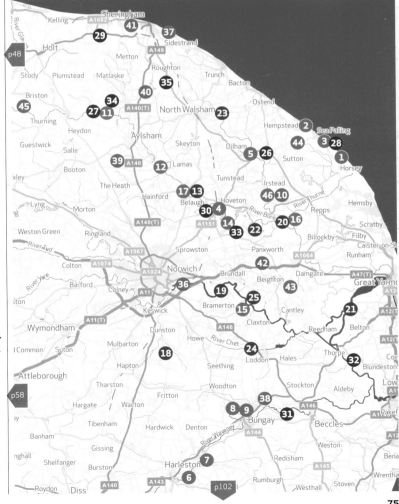

75

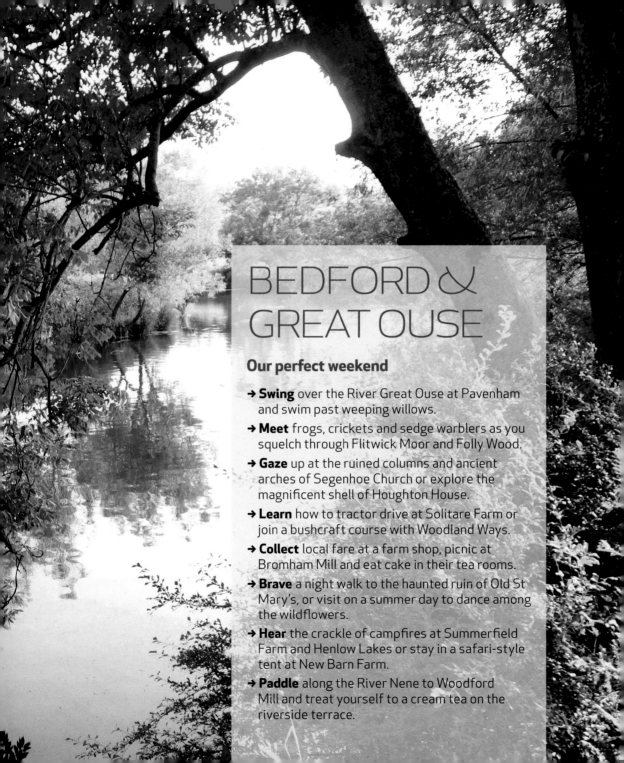

BEDFORD & GREAT OUSE

Our perfect weekend

→ **Swing** over the River Great Ouse at Pavenham and swim past weeping willows.

→ **Meet** frogs, crickets and sedge warblers as you squelch through Flitwick Moor and Folly Wood.

→ **Gaze** up at the ruined columns and ancient arches of Segenhoe Church or explore the magnificent shell of Houghton House.

→ **Learn** how to tractor drive at Solitare Farm or join a bushcraft course with Woodland Ways.

→ **Collect** local fare at a farm shop, picnic at Bromham Mill and eat cake in their tea rooms.

→ **Brave** a night walk to the haunted ruin of Old St Mary's, or visit on a summer day to dance among the wildflowers.

→ **Hear** the crackle of campfires at Summerfield Farm and Henlow Lakes or stay in a safari-style tent at New Barn Farm.

→ **Paddle** along the River Nene to Woodford Mill and treat yourself to a cream tea on the riverside terrace.

Running almost in parallel, the River Nene and Great Ouse strike diagonally across the claylands of Bedfordshire and Northamptonshire, creating two wonderful watery worlds. Dive off reed-flanked banks, paddle past forgotten mills and spy herons from peaceful hides.

Navigable along their lengths, the locks and mills along these two waterways give a glimpse into a lost world where lives and livelihoods were dependent on the river. Today, the converted grain mills at Woodford and Bromham have rustic waterside tea rooms serving delicious home-made cakes, while the mill at Great Doddington provides historic accommodation on a private River Nene island.

The waterways themselves make for exciting exploration by boat, and the River Great Ouse is particularly good for secluded swims – try the quiet waters near Felmersham and the bucolic loop near Pavenham where you can rope-swing over willow-fringed waters. Surrounding the rivers are wide floodplains, pitted with pools and wildlife-rich gravel pits.

The smallest shire in the South East, Bedfordshire's ancient woodlands were some of the first to be cleared by Neolithic farmers, who tilled the rich soils. By the 19th century this was a hub for wool and straw hat-making. Today, three quarters of the county is agricultural and any remaining ancient trees merely pepper the plains and crown any hilltops too steep to farm. The 350-year-old oak on Ickwell cricket ground is cherished by locals and, when a storm damaged a branch on 1995, local craftsmen turned the fallen wood into two village seats.

Between the Ouse and Nene stretch the soils of the Bedfordshire Plains, with the elevation of the Greensand Ridge giving distant views across rolling fields, pretty villages and country estates – scenes that were familiar to Henry VIII, who regularly visited to hunt or discuss affairs of state with his court. Slicing across the county, this escarpment has quiet footpaths to wander, peaceful places to smooth out a picnic rug, and ancient bluebell forests such as Swinehead and Spanoak to explore.

5

RIVERS & LAKES

1 SUMMER LEYS, WELLINGBOROUGH

Explore this network of wild gravel lakes along the R Nene, or take a dip in the river.

→ Find dead-end road a mile W of Wollaston, off the Hardwater Rd. There are wild lakes on R of the road or continue up to Nene river bridge ½ mile. Walk L 200m to Summer Leys lake shore and river banks. Or explore R to a smaller lake and another larger lake beyond (under pylons).

5 mins, 52.2677, -0.7007 🅿🐕🏊

2 STANWICK LAKES, R NENE

Another network of lake gravel pits (dug to build Wellingborough) with a cycle trail along old railway. Some used for fishing so continue on to the R Nene and footbridge.

→ Well-signed car park and visitor centre (NN9 6GY) off A45 Stanwick roundabout, 10 miles E of Wellingborough. Bear N through lake to find white footbridge over river.

20 mins, 52.3406, -0.5812 🅿

3 PASSENHAM, GREAT OUSE

Pretty riverside picnic area with slipway to clean waters on the upstream NW edge of Milton Keynes.

→ Between Claverton and Stony Stratford off A5 (MK19 6EW). Or from A422, go through Passenham village and turn L.

1 min, 52.0497, -0.8527 🏊🚣🏊

4 HAVESHAM RUIN, GREAT OUSE

A ruined riverside church in a quiet area of lakes on the N edge of Milton Keynes.

→ Turn L off Wolverton Rd at the canal bridge/ Black Horse Inn (MK14 5AJ, 01908 398461), a mile E of Wolverton station (or walk/cycle from the station, 2 miles). Follow track along canal, then into open fields, to find St Peter's ruin after ½ mile on L and river behind. Other lakes to L.

15 mins, 52.0776, -0.7831 🚣🏊🎣🍴🏕⛺🏊

5 OLNEY, GREAT OUSE

Shingle beach and beautiful views back to Olney church.

→ Follow the footpath behind St Peter and Paul church (MK46 4AD, Church St) and continue 200m to large beach. Continue on footpath along the river all the way to Clifton Reynes. Or park at Olney football club (MK46 4DW) on East Street - beach at end of playing fields.

5 mins, 52.1483, -0.6965 🚶🏊

6 PAVENHAM, GREAT OUSE

A wonderfully bucolic loop of the Great Ouse with willows, a deep swim and rope swings.

→ Pass the Cock pub (MK43 7NJ, 01234 822834), then L down Mill Lane and follow footpath down to the river. You can continue downstream all the way to Park End church.

10 mins, 52.1868, -0.5570 ⛺🍴🏕🏊

7 FELMERSHAM, GREAT OUSE

Easy family beach by bridge or numerous swim spots downstream for a longer swim. Very easy access for canoes.

→ Access from benches and bridge in village (Hunts Lane, MK43 7JP), or follow bridleway 300m downstream on opposite bank.

1 min, 52.2123, -0.5485 🏊🚣🏊

8 OAKLEY, GREAT OUSE

A wide, peaceful stretch of the river, deep above the weir.

→ South of Oakley (MK43 7RU) 200m, past church (Church Lane) to find path on R after bridge.

5 mins, 52.1654, -0.5316 🏊

12

17

14

9 OFFORD CLUNY, GREAT OUSE

A lovely downstream stretch of the river Ouse with many weir pools, or head upstream to bathe opposite the church.

→ Between Buckden Marina (PE19 5QS) and the narrow bridge (Station Lane), find footpath. Pass weir pool on L (swim if no fishermen) or continue, cross footbridge, and head upstream to opposite the church, ½ mile.

10 mins, 52.2874, -0.2213 🏊🏖️

10 GRAFHAM WATER

A secluded pebble beach on far side of large, warm lake. Be discreet.

→ Follow footpath from behind church in Grafham village to shore. From here explore R along wooded NE shore and return by Hill Farm, or continue another mile to picnic spot. Blue-green algae risk. Avoid sailing boats.

5 mins 52.3033, -0.3028 ❓🏖️

11 LIDLINGTON LAKE

Huge, exposed, easy-access lake, surrounded by open fields. Some sailing.

→ On lanes 1 mile NW of Lidlington village and station.

2 mins, 52.0484, -0.5677 🚴⛺🏊

RUINS & SACRED

12 SEGENHOE RUINED CHURCH

Roofless 11th-century ruin on a back road. Enter through the north porch to appreciate the elaborate columns and arches. Lots of nooks and crannies to explore. Several waymarked walks lead past.

→ Follow Eversholt Rd SE out of Ridgmont village, turn L onto Segenhoe Manor Road. Church tower visible on R from the road. Easy access through the gate.

2 mins, 52.0118, -0.5717 ✝️🖼️

13 ST MARY'S RUINED CHURCH, CLOPHILL

Eerie 650-year-old ruin that was once a place of witches' gatherings and satanic rituals. Wildflower-filled graveyard at the crest of the Greensand Ridge. Popular with ghost-hunters.

→ Head N out of Clophill (MK45 4BL) on Great Lane (signed Haynes) and find footpath after ½ mile on R.

5 mins, 52.0373, -0.4095 ✝️🖼️

14 HOUGHTON HOUSE, RUINED MANOR

Dramatic ruined 17th-century mansion combines Jacobean and Classical styles and has two Italianate loggias. Said to have been

the inspiration for House Beautiful in John Bunyan's *Pilgrim's Progress*.

→ N on B530 from Ampthill outskirts, follow signs and track to parking area (MK45 2EZ). Signed paths lead from here. House clearly visible. King's Wood ancient woodland is a 10-minute walk from here. Free.

10 mins, 52.0443, -0.4855 🖼️📍

ANCIENT WOODS & TREES

15 ICKWELL ANCIENT OAK TREE

This famous 350-year old oak stands in the 175-year-old cricket ground. Three local seats were made from a fallen branch.

→ Ickwell Cricket Club, SG18 9EF. Oak stands isolated, directly opposite the clubhouse. The Crown (SG18 9AA, 01767 627337) has low beams and seasonal food.

1 mins, 52.0957, -0.3223 📍🏠

16 KING'S WOOD, HOUGHTON CONQUEST

This SSSI woodland and meadow has spring bluebells, lily-of-the-valley, primroses, cowslips and devil's-bit scabious, plus white admiral and purple emperor butterflies. An anti-highwayman trench and Watling Street Roman road skirt the northern edge.

→ Continue on the Marston Vale Trail from Houghton House (see listing) another mile. Or ½ mile S from Houghton Conquest (MK45 3LB, Rectory Lane).

10 mins, 52.0491, -0.4755 📍🚶🖼️♿

17 BRAMPTON WOOD

One of the region's largest ancient woodlands and the best place for dormice. Also find great crested newts in the ponds, wild pear blossom and bluebells in spring. Rare butterflies and fabulous autumn fungi.

→ Follow Brampton Rd E out of Grafham village (PE28 0UR). Continue for 1½ miles after Village Hall to signed parking area on L.

5 mins, 52.3134, -0.2640 📍🚶

WILDLIFE & MEADOWS

18 SWINESHEAD & SPANOAK WOODS

Two of England's best bluebell woods, connected by a wildlife corridor. Woodpeckers are abundant – listen for the drumming of the great spotted and the laughter of the green. Ponds and rivulets sit beneath native oaks and ashes.

→ From Swineshead, turn N off High St (MK44 2AA) onto Sandye Ln. Walk to end of lane and follow track to the woods.

5 mins, 52.2876, -0.4440 📍🚶♿

19 FLITWICK MOOR AND FOLLY WOOD

Unique mosaic of wet woods, meadows and reedbeds, untouched by modern farming. Meet frogs and toads in spring, or sedge warblers and crickets in summer.

→ Head S off A507 towards Flitwick, signed off Flitwick/Maulden roundabout for Flitwick Ind Estates. Park opposite Gardener's Close, on left just before Jewson (MK45 5BT) and follow track down to the woods.

3 mins, 52.0059, -0.4841 🚶🖼️

20 EDIBLE ORNAMENTALS CHILLI FARM

PYO chillies, eat flowers in The Edible Kitchen café, join a chilli-tasting tour or stock up in the shop. Open Fri-Sun 10–4pm.

→ Roxton Rd, Chawston MK44 3BL, 01480 405663. Also signed as Cherwood Nursery.
52.1929, -0.3141 🍴🏪

21 SCALD END FARM SHOP

Café and large shop on a working farm. Fill a picnic basket with bread, meats and local wine, or sip coffee with farm views. Accommodation available in 18th-century barns. Open Thurs–Sun.

→ Mill Road, Thurleigh, MK44 2DP, 01234 772688.
52.2053, -0.4662 🍴🏪

22 SOLITAIRE FARM MEATS AND VEG

Own meats sold from a makeshift stall, plus veg and preserves. Tractor-driving and pig-keeping courses offered. Shop open 8–8 daily; shout if no-one's about. Home to England's oldest herd of Large White pigs.

→ Drove Road, Gamlingay, SG19 3NY, 01767 650884.
52.1651, -0.1976 🏪

23 WOODVIEW FARMSHOP AND CAFÉ

Try produce from the farm's sheep, chickens and Gloucester Old Spots, or buy fruit, veg and other Bedfordshire produce. Home-made cakes in cafe.

→ Mill Hill, Gamlingay, SG19 3LW, 01767 650200.
52.1436, -0.1959 🏪

24 WORLD OF BUSHCRAFT CENTRE

Stocks bushcraft equipment, open daily and runs regular Wednesday workshops on game preparation, net-making and more.

→ Priory Marina, Barkers Lane, Bedford, MK41 9DJ, 01234 351006.
52.1323, -0.4366 🛶

25 WOODFORD MILL TEA ROOMS

Working River Nene watermill and café. Boat hire and accommodation in the original mill.

→ Ringstead, NN14 4DU, 01933 623731.
52.3666, -0.5715 🛶🏠🍴

26 WOBURN COUNTRY FOODS

Excellent shop selling local and ethical goods - Woburn Abbey venison, Ouse Valley lamb, ales, dairy, veg and pickles. Open Tues–Sat.

→ Haynes West End, MK45 3RA, 01234 740300. Signed down a gravel track off London Lane.
52.0519, -0.4501 🏪

27 BROMHAM MILL CAFÉ

Attractive working mill with rustic café, gallery and home-made cakes. Water meadows with a picnic field and swimming.

→ Bridge End, Bromham, MK43 8LP. One mile from Bedford at the west end of Bromham Bridge, signposted 'watermill'. Weekends only.
52.1451, -0.5247 🛶🏊

28 JOHN O'GAUNT INN, SUTTON

Historic beamed pub with traditional games near the 14th-century Packhorse Bridge. Menu features game, meat and veg from nearby farms.

→ 30 High Street, Sutton, SG19 2NE, 01767 260377.
52.1112, -0.2161 🍺🍴

29 PARKSIDE FARM SHOP, BROOM

Lovely litte shop. Pull up in the drive and call if no-one's about. Nearby in the village, The Cock (SG18 0JE 01767 314411), serves beers direct from the tap room, while the café at Jordan's Mill (SG18 9JY) is less than a mile.

→ Southill Rd, SG18 9NN, 07803 271326.
52.0712, -0.2907 🏪

30 BEDFORD ARMS, SOULDROP

Traditional country pub with inglenook fireplace and low beams. Games room has skittles and shove-ha'penny, with petanque in the garden. Local ales and cider.

→ 6 High St., MK44 1EY, 01234 781384.
52.2447, -0.5571 🍺

31 THE PHEASANT, KEYSTONE

Thatched inn with oak beams and open fires, set in a farming hamlet. Come for Nene Valley bitter and home-made crisps, or try the local game. Veg, salad and herbs grown in the pub garden.

→ Keyston, Huntingdon, PE28 0RE, 01832 710241.
52.3654, -0.4699 🍺

32 THE BELL, ODELL

The large garden backs onto the Ouse at this thatched village pub. Low beams and open fires, with a menu that features pork from Whipsnade, Woburn lamb and venison.

→ Horsefair Lane, Odell, MK43 7AU, 01234 720254.
52.2094, -0.5885 🍺🍴🛶

33 SOUTHILL VILLAGE TEA ROOM

A real gem, the village stores stocks local produce and its quaint café has a lovely garden. Warm cheese scones and cake.

➜ 55 High Street, Southill, SG18 9JB, 01462 817430.
52.0649, -0.3166 🍴

CAMP & STAY

34 THE PADDOCK, OUTFIELDS FARM

Tranquil camping paddock almost a mile from the nearest road. Communal BBQ, gazebo area and farm shop. B&B also.

➜ Graze Hill Lane, Ravensden, MK44 2SA, 07764 565560.
52.1855, -0.4730

35 NEW BARN FARM, CARLTON

Eight safari tents on a secluded farm that's visited by muntjac, owls and badgers. Home-made food in honesty shop, horses accommodated.

➜ The Causeway, Carlton, MK43 7LX, 01420 80804. featherdown.co.uk
52.1854, -0.5943

36 ST NEOTS CARAVANNING & CAMPING

Perfect wild swimming all along this Ouse-side 180-pitch site, or bring your rod for fishing. Set beside water meadows near the town of St Neots.

➜ Hardwick Rd, Eynesbury, PE19 2PR, 01480 474404.
52.2198, -0.2745 🏊📷

37 SUMMERFIELD FARM

Lovely farm site with campfires and no fixed pitches. Bordered by golden wheat and borage in summer. White Horse pub (PE28 0JP, 01480 860764) is an easy stroll away.

➜ 58 High St, Tilbrook, PE28 0JP, 0771 821722.
52.3084, -0.4188 🔥

38 AGDEN HILL FARM, AGDEN GREEN

Pitch up on this wildlife-rich farm. Summer butterflies and wildflowers or sloes and blackberries to gather in autumn. Wooden cabin and B&B available.

➜ Great Staughton, PE19 5EX, 01480 869424.
52.2870, -0.3495

39 THE OLD PIGGERY, HAYNES

Stay in this converted pig barn on a working arable farm set upon the Greensand Ridge in a wonderfully rural location.

➜ West Park Farm, Haynes, Beds MK45 3RD, 01234 742142.
52.0629, -0.4396 🛏

40 HARDWATER MILL

Former grain mill on a private River Nene island. Mentioned in the Domesday Book – Thomas Becket hid here in 1164.

➜ Hardwater Road, Great Doddington, NN29 7TD, 01933 276870.
52.2640, -0.7180 🏊🛏

41 WARREN HOUSE, KIMBOLTON

Unique and unaltered 18th-century, timber-framed house, built for Kimbolton Castle's rabbit keeper.

➜ 01628 825925, Landmarktrust.org.uk
52.3623, -0.3781 🛏

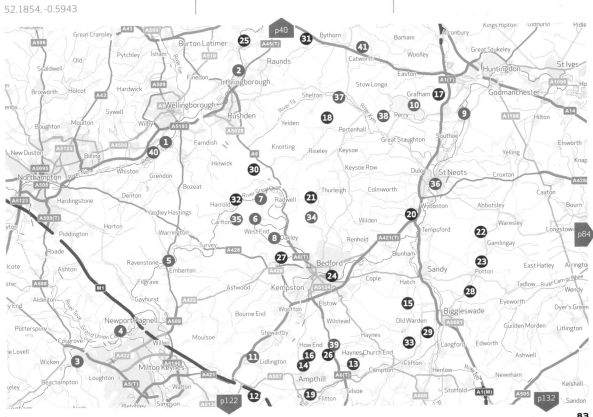

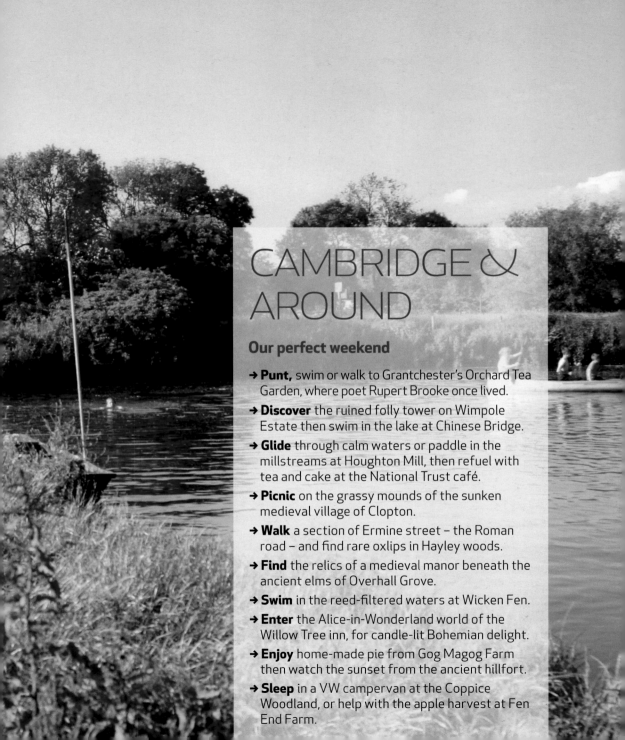

CAMBRIDGE & AROUND

Our perfect weekend

→ **Punt,** swim or walk to Grantchester's Orchard Tea Garden, where poet Rupert Brooke once lived.

→ **Discover** the ruined folly tower on Wimpole Estate then swim in the lake at Chinese Bridge.

→ **Glide** through calm waters or paddle in the millstreams at Houghton Mill, then refuel with tea and cake at the National Trust café.

→ **Picnic** on the grassy mounds of the sunken medieval village of Clopton.

→ **Walk** a section of Ermine street – the Roman road – and find rare oxlips in Hayley woods.

→ **Find** the relics of a medieval manor beneath the ancient elms of Overhall Grove.

→ **Swim** in the reed-filtered waters at Wicken Fen.

→ **Enter** the Alice-in-Wonderland world of the Willow Tree inn, for candle-lit Bohemian delight.

→ **Enjoy** home-made pie from Gog Magog Farm then watch the sunset from the ancient hillfort.

→ **Sleep** in a VW campervan at the Coppice Woodland, or help with the apple harvest at Fen End Farm.

The river Cam flows beside long grass meadows, dotted with picnic parties. Punts and canoes glide by, some heading downstream towards Cambridge's famous Backs, others heading upstream to the historic tea gardens in Grantchester. Every now and then you hear the clunk of wooden oars, the splash of punters cooling off or the giggles of carefree picnickers enjoying lazy afternoons.

On hot summer days it can seem like little has changed on this stretch of river since Edwardian times, when the charismatic graduate Rupert Brooke became a Grantchester resident in 1909 and commuted to and from Cambridge in his canoe. An age of relaxed elegance, Brooke and the young Bloomsbury Group, including Virgina Woolf, embodied a free-spirited outdoor lifestyle, taking long walks, sleeping under canvas, picnicking on the grass and skinny-dipping in the river. Their philosophy was for a simpler, gentler lifestyle, in tune with nature and underpinned by reciprocity and friendship.

Pancake-flat, Cambridgeshire makes for lazy exploration by boat, foot or bike, with gradient-free paths and gently flowing rivers, . Beyond the dreamy Cambridge fringe, chalky hills and golden fields roll south towards Bedford and Hertfordshire past meandering rivers and pockets of forest, such as the oxlip-rich woods of Hayley and Shadwell. This is an area of intriguing ruins and ancient remains, where the moongate at Gamlingay was built purely for appreciating the full moon, and the lost village of Clopton lies beneath a hillside, blanketed in turf.

Further west at Houghton and Hemingford Grey is one of the prettiest swimming sections of the River Great Ouse, with an old mill, beautiful churches and perfect picnic meadows. To the north are pepper-black fields and unbroken fens, where the reed-filtered waters near Setchel and Wicken Fens can be wonderfully pure and were once filled with juicy eels. Ely, which translates as 'island of eels' refers to this medieval past when eels were a delicacy and used as currency. Although it is no longer an island surrounded by steamy swamp, foggy mornings create an equivalent modern-day scene, with Ely cathedral, known as the 'Ship of the Fens,' rising above the mist. Appreciate it to best effect with a swim in the Ouse at Little Thetford.

5

RIVERS & LAKES

1 WICKEN FEN, UPWARE
Filtered and purified by the reed beds of the famous nature reserve, Wicken Lode is clear, clean and beautiful. Be silent.

→ Head for the Five Miles Inn in Upware near Wicken A1123 (CB7 5ZR, 01353 721654) with pleasant gardens along the River Cam (lots of river to explore along here). Turn R and after 200m take the footpath L by sluice/bridge leading to footbridge after 300m.

15 mins, 52.3033, 0.2613

2 BRAMPTON, GREAT OUSE
The river is wide and secluded with some beaches and diving spots.

→ Approaching Brampton from S on B1514, turn R down River Lane by Frosts Garden Centre (PE28 4NF). At bottom walk R upstream along riverbank.

2 mins, 52.3142, -0.2116

3 HOUGHTON MILL, GREAT OUSE
Wide meadows and calm, deep water make this a brilliant summer location in beautiful meadows. There are fun millstreams for paddling and a NT mill and café too, plus you can hire rowing boats.

→ The Mill is well signed from Houghton, on A1123 between Huntingdon and St Ives. Park at the Mill (PE28 2AZ, 01480 301494) and walk W down the path, beyond the caravan site, bearing R across the wooded mill streams to reach open riverbank. Or cross at the lock and explore the opposite bank (Hemingford Meadows), also accessible from Hemingford Abbots (PE28 9AR).

10 mins, 52.3282, -0.1171

4 NEEDINGWORTH/OVER, GREAT OUSE
The river flows through the empty meadow and lake landscape of Ouse Fen.

→ From Needingworth follow signs to The Pike & Eel (Overcote Lane, PE27 4TW, 01480 463336) then follow the path N (downstream) to find a place to dip. Or access from Over on opposite bank. Rope swing upstream.

20 mins, 52.3314, 0.0055

5 UPPER CUTS, SETCHEL FEN
In remote open countryside, the Great Ouse has shrunk as it meanders through bucolic countryside.

→ 3 miles N of Cottenham (B1049) park on track, R, just before bridge and bend, and take river footpath upstream to L, for up to 4 miles.

10 mins, 52.3215, 0.1631

6 LITTLE THETFORD, OUSE VALLEY WAY
Beautiful and wild, with 'Ship of the Fens' cathedral views to Ely.

→ Little Thetford is just S of Ely off A10. Head to level crossing, cross over and bear R down track, then follow river.

10 mins, 52.3570, 0.2537

7 GRANTCHESTER MEADOWS, R CAM
Over two miles of meadows and swimming from Sheep's Green down to the Orchard Tea Gardens in Grantchester. Deep banks make this good for diving, but it can be muddy! Some weeds but clean. Continue walk to Grantchester to find popular swimming hole next to the Orchard Tea Gardens.

→ From A603/Barton Rd take Grantchester St by lights and find footpath at bottom, L, heading to river and fallen tree 200m (Paradise Pool). Or continue on and park in the car park at bottom of Grantchester Meadows. There's a good pool within 150m on a bend, or explore riverbank 30 mins to Grantchester tea rooms (CB3 9ND). For a longer riverside walk, set out from the The Mill (CB2 1RX) at Sheep's Green in Cambridge.

5 mins, 52.1907, 0.1046

9

20

3

entrance and, 500m after, find gate on L (before SG8 0BU). Folly is 300m up hill, lake is below. Upper lake best for swimming, from next to the 'Chinese' bridge.
10 mins, 52.1504, -0.0502 🖼️⛵

11 HAYLEY WOOD AND ERMINE STREET

This SSSI is more than 700 years old and has one of the UK's largest spring oxlip populations. Also good for glow-worms and bats. From here, follow footpaths SW towards Ermine Street Roman road and East Hartley village, passing two moated sites en-route – the second has a wooden plank giving access to the raised and wooded interior.

→ Follow B1046 (CB23) from Little Gransden to Longstowe. Opposite water tower on L, follow footpath R into wood.
3 mins, 52.1662, -0.1087 🅿️🖼️🚶

12 MOONGATE, GAMLINGAY CINQUES

Created as a viewing aid to enhance the full moon, this 18th-century moon-gate stands by the edge of a field, the former grounds of Gamlingay Hall. Visit during a full moon to appreciate.

→ Heading W from Gamlingay on Drove Rd, pass Old Plough Farm (SG19 2HX). 200m further, after bungalow, find footpath on L. Follow along the field boundary for 200m.
2 mins, 52.1582, -0.2114 🖼️🌳

13 ALL SAINTS RUINED CHURCH TOWER

A ruined woodland tower pokes through the trees, part of the former village of Silverley and mentioned in the Domesday Book. The last request for a burial here was in 1564.

→ In a wooded area beside the B1063 between Ashley and Lidgate, opposite the turn-off for Upend/Kirtling. Visible from the road.
2 mins, 52.2137, 0.4930 ✝️🖼️❓

14 MUTLOW HILL, FLEAM DYKE

Large round barrow on Fleam Dyke, with Iron Age tumulus. Lovely views over arable Cambridgeshire.

→ Find Harcamlow Way footpath 100m E of Fulbourn church at CB21 5ES. Follow for 2 miles, to steps leading up Mutlow Hill (close to A11).
40 mins, 52.1660, 0.2599 🚶

15 HEYDONS DITCH

Saxon track running from Heydon to Fowlmere. Excavations unearthed the bones of headless Saxons. Legend says the ditch is haunted by warriors.

→ In Heydon village find driveway of 'Four

8 GREAT SHELFORD, R CAM

Clear river pool in the young Cam, with water lilies. Very good deli on the High Street for afterwards.

→ At far end of recreation ground. Entrance is almost opposite the deli (8a Woollards Lane, CB22 5LZ, 01223 846129).
5 mins, 52.1429, 0.1350 🏊🖼️🍴

9 WEST ROW, RIVER LARK

Head up or downstream for wild swimming. Two miles down is a popular site for traditional 'total immersion' baptisms, below Isleham, mentioned by Roger Deakin.

→ Follow the R bank paths from the Jude's Ferry pub on the road bridge (IP28 8PT, 01638 712277). Also try upstream at Temple Bridge, Icklingham (52.3280, 0.5776).
5 mins, 52.34556, 0.46101 🏊🖼️ⓘ🏕️

RUINED & ANCIENT

10 WIMPOLE FOLLY

Four-storey gothic tower and sham ruins from the 18th century, set in beautiful parkland with lake for a dip.

→ From Orwell (A603) follow signs for NT Wimpole Hall/Old Wimpole Church. Pass the

Winds' house (SG8 7QU) on Foulmere Rd. This becomes trackway, marked on OS maps as Harcamlow Way and Icknield Way Trail.
2 min, 52.0448, 0.0839 ⊡🚶

16 REMAINS OF OLD ST HELENS, COLNE

The ruined porch and overgrown graveyard are all that remains of this church, destroyed when the tower collapsed in 1895.

➔ From High Street, Colne, turn down Church Ln (PE28 3NE). Continue past houses. Ruin is in woodland on R.
5 mins, 52.3660, 0.0057 ⊡✝

17 CLOPTON DESERTED VILLAGE

Deserted in the 16th century, Clopton is now an extensive series of grassy lumps and bumps. Picnic on the high ground and look for the moat, church and roads.

➔ From East Hatley (SG19 3HU), head S towards B1042. After steep (10%) descent, find small car park on R, opposite the 'High St'. Follow Clopton Way footpath 400m to gate and info board.
5 mins, 52.1231, -0.0996 ⊡🚶

18 OVERHALL GROVE, MEDIEVAL REMAINS

The largest elm woodland in the county,

where a medieval manor once stood. Find the remains in the northern section, where badgers have dug up 11th-century pottery. Also look for ancient oaks and listen for songbirds.

➔ Footpath leads behind Church of All Saints, Knapwell, CB23 4NW.
1 min, 52.2503, -0.0399 📷⊡

19 WANDLEBURY HILLFORT & MAGOG

Highpoints which offer panoramic views over Cambridge, with no higher ground NW for 50 miles. Sledging can be good here.

Earthworks of hillfort and many trees.

➔ Signed Wandlebury off the A1307, 5 miles SE of Cambridge, after Gog Magog farm shop (CB22 3AD). Cross over the A1307 for Magog Down and Little Trees Hill tumulus viewpoint.
5 mins, 52.1544, 0.1736 📷

WILDLIFE WONDERS

20 LARK RISE FARM, SKYLARKS

Working farm that has been transformed from intensive farming to a landscape teeming with wildlife, including brown hares and the highest density of skylarks in the

county. Visit at dawn then head to Burwash Manor for breakfast (CB23 7EY).

→ Entering Barton on A603 from W, pass Haslingfield Rd on R and take next R, after 100m, down track (CB23 7AB, next to 47–49 Wimpole Rd) to fields.

5 mins, 52.1765, 0.0596

21 CHIPPENHAM FEN, MOTHS

Unusual raised fen with hay meadows, woodland and ponds. Wetland flowers include rare Cambridge milk parsley. Over 500 moth species.

→ From Tharp Arms, Chippenham (CB7 5PR) take Palace Rd dir Snailwell to Park Farm, on sharp L bend (52.2915, 0.4265). Follow footpath 600m along track to reserve (CB7 5QB).

7 mins, 52.2915, 0.4265

22 SHADWELL WOOD WILDFLOWERS

Oxlips, primroses, wood violets, orchids and bluebells are all found here.

→ From The Rose and Crown, Ashdon, (CB10 2HB), follow sign towards Saffron Walden. Pass track to Hall Farm on R, and take next R turn for Fallowden Ln. At end, follow footpath into woods on L.

1 min, 52.0474, 0.2905

SLOW FOOD

23 OLD FERRY BOAT INN, HOLYWELL FRONT

Claiming to be England's oldest pub, this thatched, whitewashed inn has an idyllic riverside setting next to rural footpaths and fens. Lovely garden. Food served.

→ Holywell Front, PE27 4TG, 01480 463227. 52.3173, -0.0315

24 SUNCLOSE FARM, MILTON

Soft fruits, asparagus and carrots sold, plus award-winning Alder Tree 'Fruit Cream Ices', farm's own honey, tomatoes and potatoes. Open daily May – late Sep.

→ Butt Lane, Milton CB24 6DQ, 01223 860522. Four-mile cycle from Cambridge. 52.2484, 0.1453

25 THE ORCHARD, TEA GARDEN

Home of Rupert Brooke and his summer visitors, Virginia Woolfe and Bloomsbury Group. Find a spot in the long grass beneath the fruit trees. Occasional outdoor Shakespeare and music performances in summer. River swimming adjacent.

→ 45–47 Mill Way, Grantchester, CB3 9ND, 01223 551125. 52.1771, 0.0959

26 THE HOLE IN THE WALL

Snug English inn run by Masterchef finalist. Focus is local and seasonal. Log fires, dark beams, rural village setting.

→ Primrose Farm Road, Little Wilbraham, CB21 5JY, 01223 812282. 52.2037, 0.2563

27 THE RED COW, CHRISHALL

Lovely pub with terracotta tiles and gnarled beams. Kitchen uses own veg and local game. Garden has views over cornfields and wildflower meadows.

→ High Street, Chrishall, SG8 8RN, 01763 838792. 52.0330, 0.1057

28 BUSHEL BOX FARM SHOP & COFFEES

Orchard fruits – apples, apricots, pears and plums – available within hours of being picked. Also asparagus, eggs and apple juice. Coffee shop uses locally roasted beans and serves own cakes.

→ 130 Station Road, Willingham, CB24 5HG, 01954 206015. 52.3033, 0.0526

29 GOG MAGOG HILLS FARM SHOP

Rustic barns with shop, cafe and outdoor 'shack' where you can bring the dog and sit undercover in your wellies, enjoying sausage rolls and hot chocolate.

→ Heath Farm, Shelford Bottom, CB22 3AD, 01223 248352. 52.1596, 0.1740

30 LA HOGUE FARM SHOP AND CAFE

Large shop and café. Supports over 100 local producers.

→ Chippenham, CB7 5PZ, 01638 751128. 52.2842, 0.4612

31 THREE TUNS, FEN DRAYTON

Olde-worlde village pub with heavy-set Tudor timbers, open fires and garden. Good grub tied to local producers. Find Fen Drayton RSPB reserve on village edge.

→ 75 High St, Great Abington, CB21 6AB, 01223 891467. 52.2960, -0.0379

32 THE WILLOW TREE, BOURN

Bohemian country pub with open-air theatre. Candle-lit rooms, open fires and country garden with a majestic willow. Local suppliers include Burwash Manor and Wimpole Hall.

→ 29 High Street, Bourn, CB23 2SQ, 01954 719775. 52.1906, -0.0627 🍴

33 THE ANCHOR INN, SUTTON GAULT

17th-century riverside inn, focusing on East Anglian ingredients. Canoe here or bream fish on the river. Four guest rooms.

→ Bury Lane, Sutton Gault, CB6 2BD, 01353 778537.
52.3962, 0.0982 🛏🍴

CAMP & SLEEP

34 THE COPPICE WOODLAND

VW camper van plus bell tent and wood-fired hot tub. Dining area cut into an alcove of trees, hammock, rustic football goals, streams and woodland. A self-sustaining eco-system, with BBQs and beekeeping.

→ 0117 204 7830 Canopyandstars.co.uk Guilden Gate, 86 North End, Bassingbourn, SG8 5PD, 01763 243960.
52.0843, -0.0607 🛶

35 LOVES LANE CAMPING, ASHWELL

Secluded spot, hosts a limited number of tents and caravans on its ¾ acre site.

→ Ashwell, Baldock SG7 5HZ, 01462 742382.
52.0429, -0.1735

36 FEN END FARM

Five-pitch orchard on organic farm, with gypsy wagon and yurt. Visit for sustainability courses and volunteer days, or help with the apple harvest in October.

→ Oxholme Drove, Cottenham, CB24 8UP, 07950 561787.
52.3123, 0.1281 🛶

37 BRAHAM FARM CAMPSITE, NR ELY

Farm campsite on a grassy lawn with views across the wheat fields to Ely Cathedral. Footpaths lead to Ely (2 miles) and River Great Ouse.

→ Little Thetford, CB6 3HL, 01353 662386.
52.3746, 0.2489

38 TREELANDER, ISLEHAM

Set in five acres of fenland, surrounded by wildlife and near the River Lark for fishing and walks. 45 min riverside walk to Isleham village.

→ 18 Prickwillow Road, Isleham, Ely, Cambs, CB7 5RG, 01353 687984.
52.3733, 0.3898

39 KARMA FARM

Eco-friendly camping, plus a yurt, tipi site and log cabin. Set on three acres of fenland countryside with a hide for wildlife viewing on the washes.

→ 8 Fen Bank, Isleham, Ely CB7 5SL, 07900 961217.
52.3577, 0.4132 🛶

40 STOKER'S COTTAGE

Simple 1840s cottage built to serve a fenland pumping station. Stands on the bank of the Old West River (Great Ouse), with lovely towpath walks.

→ Stretham, CB6 3LF. Landmarktrust.org.uk, 01628 825925.
52.3342, 0.2239 🛶

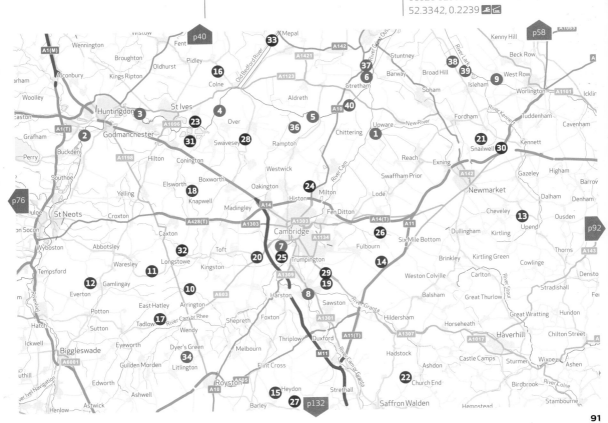

INLAND SUFFOLK

Our perfect weekend

→ **Discover** snake's-head fritillaries at Martins' Meadow, carpets of bluebells in Freston Wood and spectacular snowdrops in Priestly Wood.

→ **Hire** a canoe from Rushbanks Farm and paddle up the River Stour for a pint at The Anchor pub.

→ **Kick** back by the quay at the Butt & Oyster, and watch the boats of Pin Mill drift by.

→ **Find** the isolated folly of Belchamp Hall, or explore the remains of South Elmham Minster.

→ **Watch** for deer and hare at The Pheasant while your meal is home-smoked, plucked from the garden or drizzled with honey from the pub's own hives.

→ **Visit** Groton Wood at dawn to see hawfinch in the cherry trees, or at dusk for woodcocks.

→ **Cool** off in the river pool at Fen Bridge, in Constable's Dedham Vale.

→ **Join** foodies at Wyken Vineyard's and munch a griddled venison burger fresh from the estate.

→ **Explore** pretty Lavenham and visit the farmers' market for Suffolk cheese and wine.

A place of luxurious meadows and wildlife-rich woods, working mills and peaceful rivers, this is a deeply rural region of big skies, pretty villages and empty roads. To the south are the gentle waterways and cultivated uplands that inspired John Constable – the 19th-century landscape painter who captured the beauty of the Suffolk-Essex border on canvas.

At Dedham Vale, where the River Stour draws a line between the two counties, Willy Lott's cottage still sits by the river bank, just as Constable depicted it, the spire of Dedham church rising above the meadows, beneath a sky of purple-tinged clouds. As you explore this valley and head further north into Suffolk, pubs like the Butt & Oyster at Pin Mill and The Anchor at Nayland invite you to sit by the river and dip your toes in the water, while the River Alde at Iken Cliff can be wonderfully warm for a swim. Constable loved Suffolk from every angle and throughout the seasons, under the "stillness of noon, the depths of twilight and the dews and pearls of the morning" – scenes that moved him to tears.

From reedy riverbanks to ancient woodland and rolling heaths, this is an area rich in wildlife, with protected patches of wilderness and magnificent wildflowers. South of the historic market town of Bury St Edmunds, rare oxlips bloom in Bull's Wood, while Priestly Wood is prettied with winter snowdrops and summer orchids. Further east, the bluebells in Freston Wood are some of Suffolk's best. However, the area's most striking wild flower is the rare snake's-head fritillary, which fills four Suffolk meadows each April–May. Three of these meadows are open to the public, and at Fox Fritillary Meadow (the largest), up to 300,000 purple-and-white chequered flower heads can be seen nodding in the breeze on annual open days.

This low-lying patch of England has few high points and not one motorway to speak of. Instead, scattered between the pig farms and beet fields, are grand estates such as Elveden and Wyken, while timber-framed towns reflect the area's prosperous medieval wool industry. Just as it was back then, this region is blessed with a bounty of local produce, which you can taste in excellent eateries, such as Gestingthorpe's award-winning pub The Pheasant, or buy fresh from the atmospheric markets at Wyken Vineyard or Lavenham – the higgledy-piggledy village where Jane Taylor wrote the lullaby *Twinkle Twinkle* in 1806.

5

RIVER SWIMMING

1 LONG MELFORD, R STOUR
Follow the St Edmund Way path past the weir pool and through meadows along the river.
→ Follow Liston Ln W out of Long Melford (CO10 9RF) to find footpath on R after 200m, by weir pool. Explore on footbrigde upstream.
5 mins, 52.0728, 0.7080 ▨▨

2 SUDBURY, R STOUR
Many good spots in the meadow on the W edge of Sudbury, including this large weir pool with beach, behind the hospital and church.
→ Signed Sudbury Meadows from the main church (down Croft Rd, CO10 1HR) then explore downstream 50m to weir pool, or upstream for over a mile into meadows. Much quieter and more rural sections of the river are at Borley (52.0530, 0.7129, behind CO10 7AB).
10 mins, 52.0408, 0.7235 ▨▨▨▨

3 WISSINGTON, R STOUR
Griff Rhys Jones's favourite section of the Stour. Lovely walk past pretty church.
→ In Nayland take Wiston Rd off A134 at Nags Corner (CO6 4LS), then after a mile L signed Wiston Church. Walk past church to river and footbridge, exploring downstream all the to the weir. More remote spots 2 miles upstream at Wormingford (51.9670, 0.8000).
10 mins, 51.9628, 0.8495 ▨▨

4 NAYLAND, R STOUR
The river winds through open water meadows here, with deep sections and a waterside pub where you can land a canoe.
→ Follow the footpath from behind the lovely Anchor Inn, Court St (CO6 4JL, 01206 262313). Stroll downstream as far as the footbridge and walk back on the other bank.
10 mins, 51.9675, 0.8725 ▨▨▨▨

5 DEDHAM VALE, R STOUR
A beautiful, open and historic vale, site of Flatford Mill, where people row boats and occasionally swim. Fen Bridge is a quiet spot with deep pools and shelving access. Some weeds to watch for.
→ Park at Dedham Bridge, opposite the Boathouse (restaurant and rowing boat hire, CO7 6DH, 01206 323153). Follow footpath downstream ¾ mile (L bank) to Fen Bridge. Or 45 mins walk on the St Edmund Way from Manningtree Station via Flatford Mill.
15 mins, 51.9623, 1.0079 ▨▨▨▨▨

6 KNETTISHALL HEATH, LITTLE OUSE
Sandy beach and pretty, shallow weir pool, next to car park and fields. Perfect for picnics and little ones.
→ From A1066, 2 miles W of Garboldisham, take road S signed Gasthorpe. R at crossroads after 1 mile signed 'Country Park' to find parking and river on R after a mile.
2 mins, 52.3899, 0.8725 ▨

ANCIENT & SACRED

7 BELCHAMP HALL FOLLY
Isolated 18th-century folly near Belchamp Hall (that featured in the TV series *Lovejoy*).
→ From village pond in Belchamp Walter head E (Hall Rd) past playing field to find footpath track on R after 300m (CO10 7AS). Follow track 350m along field edges to folly. Walk on 2 miles for Gestingthorpe and The Pheasant (CO9 3AU, 01787 461196).
5 mins, 52.0319, 0.6567 ▨▨

8 ST JAMES CHAPEL & LINDSEY CASTLE
Thatched 13th-century chapel, which survived the Reformation to become a barn for nearly 400 years. Once served as a chantry to nearby Lindsey Castle, now just traces of the motte and bailey earthworks behind.

9

7

8

→ Chapel is signposted from A1141 near Kersey. Pass through Kersey then continue approx one mile further W towards Lindsey village (IP7 6QA) to find church signed on L. Find footpath to castle earthworks 500m before reaching the chapel by white cottage on L. Free entry, open year-round.
5 mins, 52.0624, 0.8836 ✝

WOODS & WILDLIFE

9 SHOTLEY MARSHES WADERS

Flanking the River Orwell, this is Suffolk's top breeding site for waders (lapwing, snipe, redshank).

→ Travel N out of Shotley Gate on the B1456. After 400m footpath on R opposite Over Hall Farm (IP9 1PW) leads 400m E to the marshes and river. For a longer walk, turn L at river and follow path 4½ miles N to Butt & Oyster pub at Pin Mill (IP9 1JW, 01473 780764). Fine views from St Marys church (IP9 1ER).
5 mins, 51.9696, 1.2717 🚫🏊🏃🚶🅿

10 CAVENHAM HEATH, NIGHTJARS

Hear the rattle of male nightjars on summer eves in this beautiful heath. Swim in the River Lark, which runs to the E.

→ In Icklingham on the A1101, pass St James

church on L (opp IP28 8PU), then take second L (West St) towards Tuddenham. At sign for weak bridge, continue on foot to bridge (½ mile) then turn immediately L (S) and follow footpath 500m to reserve. Be wary of adders March–October.
15 mins, 52.3215, 0.5869 🚫🏊🏔❄

11 GROTON WOOD, PONDLIFE

East England's most ancient woodlands, at over 2,000 years old. Rare lime and cherry trees, seasonal ponds with toads and frogs, as well as an abundance of birds, butterflies and wildflowers. Watch woodcock displays at dusk.

→ From Fox & Hounds in Groton (CO10 5ED, 01787 210474), go L following sign for Milden and Lavenham, then after 400m take R turn for Castling's Heath. At T-junction, head R for Kersey Tye and Hadleigh. Continue straight for 700m to entrance on L (before IP7 6HD).
1 min, 52.0489, 0.8805 🍴❄

12 PRIESTLEY WOOD, WILDFLOWERS

Over 100 species flower in this SSSI. See snowdrops and spurge laurel (Jan), dog's mercury (Feb), wood anemones, dog violets, primroses and false oxlips (Easter), or purple orchid, yellow archangel and herb paris

(summer). Also home to one of Suffolk's two wild pear trees (inedible).

→ Footpath leads off B1078 Barking Rd, just E of Parson's Ln (IP6 8HG). From Needham Market station head W on B1078 (dir Barking) to find footpath on L after a mile (IP6 8HG), 100m before Barking Church. Very limited space to pull off.
1 min, 52.1357, 1.0398 🅿️🚆

13 BULL'S WOOD, OXLIPS
See floods of rare oxlips (April), plus wood anemones, in this 13th-century woodland. Early purple orchids also abundant, as are butterflies, tawny owls, chiffchaffs and tree creepers. A peaceful place.

→ Turn E off A1141 for Cockfield. 500m after Cockfield Post Office (on R) turn R at dead-end road by triangular green. Follow to signed parkings at Palmers Farm, (IP30 0HD) and follow footpath 600m to wood.
4 mins, 52.1589, 0.8027 🅿️🚶

14 FRESTON BLUEBELLS & RAMSONS
The April/May bluebells are some of Suffolk's most magnificent. In spring, enjoy the gnarled and pollarded oaks while inhaling the garlicy aroma of ramson flowers.

→ Turn off B1456 for Freston, at disused

buildings and car park (IP9 1AB), opposite red postbox in wall. Concealed footpath on R at sharp L-hand corner by St Peter's church.
1 min, 52.0138, 1.1637 🚶

15 ARGER FEN & SPOUSE'S VALE
Ancient wildwood famous for bluebells and wild cherry. Bats, badgers, lizards and grass snakes.

→ Leave Assington S in dir Bures. Turn L at sign to Arger Fen (by CO10 5ND) and follow road S for approx 1¼ miles to reserve entrance on L.
10 mins 51.9821, 0.8094 🚶

MEADOWS

16 MARTINS' MEADOWS
Suffolk is one of the UK's best places for fritillaries. Rare, undrained, unfertilised, flower-rich hay meadows. Orchids and snake's-head fritillary. Reserve has two fruit orchards with local varieties.

→ With Monewden Church on your left, turn R for Clopton at T-junction. Follow Rookery Rd round sharp R-hand bend to junction, and turn L for Clopton. After less than a mile, past IP13 7DF, find signed entrance by black barns on L.
1 min, 52.1682, 1.2540 🚻

14

17 FOX FRITILLARY MEADOW
One open day per year in April. Visit to see up to 300,000 flowers.
→ Call 01473 890089 for open day details. Nr junctions of A1120 and B1077, 2 miles S of Debenham. Other public snake's-head fritillary sites are Mickfield Meadow (52.2261, 1.1334) and Martin's Meadow (see above).
1 min, 52.2006, 1.2006 ⚙️🚗❓

SLOW FOOD

18 LAVENHAM FARMERS' MARKET
A much-loved Suffolk market, more than 30 producers set up stall in this undulating timbered village, which has independent shops and eateries. (Fourth Sunday of month, 10am–1.30pm).
→ Lavenham Village Hall, CO10 9QT.
52.1051, 0.7935 🍴

19 GIFFORDS HALL VINEYARD
Family-run vineyard and café also sells own lavender products, fleeces from their sheep and juice from the orchard.
→ Hartest, IP29 4EX, 01284 830799 (drive past Hartest sign to the black barns).
52.1308, 0.6939 🍴

20 WHITE HORSE INN & CAMPING,
Rural pub with eco-credentials, own brewery and camping field. Uses local suppliers and own veg garden. Simple interior.
→ Mill Green, Edwardstone, CO10 5PX, 01787 211211.
52.0499, 0.8437 🍴

21 THE CROWN, HARTEST
Has own five-barrel brewery and smoker. Some meals cooked on the open fire. Take-away fish & chips (Fridays), outdoor play area.
→ The Green, Hartest, IP29 4DH, 01284 830250.
52.1392, 0.6784 🍴ℹ️🛏

22 LONGWOOD FARM SHOP
Organic farm shop selling meat, veg/fruit and groceries. Open Fridays and Saturdays.
→ Longwood Farm, Tuddenham St. Mary, IP28 6TB, 01638 717120.
52.3163, 0.5519 🍴

23 WYKEN VINEYARD & LEAPING HARE
Artisan food market held weekly on secluded estate. The café/restaurant serves the estate's produce in a 400 year old barn.

→ Wyken Road, Stanton, IP31 2DW, 01359 250287.
52.3082, 0.8783 🍴

24 THE WHITE HORSE, WHEPSTEAD
Beautifully restored pub with original dark beams and antique floor tiles. Menu focuses on Suffolk produce. Peaceful setting on village edge.
→ Rede Rd, Whepstead, IP29 4SS, 01284 735760.
52.1936, 0.6701 🍴

25 BARDWELL WINDMILL
Climb inside this working 1820s mill and buy milled flour and jams in the little shop (leave money in trust box). Open all year with bread-making days in summer. On the 23-mile Miller's Trail cycle route.
→ School Lane, Bardwell, IP31 1AD, 01359 251331.
52.3281, 0.8470 🍴

26 THE OLD CANNON BREWERY
Sink a pint while beer is brewed beside you at this smart freehouse. Adjacent restaurant serves beer-infused dishes and Suffolk specialities. On-site smokery and accommodation.
→ 86 Cannon Street, Bury St Edmunds IP33 1JR, 01284 768769.
52.2497, 0.7146 🍴

27 ELVEDEN ESTATE
Historic working estate with smart café and large shop selling own/local produce. Their pub, Elveden Inn, sits near the estate entrance, serving Elveden specialities such as venison, wood pigeon and foraged mushrooms.
→ London Road, Elveden, IP24 3TQ, 01842 898060.
52.3891, 0.6752 🍴

28 THE DELI CAFE, CHILLI FARM
Stocks Suffolk specialities and has a homely café with a focus on chillies.
→ Chilli Farm, Norwich Rd, Mendlesham, IP14 5NQ, 01449 766344.
52.2420, 1.1020 🍴

29 THE LINDSEY ROSE
This 15th-century inn sources meat from its own farm. A short walk S are the earthworks of Lindsey Castle and 12th-century St James's chapel.
→ The Tye, Lindsey, IP7 6PP, 01449 741424.
52.0750, 0.8915 🍴

30 HALL FARM
Award-winning butchers and deli with café in an old cattle byre. Views over the Dedham Vale, farm trail for kids, lovely picnic spots.
→ Church Rd, Stratford Saint Mary, CO7 6LS, 01206 322572.
51.9718, 0.9850 🏊

31 THE PHEASANT, GESTINGTHORPE
Exceptional foody pub with veg garden, smokery and bee hives. Serene views over the Stour Valley from garden. Low beams and fireplace inside. Boutique accommodation.
→ Gestingthorpe, Halstead, CO9 3AU, 01787 461196.
52.0069, 0.6404 🍴🛏

32 THE VEGGIE RED LION
Exclusively vegetarian pub serving meat-free and vegan meals using locally grown veg.
→ Greenstreet Green, Gt Bricett, IP7 7DD, 01473 657799.
52.1104, 0.9790 🍴

33 ANCHOR INN, NAYLAND
Set by the Stour (you could paddle here). Focuses on local produce, with on-site smokehouse and local ales. Does take-away fish & chips.
→ Nayland, Colchester, CO6 4JL, 01206 262313.
51.9699, 0.8725 🍴

34 ASSINGTON MILL RURAL COURSES
Runs rural/traditional courses, such as beekeeping, wild-meat butchery, bread-making and wild medicine harvesting. Accommodation on site.
→ Assington, CO10 5LZ, 01787 229955. Follow the brown signs.
51.9966, 0.8183

35 DEPDEN FARM SHOP & CAFÉ
Everything is home-grown/reared or sourced locally, with dirt-on veg outside in the 'Veg Shed.' Small café and terrace. Occasional supper clubs. Open Tues–Sun.
→ Rookery Farm, Bury St Edmunds, IP29 4BU, 01284 852525.
52.1798, 0.6053 🍴

36 THE BUTT AND OYSTER, PIN MILL
Historic bargemen's pub beside the R. Orwell. Focus on fresh fish.
→ Pin Mill, IP9 1JW, 01473 780764.
51.9964, 1.2127 🍺

12

23

37 POLSTEAD COMMUNITY SHOP

England's second-oldest community shop is welcoming and well-stocked. Pretty village setting with the Cock Inn and Vintage Tea Room opposite.

→ The Green, Polstead, CO6 5AL, 01206 263464.
52.0077, 0.9020 🍴

CAMP & SLEEP

38 COBBS COTTAGE

17th-century thatched cottage with chocolate-box charm. Located down single-track lane on an ancient estate overlooking the Box River valley. Stands beside a larger cottage.

→ Stoke Tye, Stoke-by-Nayland, CO6 4RP, 01787 211115.
52.0018, 0.8818 🏕 ·

39 HENRY'S LAKE, RATTLESDEN

Three miles from the nearest village, the stargazing at this small camping and caravanning site can be fantastic. Fishing lake, electric hook-ups and honesty shop.

→ High Town House, Rattlesden, IP30 0SZ, 01449 736600.
52.1670, 0.8825

40 RUSHBANKS FARM, R STOUR

Simple riverside campsite with jetty and canoe hire.

→ Two miles W of Nayland near Wissington. CO6 4NA, 01206 262350.
51.9644, 0.8373 🏕🛶🚣

41 SPENCERS FARM SHOP CAMPSITE

Small, peaceful site with PYO, farm shop and café. Village pub and shop five-min walk.

→ Wickham Fruit Farm, Wickham, CO9 2PX, 01787 269476.
51.9906, 0.6710 🏕

42 PURTON GREEN

Carry your luggage by wheelbarrow to this thatched medieval cottage – all that's left of the lost village of Purton Green. 13th-century features, surrounded by rural Suffolk views. A real treat.

→ Stansfield, 01628 825925. Exact address given on booking. Landmarktrust.org.uk
52.1512, 0.6041 🏕

43 FRESTON TOWER

Striking six-storey Tudor folly with great views over the River Orwell. Set in undulating parkland.

→ Nr Freston, 01628 825925. Exact address given on booking. Landmarktrust.org.uk
52.0126, 1.1722 🏕

44 SWATTESFIELD CAMPSITE

Secluded seven-acre site with back-to-basics feel. Fire pits and pizza oven, with bell tents, pixie hut and shepherd's hut available. Near Thornham Estate gardens and parkland.

→ Gislingham Road, Thornham Magna, IP23 8HH, 01379 788558.
52.3030, 1.0592 ⛺

45 BADWELL ASH LODGES

Four waterside timber lodges set beside fishing lakes. Each has private hot tub and veranda. Adults only.

→ Hunston Road, Badwell Ash, IP31 3DJ, 01359 258444.
52.2805, 0.9112 🏕

46 STANSTEAD CAMPING

Camping field overlooking a pond and arable fields. Farm produce sold. Adults only. Farmhouse B&B also here.

→ Stanstead Hall, Hitcham, IP7 7NY, 01449 740270.
52.1450, 0.8911

47 TWEE GEBROEDERS

This restored 1897 Dutch sailing barge is quite unique. Nostalgic interior with riverside walks and wildlife-watching from the deck.

→ Pin Mill, 200 yards L of Butt & Oyster pub (IP9 1JW), 01394 410597 (or 0117 204 7830 via canopyandstars.co.uk).
51.9967, 1.2120 🏕

48 MILL HOUSE CAMPING

Smallholding with six-pitch camping site. Open-air shower, sustainable and self-sufficiency ethos, own produce often available.

→ Mill Hill, Earl Soham, IP13 7RP, 01728 684312.
52.2184, 1.2573 ⛺

49 LING'S MEADOW

Wildlife-rich camping meadow on an 80-acre wheat and barley farm. Vehicle-free site, with wheelbarrows for luggage. Bell tents available.

→ Stanton Road Farm, North Common, Hepworth, IP22 2PR, 01359 250594.
52.3403, 0.8911 ⛺

47

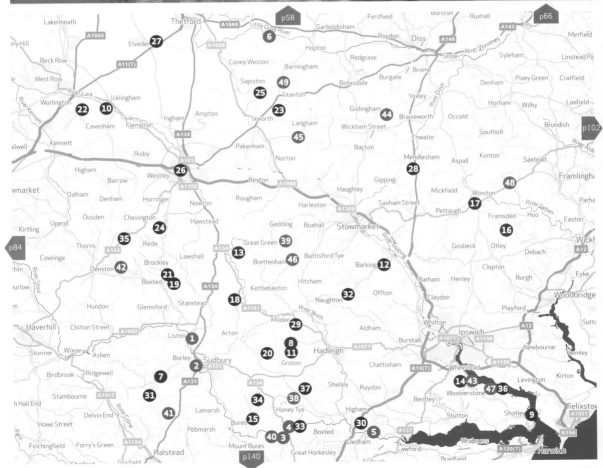

SUFFOLK COAST

Our perfect weekend

→ **Wander** through the marshes at Walberswick, take a dip in the sea and retreat to The Anchor.

→ **Explore** the huge shell of Covehithe ruined church and swim at the secret beach.

→ **Canoe** the remote Debden estuary, wild camping on the shore.

→ **Venture** into primeval woodland at The Thicks, home to contorted oaks and giant hollies.

→ **Discover** the warm tidal backwaters of Iken Cliff, hire a canoe and camp at the fruit farm.

→ **Swim** in the mere beneath Framlingham Castle.

→ **Buy** freshly smoked bloaters from Southwold Harbour Huts or visit Mrs Brinkley for fresh fish.

→ **Sleep** snug as a bug in Suffolk's most northerly Martello tower, while waves pound the walls.

→ **Boat** across to Orford Ness to discover secret ruins and experience the rare wildlife.

→ **Feed** the chickens at Alde Garden campsite.

→ **Dusk-walk** through Westleton Heath while glow-worms light the way.

Suffolk's sand-and-shingle coastline is one of the least developed in England, while its villages and resorts are set among wildlife-rich woods and marshland, and have an unspoilt charm and eccentric air.

One of the prettiest places is Orford, where Europe's largest shingle spit, Orford Ness, is still extending a long tentacle southwards to support a precious ecosystem of sea lavender and sea kale. Walks radiate along the tidal creeks, with the most westerly path leading to Butley Creek, where you can summon a rowing boat to cross the water, or swim between the wooden pontoons. On your return, you could buy fresh fish in Orford from Mrs Brinkley or scoff piles of seafood in Butley Orford Oysterage.

Looking out to the southern tip of the Ness is Shingle Street, where a string of defensive Martello towers built during the Napoleonic Wars dot the otherwise empty beach between Bawdsey and Aldeburgh. While many of Suffolk's Martello towers have been destroyed or washed away by the sea, a stroll along this stretch of coastline passes no fewer than six, with the converted tower at Aldeburgh a spectacular spot to spend the night.

Suffolk has England's most eroded coastline, and parts are being lost at a rate of more than a metre a year. This fragile beauty is most apparent at the crumbling cliffs of Covehithe, where the road to the magnificent ruined church ends abruptly and runs over the cliff – or at the lost village of Dunwich, where The Ship, Greyfriars Priory and a handful of houses are all that remains of the once-thriving port city that now lies beneath the waves.

Today at Dunwich, two miles of sand and dunes back onto heathland, where marsh harriers hover and bitterns 'boom'. A purple sea of heather in summer, visit it at dusk on a warm evening to see glow-worms winking in the grass and hear nightingales singing from the scrub. Where heathland gives way to sand dunes and beach, little terns nest in a protected area and water voles swim in the adjoining ponds. At low tide beneath an evening sky, with the surf rushing over the sand and the sea fading into pink and mauve, this is a mesmerising place for a swim.

WILD BEACHES

1 DUNWICH HEATH, MINSMERE BEACH

Beautiful sand and shingle beach bordered by lagoons, heather and birdlife. Vivid with pinks and purples in summer, this tranquil heathland supports nightjars and the rare Dartford warbler – listen for both around the gorse bushes on a summer's eve. Also look for deer, rare ant lions and adders, or visit in winter for short-eared owls.

→ ¾ mile W of Dunwich (Ship Inn IP17 3DT, 01728 648219) turn L signed Dunwich Heath. Continue 1½ miles past Beach View/Cliff House camping (IP17 3DQ, 01728 648282) to NT car park (£8) with tea room (01728 648501). Or walk in from Dunwich along the beach (30 mins).

5 mins, 52.2506 1.629

2 WESTWOOD MARSHES, WALBERSWICK

Beautiful walk across Tinkers marsh and fens, passing derelict 18th-century pumping mill and Dunwich river, to arrive at a remote section of Walberswick beach. Walberswick itself has a sandy village beach with dunes, seasonal beach camping and crabbing, or explore the River Bylth.

→ From Walberswick, head W on Lodge Road at IP18 6UN for ½ mile to Nature Reserve signs and Hoist Covert car park on R. Follow path opp SE through trees, turning L at end towards sea and stump of wind pump. Turn R at river and eventually cross dyke L on footbridge to beach. Back in Walberswick, crabbing competitions take place in the shallow channels behind the beach (where you may find seasonal camping). Swim in the Blyth upriver from the row-boat ferry jetty, riding up or downstream with the tidal current. The Anchor is the best pub with excellent beer and food (IP18 6UA, 01502 722112).

20 mins, 52.2982, 1.6478

3 THE HAVEN, ALDEBURGH

Aldeburgh's beautiful shingle beach is never too crowded and offers great food. Or head N for a long strand of wild shingle beach and the scallop-shell metal sculpture, fun to climb.

→ Head 1 mile N by road from the monument on Aldeburgh seafront (IP15 5BE, sculpture ½ mile). Funky Thorpeness is 2 miles N. 1 mile S by road to the Martello tower beach. For fish and chips try at 226 High Street (IP15 5DB).

2 mins, 52.1606, 1.6057

4 SHINGLE STREET, HOLLESLEY

A remote shingle beach with coastguard cottages and Martello towers. Strong currents at river mouth.

→ From Hollesley (near Sutton) follow narrow lanes 2 miles signed to Shingle Street (IP12 3BE). The first beach, before the cottages, has currents, so continue on and park closer to the Martello tower (700m).

5 mins, 52.0331, 1.4516

RIVERS, CREEKS & LAKES

5 METHERSGATE QUAY, SUTTON, DEBEN

Remote old stone quay with ladder and beach. Provides a simple but peaceful place for a swim, perhaps even a jump at high tide. Best reached by canoe. No mooring.

→ Take footpath opp Sutton church (IP12 3DU) ¾ mile to Cliff Farm. Bear R towards Methergate Hall, and L to shore after ½ mile (30 mins). Approx ½ mile downstream also find The Ham and The Tips, other small spits for canoe landing or wild camping.

40 mins, 52.0690, 1.3298

6 IKEN CLIFF, SNAPE

Old-world tidal backwater with lagoon, beach and riverside church. High-tide swimming in

water warmed over mud flats. Canoe hire.
→ Turn off B1069 just S of Snape Maltings, signed Orford. Then L after a mile (Iken), then first L to picnic parking (IP12 2EN). Ikencanoe. co.uk (Apr–Oct, 01728 688267).
2 mins, 52.1511, 1.5110

7 BUTLEY RIVER, ORFORD
Row boat ferry crossing with jetty to jump from at high tide. Tidal creek among fields.
→ Pass castle in Orford on R, take next R signed 'Gedgrave Only No Through Road'. After 1½ miles take footpath on R (cycle path sign, just past IP12 2BX) down to Butley River bank (500m). Then turn L along bank to ferry.
15 mins, 52.0804, 1.4905

8 FRAMLINGHAM MERE AND RUINS
Beautiful lake below the ruins of Framlingham Castle.
→ Take New Rd N from the mini-roundabout in Well Close Square (IP13 9DS) then find footpath on R after 300m. Gastro food at the Crown Hotel (IP13 9AP, 01728 723521).
3 mins, 52.2252, 1.3416

RUINS & ANCIENT

9 MARTELLO TOWERS, BAWDSEY
During the 19th-century Napoleonic Wars, these circular forts were built to defend the coastline. Eleven remain in Suffolk and you can follow a line of four by walking along the empty stretch of coastline between Bawdsey and Shingle Street. Take a picnic.
→ From Bawdsey beach carpark (East Ln, beyond IP12 3AP), looking out to sea, the first tower is to your R. Approx 1½ miles N along South Coast Path to the fourth tower at Shingle St.
5 mins, 52.0087, 1.4337

10 SOUTH ELMHAM MINSTER
Atmospheric, late-Saxon ruins built on the site of a 7th-century minster and set within a tree clump. It's possible that this was the bishop's main seat during the 9th century.
→ Follow signs from St Cross South Elmham, which lead you out SE onto Hall Rd. Follow for ½ mile to find byway on R. After 250m on byway, turn L onto footpath and follow for 500m to find the tree-shrouded minster on R.
12 mins, 52.3933, 1.3898

12

11 COVEHITHE RUIN AND BEACH

Medieval ruin with 14th-century tower, set back from cliffs. Smaller church sits inside the crumbling shell. A wild, eroded coastline, much of Covehithe has been lost to the sea. Remote beach with lake is a short walk away.

→ From A12 in Wrentham turn off for Covehithe and continue to church (NR34 7JW). Footpath 100m before church leads to beach (10 mins – follow field edge to cliff and down to Covehithe Broad). Difficult parking.

1 min, 52.3767, 1.7052 ✝️ 📧

12 GREYFRIARS PRIORY, DUNWICH

The once-thriving port city of Dunwich lies beneath the waves. A café, The Ship Inn and the striking ruins of Greyfriars Priory are all that remains.

→ Signed on Monastery Hill, Dunwich (IP17 3DT).

5 mins, 52.2755, 1.6306 ✝️ 📧

13 ALL SAINTS CHURCH, RAMSHOLT

Round-towered church with views over the pines to the River Deben. Locally sourced food at the riverside Ramsholt Arms.

→ Turn S off B1083 between Shottisham and Alderton, at signs just SE of IP12 3EW for Ramsholt Arms (IP12 3AB, 01394 411209).

Lane to church signed on R. Walk NW along the shore path to find a lagoon for swimming.

10 mins, 52.0294, 1.3619 📷 ✝️ 🛈 🏊

14 ORFORD NESS SHINGLE SPIT

This remote and internationally rare, vegetated shingle spit is Europe's largest. Former MOD testing ground, with many old military buildings.

→ Access by NT boat in season only (call 01728 648024). Boat leaves every half hr 11am–2pm (Saturdays in spring and autumn and Tues-Sat in summer), from jetty at end of Quay St, Orford (IP12 2NU).

2 mins, 52.0828, 1.5534 🏖️ 🏞️

WOODLAND & WILDLIFE

15 DINGLE MARSHES & DUNWICH FOREST

A wilderness of reed beds – part of Britain's largest – nurtures bitterns and marsh harriers. Visit in May for the best of both. Also look for sea otters and the rare starlet sea anemone.

→ From The Ship (Dunwich, IP17 3DT), walk N along the beach to find marshes to L or skirt the E edge of Dunwich Forest along the South Coast Path.

5 mins, 52.2787, 1.6331 🐑

18

16 TRIMLEY MARSH, BIRDS

Mosaic of traditionally managed wetland habitats. Huge numbers of coots, cormorants, avocets and waders.

→ Exit Trimley station (IP11 0UD), and follow the road SW out of town to obvious parking area and footpaths, where road narrows to a lane. Walk a mile to river and R to start of marshes and hides.

20 mins, 51.9726, 1.2918 🚣 🐕 🚶

17

MAZAWATTEE TEA

24

EMMETT'S STORE

24

17 THE THICKS, STAVERTON PARK

Primeval woodland with gnarled, twisted and ivy-clad trees. More than 4,000 pollarded oaks, some of Britain's largest holly trees and the oldest oaks in East Anglia.

→ ½ mile SW of Butley (IP12 3PU) on B1084, dir Woodbridge, find footpath on R. Difficult parking. Continue straight into woods.
1 min, 52.1028, 1.4451 🍷

18 WESTLETON HEATH GLOW-WORMS

Suffolk's best surviving tracts of medieval heathland, with nightingale song and glow-worms on summer eves. Also experience nightjars, woodcocks and butterflies.

→ Dunwich Rd runs E off the B1125 at Westleton through the reserve to Dunwich (IP17 3DT). Car park L 1 mile from Westleton.
1 min, 52.2720, 1.5998 🏃

SLOW FOOD

19 BOATHOUSE CAFE

Eat local crabs and smoked prawns, or munch scones and jam, with fruit scrumped from the hedgerows. Veranda overlooks the River Deben. Open daily May–Oct, Fri–Sun in Nov.

→ The Quay, Bawdsey, IP12 3AZ, 07900

811826. Postcode is misleading, follow B1083 through Bawdsey all the way to the end.
51.9898, 1.3944 🍴

20 SOUTHWOLD HARBOUR HUTS

Buy everything from fresh fish to cake at these rustic harbour huts. Sole Bay Fish Co is open year-round and has a café/restaurant, Harbour Inn does good fish. Similar fish huts in nearby Aldeburgh also good.

→ Southwold Harbour, Blackshore. Sole Bay Fish Co, Shed 22e, IP18 6ND, 01502 724241. Harbour Inn, IP18 6TA, 01502 722381.
52.3174, 1.6672 🍴

21 WATERFRONT CAFE, THE GRANARY

300-year-old former granary, overlooking the River Deben. Open seasonally. They also own Woodbridge Fine Food Co (2a New St, IP12 1DT) – perfect for picnic fodder.

→ The Granary Building, Tide Mill Way, Woodbridge, IP12 1BY, 01394 610333.
52.0902, 1.3209 🍴

22 BUTLEY ORFORD OYSTERAGE

No-frills local institution serving fresh oysters and fish, mostly hauled in and smoked by the owners. Open daily until 4ish.

Also Pinney's fish shop (Quay St, IP12 2NU).
→ Market Hill, Orford, IP12 2LH,
01394 450277.
52.0945, 1.5332 🍴

23 FOX AND GOOSE INN
16th-century, timbered pub in lovely Suffolk village. Much of the food sourced from six-mile radius.
→ Church Road, Fressingfield, Suffolk IP21 5PB, 01379 586247.
52.3486, 1.3182 🍴🛏

24 EMMETT'S OF PEASENHALL
Traditional store, café and smokehouse in pink-washed village that hosts the World Pea Podding Championships (June). Buy smoked pork, unpasteurised cheese, or stop for coffee.
→ Peasenhall, Saxmundham, IP17 2HJ, 01728 660250.
52.2722, 1.4527 🍴

25 THE SHIP, DUNWICH
Former smugglers' inn near the beach and marshes. Large garden with 300-year-old fig tree. Independent ales, cream teas and local meats.

→ St James St, Dunwich IP17 3DT,
01728 648219.
52.2773, 1.6312 🍴🛏

26 SHAWSGATE VINEYARD
Full range of wines produced and sold. Self-guided tours with maps an option, or 90-min tours given on Wed eves in summer.
→ Badingham Rd, Framlingham, IP13 9HZ, 01728 724060.
52.2338, 1.3636 🍴

27 THE KING'S HEAD, LAXFIELD
Thatched pub with low ceilings and no bar. Serves seasonal produce. Frequented by Morris dancers and the local horse and trap in summer.
→ Gorams Mill Lane, Laxfield, IP13 8DW, 01986 798395.
52.3024, 1.3674 🍴

28 METFIELD STORES
Volunteer-staffed community shop with local produce. Perfect place to buy lunch stuff. Picnic tables on grass beside the shop.
→ The Street, Metfield, IP20 0LB, 01379 586204.
52.3707, 1.3698 🍴

29 THE ANCHOR, WALBERSWICK
Award-winning pub, with food sourced from own garden, local butchers and organic veg growers. Sun terrace overlooks beach huts, and there are occasional summer BBQs. Chalet accommodation.
→ The Street, Walberswick IP18 6UA, 01502 722112.
52.3133, 1.6627 🍴🛏

30 THE FROIZE INN, CHILLESFORD
Food miles and fair trade are core principles of this relaxed rural restaurant.

→ The Street, Chillesford, IP12 3PU,
01394 450282
52.1167, 1.4887 🍴

31 SWEFFLING WHITE HORSE

200-year-old pub with wood fires. Serves
Suffolk ales and ciders from the cask.
Simple, home-made food includes pies in
winter and ploughmans in summer. Has Alde
Garden camping adjacent.

→ Low Road, Sweffling, IP17 2BB (on the
B1119), 01728 664178
52.2267, 1.4314 🍴

32 THE SHIP INN, BLAXHALL

Join in with local folk singing at this rural
village pub. Local and seasonal food served.
Accommodation available.

→ School Road, Blaxhall, IP12 2DY,
01728 688316
52.1597, 1.4593 🍴

33 SEASHORE FORAGING WITH JON TYLER

Join wild-food expert Jon Tyler and learn how
to identify, harvest and prepare or preserve
wild food such as samphire, sea beet and
sea purslane. Wild-cooking and sea-foraging
events often held at Rendlesham Forest or
along the coast.

→ Jon Tyler, 07896 678956. See
wildforwoods.co.uk for upcoming group
events or contact Jon for tailored activities.
52.0990, 1.4134 🍴

34 BRINKLEY'S FISH SHED

With no electricity, Mrs Brinkley puts
the fish Mr B catches on ice. Stoke up a
driftwood fire and eat on the beach outside.

→ Orford Foreshore, Orford Quay, 07530
911458. Near Riverside Tea Rooms (IP12 2NU).
52.0909, 1.5388 🍴

35 WHITE HORSE, SIBTON

Award-winning rural pub where locals trade
produce for meals. Inglenook fireplace, horse
brasses on the walls, big garden.

→ Halesworth Rd, Sibton, IP17 2JJ,
01728 660337.
52.2792, 1.4548 🍴 🛏

36 EELS FOOT INN, EASTBRIDGE

Cosy pub near RSPB Minsmere. Serves
Suffolk fish and meat from surrounding
farms. Offers bike hire, camping and B&B.

→ Eastbridge, Leiston, IP16 4SN,
01728 830154.
52.2389, 1.5905 🍴 🛏

37 THE GREYHOUND INN, PETTISTREE

Strong emphasis on local food, with
everything made from scratch. Village
setting by church.

→ The Street, Pettistree, IP13 0HP,
01728 746451.
52.1437, 1.3597 🍴

CAMP & SLEEP

38 NEWBOURNE WOODLAND CAMPSITE

Woodland camping in forest clearings on
20-pitch site. Picnic shed with woodburner.
Adults only.

→ Jackson Rd, nr Newbourne, IP12 4NR,
01473 736201.
52.0336, 1.3015 🚿 ⛺

39 THE BARNS AT BELLE GROVE

Treat yourself to a luxurious yet rustic
escape. Five very unique, converted barns
with Alice-in-Wonderland style interiors.
Spellbinding but expensive.

→ Lower Common, Westhall, IP19 8QU,
01986 873124.
52.3741, 1.5277 🏠

40 SUFFOLK YURT HOLIDAYS

Five yurts set in wildflower meadows,
surrounded by ancient trees. Wood stoves
and eco-shower block, hand-crafted interiors
and communal campfires.

→ Oak Cottage, Ufford Road, Bredfield, IP13
6AR, 07907 964890.
52.1255, 1.3223 🏠 🚿

41 CHURCH FARMHOUSE B&B

Grade II listed farmhouse in three acres of
orchard and garden. Views of rolling fields.

→ Uggeshall, NR34 8BD, 01502 578532.
52.3665, 1.6064 🏠

42 POTTON HALL CAMPSITE

Very basic, adults-only site for a few tents and caravans. A tranquil place.

→ Blythburgh Road, Westleton, IP17 3EF, 01728 648265.
52.2837, 1.5937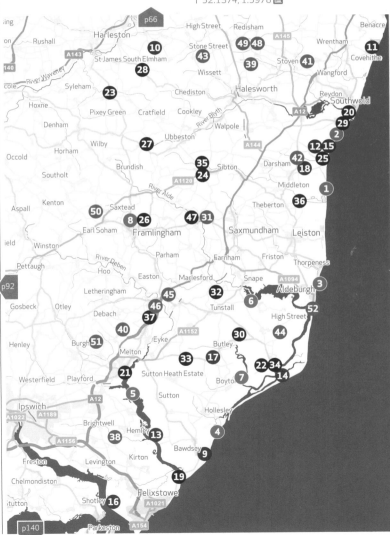

43 GREEN HAVEN

Simple, 10-tent eco-campsite within reach of the coast and village. Local produce sold. Also allows caravans.

→ The Street, Rumburgh, Halesworth, IP19 0NL, 01986 781132.
52.3800, 1.4599

44 HIGH HOUSE FRUIT FARM

Small and simple campsite (15 people max) on PYO fruit farm. Sells home-made apple juice and jams.

→ Sudbourne, IP12 2BL, 01394 450263.
52.1194, 1.5464

45 BRICK KILN FARM

Meadow for large pitches and orchard for single pitches. VW campervans and bell tents available. Communal stables for cooking.

→ Campsea Ashe, IP13 0QL, 07807 181602.
52.1599, 1.3934

46 THE ORCHARD CAMPSITE

Choose a woodland, pond-side or meadow spot. Pitch your own tent or choose glamping. Shop with off-licence.

→ 28 Spring Lane, Wickham Market, IP13 0SJ, 07818 034729.
52.1530, 1.3702

47 ALDE GARDEN

Tranquil family campsite by the adjoining Sweffling White Horse pub. Range of unique glamping huts and bikes also available.

→ Low Road, Sweffling, Suffolk IP17 2BB, 01728 664178.
52.2269, 1.4308

48 IVY GRANGE FARM YURTS

Yurts on a private farm setting. With woodland showers, games barn and PYO salad/veg. Adjacent to Gypsy Hollow site.

→ Butts Road, Westhall, IP19 8RN. Ivygrangefarm.co.uk.
52.3909, 1.5189

49 GYPSY HOLLOW

Traditional gypsy wagon on a farm, with summerhouse and spa. They'll collect you in a horse and cart from Bungay train station.

→ Vallley Farm, Butts Rd, Westhall, IP19 8RN, 01986 780995.
52.3912, 1.5183

50 WINDMILL LODGES

Seven luxury lodges with hot tubs, set around a fishing and wildlife lake. Private rural setting with swimming pool in summer.

→ Red House Farm, Marlborough Rd, Saxtead, IP13 9RD, 01728 685338.
52.2352, 1.2933

51 SECRET MEADOWS

Off-grid farm stays in luxury lodge tents, gypsy caravans and 'hobbit box.' Organic towels, handmade soap. Option of bushcraft courses.

→ White House Farm Wildlife Site, Hasketon, IP13 6JP, 01394 382992.
52.1190, 1.2821

52 MARTELLO TOWER, ALDEBURGH

Converted Martello tower that's England's most northerly. Waves crash against the walls at high tide. Vaulted ceilings, military feel, rooftop views.

→ Aldeburgh beach. 01628 825925 (Landmarktrust.co.uk).
52.1374, 1.5978

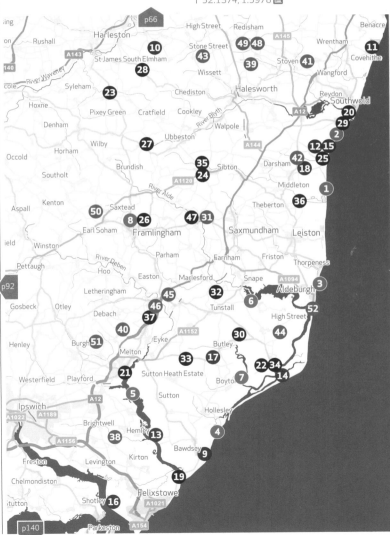

OXFORD &
COTSWOLDS

Our perfect weekend

→ **Swing** from the trees at Buscot weir, picnic in
the grass then canoe up to Cheese Wharf.

→ **Visit** tiny St Oswald's church, then swim in the
River Windrush past the ruins of Minster Lovell.

→ **Commune** with the megalithic Rollright Stones
and the mysterious Hoar Stone, rumoured to
protest if anyone tries to move them.

→ **Camp** on an island in the River Thames at Pinkhill
Lock or in the meadows at Northmoor Lock.

→ **Discover** the ruins of Hampton Gay Manor, a
roofless shell at the site of a lost village.

→ **Walk** and swim at Port Meadows, stopping for
refreshment at The Perch or The Trout Inn.

→ **Breeze** through the bluebells in Foxholes nature
reserve and feel butterflies flutter past in
Piddington Wood.

→ **Tuck** in at The Feathered Nest, try Michelin-
starred home-smoked salmon at The Nut Tree
or admire the views from the Mole and Chicken.

The young Thames is a quiet river, rising in the Cotswold Hills and flowing peacefully through the Oxfordshire plains. Distant church spires peek over billowing wheat fields and wild flowers wave in the hedgerows.

The lower Cotswolds flank the meadows of the upper Thames, tumbling east to melt into Oxfordshire, the South East's most rural county. An escarpment of fossil-rich Jurassic limestone, these rolling hills provide the golden stone that characterises Cotswold villages such as Nether Westcote, where the Feathered Nest Inn sells local produce from the pantry, or Little Barrington where the Fox Inn sits prettily beside the River Windrush.

Taking its name from the rushes that whisper along its course, the Windrush snakes through the Cotswolds to meet the Thames near Oxford, flowing past the isolated church of St Oswald, and the remains of a 15th-century manor at Minster Lovell. Here, alongside arches and ruined walls, you can bathe in the blue-tinged waters and catch crayfish big enough for supper.

A little way to the north, running parallel to the Windrush, the River Evenlode passes ancient Wychwood Forest, the bluebells of Foxholes woodland and the shallow paddling spots by the footbridge in Stonesfield, where the world's first identified dinosaur remains were discovered in 1824. Where the Evenlode joins the Thames near Cassington, the island campsite at Pinkhill Lock is wonderfully secluded or, further upstream, you can camp at Rushey Lock, near the Trout Inn at Tadpole Bridge, then paddle or stroll to the peaceful swim spots near Chimney Meadows reserve.

The Thames enters Oxford along Port Meadow, England's largest and oldest continuous meadow, recorded in the 1086 Doomsday Book. A popular Oxford stroll involves walking through the meadows to The Perch at Binsey, then continuing to The Trout at Wolvercote for lunch and another pint. Port Meadow has never been ploughed, and is older than any building in Oxford. At the northern end near Wolvercote you can swim beneath the weir, with grand views of Oxford's dreaming spires. This is the setting and inspiration for the opening lines of *Alice in Wonderland* who was 'beginning to get very tired of sitting with her sister on the bank…' – and the closing lines where Alice sees 'an ancient city and a quiet river winding near it along the plain'.

RIVER SWIMMING

1 SHERBORNE PARK, R WINDRUSH
Totally secluded, secret river pools in woods.
→ 1¾ miles S of Clapton-on-the-Hill (GL54 2LG) car park R at Northfield Barn. Walk S past farm, take track L down to cross river, over bridges then upstream for 10 mins, through two fields.
35 mins, 51.8409, -1.7283

2 BURFORD, R WINDRUSH
Water meadows and pool by old willow.
→ A mile E downstream of Burford (OX18 4SN) on Witney Street. Find footpath on L after ½ mile. Or reach from pretty Widford (OX18 4DU), upstream on footpath.
5 min, 51.8008, -1.6175

3 ASTHALL, R WINDRUSH
More fields and swimming/paddling. Also a lovely pub.
→ Signed from A40 2½ miles E of Burford at roundabout (B4047 then immediately L). Pass the lovely Maytime Inn (OX18 4HW, 01993 822068) to find river bridge. Follow footpath downstream.
3 mins, 51.8021, -1.579

4 MINSTER LOVELL, R WINDRUSH
Romantic ruins beside the River Windrush, built in 15th century by the seventh Lord Lovell, once one of the richest men in England. Abandoned in the 18th century. Clear, pretty Cotswold river running through the grounds is just deep enough to swim. Deeper section downstream at footbridge.
→ Follow the signs for the church (OX29 0RR) to find Minster ruins down a path behind. Good for crayfishing.
5 mins, 51.7991, -1.5295

5 STONESFIELD, R EVENLODE
Pretty footbridge with paddling. Grassy banks below gentle Cotswold escarpment. Site of the first conclusive dinosaur fossil find. Roman villa up hill.
→ From Stonesfield village (OX29 8QZ) follow Church St and then Brook Ln (track) S, down to the stream (500m beyond cemetery R).
10 mins, 51.8453, -1.4304

6 LECHLADE PARK, R THAMES
A popular stretch of common land and river upstream. Easy parking and a nice pool below wooden footbridge. Watch kids jump from the Ha'penny Bridge (they're not meant to).

→ Large car park 450m S of the Ha'penny town bridge (Swindon road). Continue upstream ¾ mile for pool above the footbridge, near the Round House and junction of R Coln. Also from pretty little Inglesham (SN6 7RD).
15 mins, 51.6885, -1.7042

7 CHEESE WHARF, R THAMES
Old cheese-loading wharf, now a little wooded road-side picnic area with good swing.
→ Head E from Lechalde (A417, dir Buscot) past the Trout Inn (GL7 3HA, 01367 252313), continue for ½ mile to find parking on L.
1 min, 51.6839, -1.6765

8 BUSCOT WEIR, R THAMES
A wonderful large, deep weir pool with trees, rope swings and lawns in pretty NT hamlet.
→ Continue S from Cheese Wharf and turn L in Buscot to find car park (SN7 8DA) after 150m.
2 mins, 51.6809, -1.6683

9 KELMSCOTT, R THAMES
Wild open stretch of Thames downstream from famous gardens and tea room.
→ From lovely Kelmscott (charming Plough Inn, GL7 3HG, 01367 253543) go right to pass

12

10

19

the Manor onto trackway, parking at very end. Follow the river 2 miles downstream through endless open fields and many riverbank pools, all the way to remote Grafton Lock (weir pool, road access, 51.6920, -1.6079) and on to Radcot Bridge (campsite on island opposite the Swan Inn, OX18 2SX, 01367 810220).
20 mins, 51.6857, -1.6303 ▲⚐♨✦☎ 🍴

10 CHIMNEY MEADOWS, R THAMES
Meadows and nature reserve bordering a remote stretch of the Thames.
→ Walk 2 miles downstream from Trout Inn at Tadpole Bridge (SN7 8RF, 01367 870382). Or access via Chimney. You might also like to seek out the secret shallow glade pool and ford at Duxford, on opposite bank (51.6990, -1.4660).
40 mins, 51.6945, -1.4900 🚶♨⚐🍴☎✿

11 SWINFORD BRIDGE, R THAMES
Beautiful meadows and quiet river, just outside Oxford. Peer into a secret wood or camp on an island.
→ Explore downstream to the edge of secret Wytham Great Wood (SSSI, permits needed to walk here Wytham.ox.ac.uk) or upstream, all the way beyond Pinkhill Lock (OX29 4JH, island with camping) by Farmoor Reservoir.
10 mins, 51.7746, -1.3594 ▲⚐♨

12 PORT MEADOW, R THAMES
Oxford's largest area of grazing common land. Two miles of river with beaches and grassy meadow on both banks, burial mounds and migratory birds. Two pubs.
→ Park near the Trout Inn (OX2 8PN, 01865 510930). There's a popular pool and rope swing under the bridge. Or from Oxford train station at S end, turn R onto main road and after 300m drop down to Thames footpath on R. Follow for ¾ mile upstream. First footbridge leads to W bank (open meadow), next leads to E with path and access to The Perch inn (OX2 0NG, 01865 728891).
15 mins, 51.7698, -1.2881 🍴♨⚐🚶♨🍴

13 APPLEFORD, R THAMES
Open field and quiet beach behind a church, just a short walk from station.
→ Follow footpath behind church (near OX14 4NT) 200m, or continue on to Little Wittenham. Also Sutton Pools upstream (51.6466, -1.2739).
2 mins, 51.6411, -1.2327 🚶♨⚐

14 CLIFTON HAMPDEN, R THAMES
A pretty bridge and pub, frequented by Jerome K. Jerome. Downstream for many miles there are sandy bays shelving to

20

deeper water bordered by open meadows.

→ Off A415 between Abingdon and Wallingford. Park opposite Barley Mow pub (OX14 3EH, 01865 407847) and riverside campsite (01865 407725). Continue downstream on river's S bank for up to 2 miles through meadows towards Dorchester.
2 mins, 51.6551, -1.2099 🚶🏕🚶🛶🏊

15 PARSON'S PLEASURE, R CHERWELL
Historic university river-bathing pool, though water quality can be variable.
→ Take cycle path at lights on corner of St Cross Rd and South Parks Rd by Linacre College (OX1 3JA) and continue behind college 200m to the punt rollers, or anywhere upstream.
5 mins, 51.7606, -1.2458 🏊

16 KIDLINGTON, R CHERWELL
Remote and meandering, through meadow and common land with many kingfishers.
→ Cycle route 51 E from Kidlington church (OX5 2AZ).
10 mins, 51.8290, -1.2673 🚴🏊

17 SHABBINGTON, R THAME
Pub with paddling and deeper swims downstream.

→ Opp The Old Fisherman, Mill Road (HP18 9HJ, 01844 201247).
5 mins, 51.7538, -1.0330 🚶🛶🏊

ANCIENT & SACRED

18 GODSTOW NUNNERY
Ruined abbey, founded as a nunnery in the 12th century. Originally built on an island, it was converted to a house following the Dissolution. Occupied until 1645.
→ From the Trout Inn (OX2 8PN, 01865 510930), cross the bridge over the Thames. Abbey obvious on L.
1 min, 51.7782, -1.2993 🚗✝🅱

19 ST OSWALD'S CHURCH, WIDFORD
Small, isolated church set amid arable fields. Interior features 14th-century paintings and a 15th-century pulpit.
→ From A40 Burford go E. Take hairpin L after 1½ miles (OX18 4EX), signposted Widford. Take first R, then L at the stone house (signposted as a dead end) over river. Park in layby, cross cattle grid to follow footpath to ruin.
5 mins, 51.8068, -1.6051 ✝🚗

18

20 THE ROLLRIGHT STONES
Famous stone circle (King's Men) constructed from local limestone 2,000 years ago. Also King Stone and Whispering Knights burial chambers adjacent.
→ Signed 'The Rollrights' off A44, 3 miles NW of Chipping Norton. Find entrance opp caged stone (OX7 5QB). £1 entry (put in collection box if not wardened). Wyatt Farm Shop (OX7 5SH, 01608 684835) nearby for coffee/lunch.
1 min, 51.9755, -1.5709 ✝🍴

23

22

25

21 HOAR STONE, ENSTONE

Three impressive large stones are the ruins of a Neolithic tomb. Three metres high, the largest is Old Soldier. Legend says they return to their original places if moved.

→ Leave Neat Enstone (OX7 4LF) on Cox's Ln, dir Fulwell. Cross B4022 onto unnamed road. Stones are to your R behind drystone wall.
1 min, 51.9096, -1.4519 ✚

22 HAMPTON GAY MANOR RUIN

16th-century manor beside the Oxford Greenbelt Way (50-mile circular footpath). Striking roofless shell that was once part of a larger village. In a precarious state – take care.

→ Hampton Gay, OX5 2QH. From Bletchingdon (OX5 3BZ) take Oxford Rd dir Hampton Poyle. After ½ mile follow signs for 'Hampton Gay only.' Continue to gate, cross style at end of road and bear R. Ruin in next field, behind the first big tree.
5 mins, 51.8450, -1.2946 🏞 V

WOODLAND & MEADOW

23 FOXHOLES RESERVE, BLUEBELLS

Spectacular bluebell wood which slopes to the River Evenlode. Once part of Wychwood Forest. Yellow primroses and purple violets abundant in spring, around 200 species of fungi in autumn.

→ From B4450 or Kingham station in Bledington, turn L for Foscot (OX7 6RL). Take second L down dead-end road signed 'Foxholes Only.' At the end, follow R-hand footpath into wood.
5 mins, 51.8859, -1.6304 🏞🚶🚻

24 PIDDINGTON WOOD, BUTTERFLIES

One of the area's few ancient woods that hasn't been planted with conifers. A haven for summer butterflies. Bring binoculars.

→ From A41 at take B4011 for Blackthorn. At turnoff for HM Prison Bullington (OX25 1PZ) continue S dir Oakley for ½ mile. Enter via metal kissing gate, layby on R.
1 min, 51.8421, -1.0849 🏞

25 BERNWOOD MEADOWS

Traditional hay meadows, bursting with wild flowers April–July. Cut from mid-July to encourage growth. Adjacent, Bernwood Forest was a favourite of Edward the Confessor's.

→ From Horton-cum-Studley village (OX33 1BE) head SE past OX33 1BJ and turn L for Bernwood Forest carpark (51.8008, -1.1154).

Head SW along the butterfly trail and turn R at the grassy crossroads. Follow path as it bears L to sign for meadow on R.
10 mins, 51.7934, -1.1176 🔲🚻🧍

26 WYCHWOOD FOREST NNR
Often referred to as 'the secret forest' for its magical quality, this is the largest continuous woodland in West Oxfordshire.
→ From Charlebury station (OX7 3HH), follow the B4437 W (dir Burford). Turn L after a mile for Leafield and continue to stables on R after ¾ mile. Footpath into woods on L.
1 min, 51.8591, -1.5141 🅿️🚉

SLOW FOOD

27 WORTON ORGANIC GARDEN & SHOP
Smallholding and café with veg and flowers and down-to-earth appeal. Open Fri–Sun.
→ Worton, nr Cassington, OX29 4SU, 07718 518964.
51.8009, -1.3248 🍴

28 WYATT'S PLANT CENTRE & CAFÉ
Near to the Rollright Stones, this rural garden centre has a café, butcher, deli and groceries.

→ Hill Barn Farm, Great Rollright, OX7 5SH, 01608 684835 Signed on road E from Rollright Stones (see listing).
51.9815, -1.5455 🍴

29 THE FOX INN, LITTLE BARRINGTON
Cotswold stone pub set beside the River Windrush. Exposed beams and log fires, with meats, trout, honey and more sourced locally. Accommodation available.
→ Little Barrington, OX18 4TB, 01451 844385.
51.8162, -1.7047 🍴

30 THE NUT TREE INN, MURCOTT
Home-smoked organic salmon and pork from the pub's own rare-breed pigs are on the Michelin-starred menu at this 15th-century, thatched village pub.
→ Main Street, Murcott, OX5 2RE, 01865 331253.
51.8362, -1.1497 🍴

31 THE TROUT AT TADPOLE BRIDGE
Thames-side inn with lovely garden. Game supplied by local shoots, trout from local fishermen, meat and veg from local estates and farms.

→ Buckland Marsh, Faringdon, SN7 8RF, 01367 870382.
51.7009, -1.5170 🍴

32 THE FEATHERED NEST INN
Eat beneath the sycamore or sit by the fire inside this restored malthouse. Menu is true to the seasons with local fare available to buy.
→ Nether Westcote, OX7 6SD, 01993 833030.
51.8816, -1.6725 🍴🛏️

33 THE SWAN INN, SWINBROOK
Historic riverside pub with flagstone floors and own chickens. Owner's family rears Aberdeen Angus, while gamekeepers and local farmers help stock the kitchen.
→ Swinbrook, Near Burford, OX18 4DY, 01993 823339
51.8047, -1.5921 🍴🛏️

34 THE PERCH AND THE TROUT
Two popular riverside pubs on the edge of Port Meadow, Oxford. From the station it's a 20–30 mins walk across Port Meadow to The Perch Inn, followed by a further 20–30min stroll back via The Trout Inn, which featured in the *Inspector Morse* series.
→ The Perch, Binsey Lane, Binsey, OX2 0NG,

01865 728891; The Trout, Godstow Road, Wolvercote, OX2 8PN, 01865 510930. Start at Walton Well Rd carpark OX2 6ED and walk around the meadow's western edge, or from the station (see Port Meadow swim).
51.7623, -1.2743

35 THE MOLE & CHICKEN, EASINGTON

Ridge-top country pub with stunning views from the garden. Inside, it has gas lamps, antique furnishings and open fires. Not cheap, but the food is good.
→ Easington, HP18 9EY, 01844 208387.
51.7860, -1.0053

36 UPTON SMOKERY

Family-run smokehouse set in rolling countryside. Specialises in curing and smoking meat, game and fish in a traditional way, using traceable raw materials.
→ Upton Downs Farm, Burford, OX18 4LY, 01993 823699. Signed on B4425.
51.8044, -1.6707

37 LILY'S FARM SHOP AND TEA ROOM

Small, family-run tearoom and shop in 16th century building, uses and sells own organic produce. Set in pretty village that's often used as a location for 'Midsommer Murders' series. Open 10am–5pm, closed Tues and Sun.
→ 28 High Street, Dorchester, OX10 7HN, 01865 340900 .
51.6449, -1.1663

38 THE WILD RABBIT, KINGHAM

Part of the Daylesford Organic family — this chic pub has rustic rooms and food is sourced from the garden and local farms.
→ Church Street, Kingham OX7 6YA, 01608 658389.
51.9128, -1.6238

STAY AND CAMP

39 TURKEY CREEK, BAMPTON

Woodland campsite with fire pits on a farm at the edge of the Cotswolds. Log cabin and yurts available.
→ Westmoor Farm, Buckland Road, Bampton, OX18 2AA, 01993 851364.
51.7238, -1.5377

40 GLAMPING THORPE

Stay in a shepherd's hut, gypsy wagon, horse lorry or 'love shack' on this Georgian farm.
→ Banbury Ln, Thorpe Mandeville, OX17 2HA, 07973 294495.
52.0984, -1.2246

41 NORTHMOOR LOCK, APPLETON

Rugged site with meadows, willow trees and nearby weir for swimming/fishing. Two camping fields with firepits. Log huts and bell tents available.
→ Appleton, OX13 5JN, 07961 514043.
51.7116, -1.3639

42 COTSWOLDS CAMPING, CHARLBURY

Pine-fringed, 18-pitch campsite with views of the Evenlode Valley. Some caravans.
→ Spelsbury Rd, Charlbury, OX7 3LL, 01608 810810.
51.8855, -1.4899

43 LYNEHAM LAKE, CHIPPING NORTON

Eight pitches, back-to-basics camping on a lakeside site.
→ Churchill Heath, Kingham, OX7 6UJ, 01608 658491.
51.8996, -1.6087

44 SANDY LANE FARM CAMPSITE

Open 28 days a year, this organic farm cuts its hay meadow in late June, creating an exclusive site for parties of 10–150. There is water but no showers or loos.
→ Eight miles outside Oxford, 01844 279269. Exact location given on booking.
51.7339, -1.0632

45 RUSHEY LOCK, TADPOLE BRIDGE

Peaceful riverside camping field with apple trees. Footpaths lead along the river and to local villages. Ideal for kayaking and swims.
→ Tadpole Bridge, Buckland Marsh, nr Faringdon, SN7 8RF, 01367 870218.
51.7014, -1.5171

46 PINKHILL LOCK, WITNEY

The only things on the island at Pinkhill Lock are the lock-keeper's house and this five-pitch campsite. Not accessible by car – arrive by foot, boat or bike.
→ Eynsham, Witney, OX29 4JH, 01865 881452.
51.7611, -1.3632

47 THE PIG PLACE, ADDERBURY

Basic 'festival-style' camping on a smallholding by the Oxford Canal with moorings available. You can buy the farm's own produce for your own breakfasts.
→ Aynho Road, Adderbury, OX17 3NU, 07892 879447.
52.0092, -1.2905

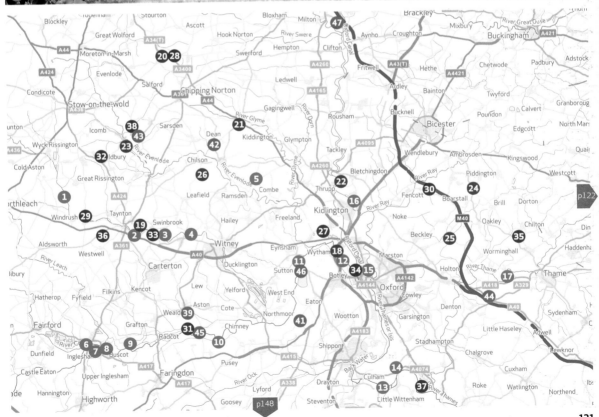

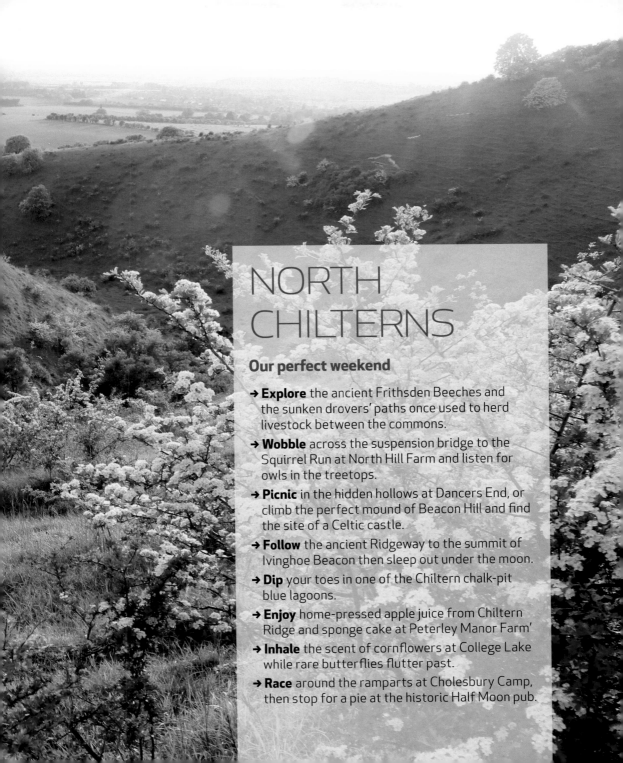

NORTH CHILTERNS

Our perfect weekend

→ **Explore** the ancient Frithsden Beeches and the sunken drovers' paths once used to herd livestock between the commons.

→ **Wobble** across the suspension bridge to the Squirrel Run at North Hill Farm and listen for owls in the treetops.

→ **Picnic** in the hidden hollows at Dancers End, or climb the perfect mound of Beacon Hill and find the site of a Celtic castle.

→ **Follow** the ancient Ridgeway to the summit of Ivinghoe Beacon then sleep out under the moon.

→ **Dip** your toes in one of the Chiltern chalk-pit blue lagoons.

→ **Enjoy** home-pressed apple juice from Chiltern Ridge and sponge cake at Peterley Manor Farm'

→ **Inhale** the scent of cornflowers at College Lake while rare butterflies flutter past.

→ **Race** around the ramparts at Cholesbury Camp, then stop for a pie at the historic Half Moon pub.

From the ridge of the Dunstable Downs, the highest point on the northern Chilterns, the Vale of Aylesbury unfolds beneath you. While chalk escarpments march east and west, sculpting the landscapes of West Herts and Bucks into rolling peaks, deep clefts and wooded holloways.

This is an ancient land of tree-tunnel lanes and chalky white trails that lead to high points crowned with hillforts or exposed lookouts, like the panoramic peak of Ivinghoe Beacon or the site of Cymbeline's Castle on Beacon Hill. From here, Britain's oldest trackway, The Ridgeway, begins its 87-mile journey towards Wiltshire – a route which herdsmen, soldiers and travellers have followed throughout the centuries. Alternatively, for a flatter, modern-day routeway, the serene towpaths beside the Grand Union Canal make for easy bike rides on lazy days.

Where the precious chalk has long been worked out, old quarries have filled with spring water to become blue lagoons. Some, like College Lake, have returned to nature, and are riotous with displays of cornflowers each spring, while the others at Pitstone and Charndon are good for cooling off on hot summer days.

In the lower foothills, silent woods fill the valley bottoms where gnarled beech trees once supplied a thriving furniture industry and the Chilterns' famous 'bodgers' or woodturners. The Tolkien-esque trees that survive today can be seen at their best in the enchanting woodlands of Frithsden Beeches, where you can snap and crackle your way over fallen branches and crispy autumn leaves. Nearby, in the working commons of Ashridge Estate, sunken drovers' paths wend beneath the canopy and, if you're prepared to help out with local conservation tasks, you can sleep in the bunkhouse or camp beneath the trees.

Ancient pubs abound between these woodlands. At Frithsden and Long Crendon, smoke billows from the chimneys of local inns, and thatched cottages cluster around perfect village greens. Or you might just make out the streets where the BFG blew his dreams, or the mound marking Mr Fox's den, as you stroll through Roald Dahl countryside to Peterley Manor Farm for strawberries and cream in summer.

6

RIVERS AND LAKES

1 CHESHAM LAKE, CHESHAM TUBE
Little oasis of silky water and calm near a London tube. Grassy banks. Occasional fishermen.

→ From Chesham station, head SE along Waterside and Latimer Rd. Opposite Hill Farm Rd (park here, HP5 1QT) find trackway. Follow this past weir to lakeside. Or a pleasant 30-min walk along the river Chess from the tube (footpath starts on Moor Rd).
3 mins, 51.6928, -0.5953 🖼🏊

2 CALVERT JUBILEE LAKE, CHARNDON
Quiet, remote wildlife-reserve lake, once a clay pit, now with blue waters.

→ ½ mile NE of Charndon (Steeple Claydon road) turn L at junction (OX27 0BQ). 100m N of entrance to Great Moor Sailing Club find small parking on R. Be discreet and avoid if birdwatchers in hides. NT Claydon House close by.
5 mins, 51.9208, -1.0085 ❓🚶

3 WILSTONE RESERVOIR
Largest of the three historic reservoirs that supply the Grand Union Canal. Exposed and shallow, it does dry out in summer, leaving mud and the sandy ridge bars of medieval strip farming.

→ E of Ashton Clinton (A41), dir Marsworth on B489, find car park on R. Fishermen, concrete embankment. HP23 4NW.
5 mins, 51.8112, -0.6920

4 TRING BLUE LAGOON, FOLLY FARM
This deep, beautiful chalk pit has clear water and is very popular with locals. Often litter, so please take some away.

→ Sometimes people park by roundabout of B488 with Northfield Rd (HP23 5QJ) between Pistone and Tring station. Enter through woods. Or a lovely walk from Tring via Pitstone Hill. Nearby notorious Chinnor pit lakes are amazingly azure, but fenced off (51.6919, -0.9055).
5 mins, 51.8182, -0.6336 ❓

5 WEST WYCOMBE PARK
Downstream of these famous lakes, through the parkland, is a secret river pool.

→ National Trust property (HP14 3AJ), with entrance fee. Drop down to the meadow, by the waterfall and haha. Follow the stream to the footbridge at the bottom.
10 mins, 51.6421, -0.7942 ❓🖼

6 HUGHENDEN, RIVER WYE
Lovely paddling in meadow, with deeper sections and a larger lake just downstream. The NT estate also contains the largest horse chestnut in the UK, and was once home to Benjamin Disraeli.

→ Signed off the A4128 ½ mile N of High Wycombe outskirts. As you enter the estate (HP14 4LA) the stream is to your left, and you can park and walk down from the church.
10 mins, 51.6497, -0.7512 🧍🏊🚶

ANCIENT & SACRED

7 MARLIN CHAPEL RUIN, BERKHAMSTED
Overgrown 13th-century ruin also known as St Mary Magdalene. Near to a moated, haunted farm with ancient walls. Footpaths continue to Hockeridge Wood for ancient trees and wildflowers.

→ From A416 (S of Berkhamsted/A41) turn R at Ashley Green, onto Hog Lane. Turn L dir Hawridge, then R onto Northchurch Ln, then immediately L (dead end) at cottage, to bottom of lane. Footpath leads R, past Marlin Chapel farm (HP4 3UQ) to ruin.
10 mins, 51.7546, -0.6065 🖼🌳🏕🏞

19

8

12

8 DINTON CASTLE

Ruined 18th-century folly standing on a
Saxon burial ground and reputedly haunted
by King Charles I's executioner. Sir John Van
Hatton built his fossil collection into its
limestone walls, and some still remain.

→ On A418, 2 miles SW of Aylesbury. 100m
before Dinton turning (HP17 8UX) find layby
on R with footpath and ruin visible.
1 min, 51.7973, -0.8914 🚗

9 CHOLESBURY CAMP

The Chilterns' most impressive hillfort, with
beech-crowned ramparts. Find tree swings in
the surrounding woods.

→ Info board and signed footpath leads to
the ring from Cholesbury village hall (51.7549,
-0.6538, near HP23 6ND). Good tree swings
near the stables on Shire Ln, behind the ring.
Finish with a pint at the Full Moon (HP5 2UH,
01494 758959).
2 mins, 51.7565, -0.6528 🚶

10 HASTOE HOLLOWAY, TRING

Around 1,000 years old, this ancient roadway
runs N to Tring along the Bucks/Herts
boundary. Woods fringe the path and there
are twisted roots on the steep banks.

→ From Hastoe (HP23 6LX), follow Gadmore
Ln W. After 100m find trackway on R as road
bends sharply L. Follow trackway downhill.
1 min, 51.7740, -0.6765 🚗🚶

11 TOTTERNHOE CASTLE

Unusual motte and bailey site with two
baileys and a wide ditch, surrounded by a
chalk grassland reserve. Lovely views across
Dunstable Downs.

→ Castle Hill, Totternhoe, opposite the Cross
Keys pub (LU6 2DA).
5 mins, 51.8887, -0.5789 🚗

CAVES & FOLLIES

12 CAPTAIN COOK MONUMENT

Charming memorial to British explorer
Captain Cook. Sits on grassy island with
wooden plank over water-filled moat. Set in
private estate with public access.

→ From A413 NE of Chalfont St Giles go 550m
on the B4442, take the Vache Mews drive on L,
opposite Gorelands Ln (signed Chilterns Open
Air Musuem). Park and walk 400m down to
Vache Estate entrance gate (HP8 4UT), where
green sign and stile lead to the footpath.
Follow 500m to monument.
15 mins, 51.6434, -0.5618 📷

(18)

13 HELL-FIRE CAVES
Atmospheric network of man-made chalk and flint caverns hand-dug in 1748. Gothic entrance and former meeting place of the Hell-Fire Club.

➝ Signed from West Wycombe village on the A40 (HP14 3AH). Surrounded by lovely walks, hill-top views and red kites. Entry fee to caves but free parking.

2 mins, 51.6458, -0.8026 🔌B

SUNSET HILLTOPS

14 THE COP, GREAT BLEDLOW WOODS
Admire chalk grassland and wildflowers at Chinnor Hill Nature Reserve, then climb the hill to find the site of Iron Age village, 'The Cop'.

➝ Climb Chinnor Hill from Tring for a mile. After the sharp L bend take Hill Top Ln to the car park (OX39 4BH, 51.6957, -0.8922). Continue straight on the footpath through the reserve, past ancient barrows, then bear R for climb to The Cop.

30 mins, 51.7006, -0.8818 🚶🖼🔌

15 WHITELEAF CROSS
80ft cross cut into chalk hillside with stunning views. Woods, grassland and ancient burial grounds surround. Adjacent,

Brush Hill reserve has glow-worms, tawny owls and sunken paths.

➝ From Monks Risborough Primary School in Princes Risborough (A4010/Aylesbury Rd, HP27 9LZ), take Peters Ln (signed Whiteleaf Cross & Hill) and find car park after a mile on L.

10 mins, 51.7290, -0.8115 🚶🖼🔌

16 COOMBE HILL, WENDOVER
Rising above the woodland, Coombe Hill monument has one of the best views in the Chilterns, with lovely walks to Bacombe Hill.

➝ Take Lodge Hill S from Butler's Cross, then turn L signed Dunsmore to find car park after ½ mile (HP17 0UR). Bear L to the monument (10 mins) or straight on to Bacombe Hill Nature Reserve (20 mins).

10 mins, 51.7526, -0.7715 🚶🖼

17 IVINGHOE BEACON
This prominent and famous green wedge gives panoramic views over the Vale of Ayelsbury and Ashridge Estate. End point of Ridgeway walk and start of Icknield Way.

➝ From Ivinghoe, take B489 dir Dunstable. Take first R, signed Ivinghoe Beacon. Footpaths lead L off the road. Take the footpath R 300m for quieter Steps Hill (great spots to bivvy-out and stargaze) or continue

(13)

on lane to find lots of parking and picnic spots (51.8327, -0.6085). The cover photo of this book was taken here.

5 mins, 51.8416, -0.6068 🚶🖼B🔌

18 BEACON HILL, ELLESBOROUGH
This perfectly shaped hill is quieter than many other high-tops in the area. A lovely short walk with excellent views. On its western flank is the site of Cymbeline's Castle, fondly held to be the seat of an ancient Celtic king.

→ A footpath leads up the hill from opposite Ellesborough church (HP17 0XG) – not the track, but the path by the telegraph pole. The Prime Minister's Chequers is just behind the hill.
10 mins, 51.7490, -0.7925

19 DUNSTABLE DOWNS RIDGE

Highest point in Bedfordshire, with stunning views towards Oxfordshire. The surrounding sunken pathways are a good place to find orchids. Take a kite.

→ Car park a mile W of Whipsnade (LU6 2LF) on the B4540 on the R. Follow path uphill and then NE away from road.
15 mins, 51.8576, -0.5532

20 WATLINGTON HILL

Panoramic views over the Oxfordshire Vale. Sunken lanes and ancient yews. Look for red kites and summer butterflies.

→ Leave Christmas Common dir Watlington (W). Find car park and footpath access on L, opposite Watlington Hill Farm (OX49 5HS). Try the Fox & Hounds in Christmas Common for refreshment (OX49 5HL, 01491 612599).
1 min, 51.6359, -0.9791

21 DANCERS END, FUNGI

Rugged reserve tucked deep in the Chilterns and surrounded by sunken tracks. Overgrown hollows are filled with autumn fungi, and the rich wildlife includes tawny owls.

→ Follow B4009 ½ mile W (dir Wendover) from A41 Tring junction. Take first L (signed Dancers End). Follow 1.8 miles to the old pumping station on L (Bottom Rd, HP23 6LB). Signed trails lead from here.
1 min, 51.7708, -0.6902

22 FRITHSDEN BEECHES, ASHRIDGE

These magnificent knotted beech trees feauture in several Hollywood films, including *Harry Potter*. Beyond, sunken drovers' paths wind through the woods and commons of Ashridge Estate. Bluebells in spring, butterflies in summer, rutting deer in autumn.

→ From Berkamstead Golf Club (HP4 2QB) drive dir Ashridge and Frithsden, passing a memorial on your R. Follow managed footpath (the Chiltern Way) on L for ¾ mile to the beeches.
10 mins, 51.7810, -0.5551

23 NAPHILL COMMON

Open glades, veteran trees and flora-fringed ponds. Find deer, rare fungi and earthworks. Popular with horse riders.

→ Several access points to the S of Main Rd, Naphill, including footpaths behind the Black Lion (HP14 4SH, 01494 563176).

5 mins, 51.6660, -0.7866

24 HOLEY OAK, PENN WOOD

Listen for woodpeckers and tawny owls at the ancient Holey Oak and Penn Pollard, and watch for hawfinches with huge bills. Fungi foraging in autumn.

→ Footpath beside Holy Trinity Church (Penn Street, HP7 0PX, between Amersham and High Wycombe) leads towards Holey Oak. Branch W to Penn Pollard, near wood's northern edge.

2 mins, 51.6581, -0.6702

MEADOWS & WILDLIFE

25 ALDBURY NOWERS BUTTERFLIES

Find delicate wildflowers and over 30 butterfly species on these two hillsides. Look for common milkwort (violet petals) and scarce grizzled skippers (brown & white checked wings). Beautiful beeches overhang the surrounding paths.

→ Pass Tring station (HP23 5QR) heading E, turn L onto Northfield Road (dir Pitstone) and drive 500m to lay-by on R (51.8061, -0.6240), where trees meet the road. Take footpath through hedge and into trees, taking sharp L fork where path splits. Reserve fringes the wood on your R.

10 mins, 51.8092, -0.6243

26 ASTON CLINTON RAGPITS ORCHIDS

10 species of orchids and 25 species of butterfly thrive at this former chalk pit each summer, among fragrant cowslip and horseshoe vetch. Also find grass snakes, slow worms and huge Roman snails.

→ S of Aston Clinton, turn L off B4009 (Upper Icknield Way) dir St Leonards/Wendover Woods road (near HP22 5NH). Enter via gate on L.

3 mins, 51.7893, -0.7152

27 COLLEGE LAKE CORNFLOWERS, TRING

Hides overlooking flooded chalk pit nature reserve with water birds. Seas of cornflowers in spring/summer.

→ Visitor centre signed off B489 (HP23 4PA). Or walk in on the bridleway track from Marsworth to explore the lake's more remote, meadowed W corner.

20 mins, 51.8158, -0.6465

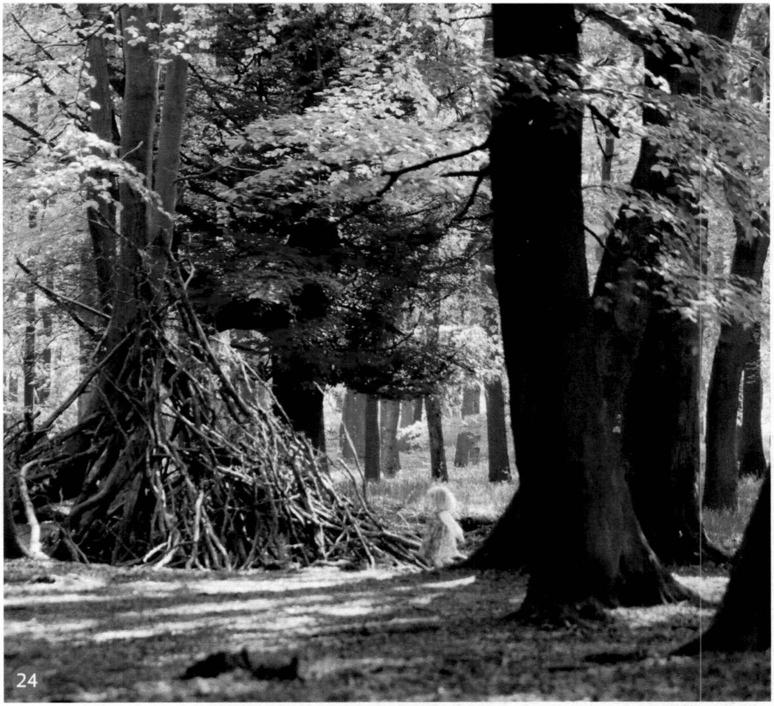

24

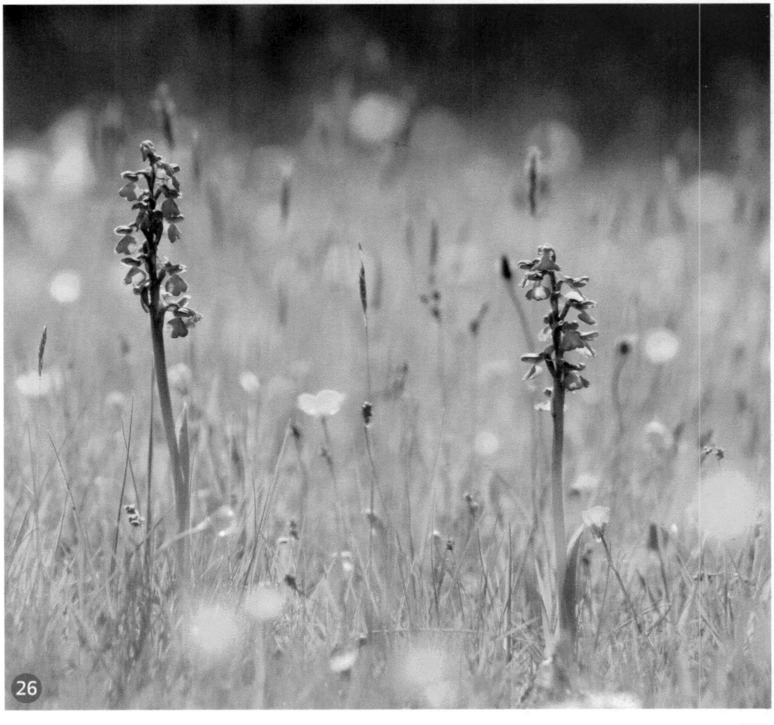

26

34

31

36

28

41

EAT LOCAL

28 PETERLEY WILD STRAWBERRY CAFE

Fill a picnic basket with products from over 20 local suppliers, pick your own organic fruits or have coffee in the Wild Strawberry café yurt (summer only).
→ Peterley Lane, Prestwood, Great Missenden, HP16 0HH, 01494 863566.
51.6867, -0.7271 ⊞

29 THREE HORSESHOES, BENNETT END

Tucked into the Chiltern Hills, this 18th-century inn has beautiful countryside views. Try local meats and ales while logs crackle in the inglenook fireplace.
→ Horseshoe Rd, Bennett End, HP14 4EB, 01494 483273.
51.6688, -0.8693 ⊞

30 PYO GROVE FARM

Pick up to 30 seasonal fruits and veg, including salads and garlic. Baskets, wheelbarrows and forks provided, picnic area and drinks available. Children very welcome. Open June–mid-October.
→ Great Gap, Ivinghoe, LU7 9DZ. From Leighton Buzzard head to Ivinghoe and look for the entrance and signs on the L, just before you get to the village outskirts.
51.8427, -0.6380 ⊞

31 ALFORD ARMS, FRITHSDEN

Local produce is a firm feature of this award-winning rural pub. Try ales from Potten End and Tring breweries, free-range chicken from Potash Farm and eggs from Ashley Green.
→ Frithsden, HP1 3DD, 01442 864480.
51.7778, -0.5279 ⊞

32 CHESHAM FARMERS' MARKET

Britain's greenest market fills Chesham market square fourth Saturday of the month (general markets other Saturdays). Berkhamsted farmers' market is also excellent (third Sunday each month). Both 10am–2pm.
→ Chesham High Street, HP5 1EP/ Berkhamsted High Street, HP4 1HU.
51.7037, -0.6133 ⊞

33 GRAND JUNCTION ARMS

Great canal-side setting with large garden, tree-planting garden and home-cooked food.
→ Bulbourne Rd, Bulbourne, HP23 5QE, 01442 891400.
51.8134, -0.6480

34 CHILTERN RIDGE FARM

Buy apple-fed pork, free-range eggs, chicken, lamb and home-pressed apple juice from the little shop-shed at this home-run farm. B&B in a converted stables.
→ Old Sax Lane, Chartridge, HP5 2TB, 01494 776309.
51.7233, -0.6431 ⊞

35 CHILTERN BREWERY

Oldest independent brewery in the Chilterns (established 1980), open six days a week. Brews natural beers using class-A malt and hops.
→ Nash Lee Road, Terrick, Aylesbury, HP17 0TQ, 01296 613647.
51.7685, -0.7805 ⊞

36 FRITHSDEN VINEYARD

English vineyard in the Chilterns foothills. Shop and terrace café open March–October. Visit for tours, vineyard walks and tastings.
→ Frithsden, Hemel Hempstead HP1 3DD, 01442 878723.
51.7790, -0.5263 ⊞

37 EIGHT BELLS, LONG CRENDON

Excellent local and seasonal gastro-pub grub. Lovely little garden and pretty village setting.
→ 51 High Street, Long Crendon, Bucks, HP18 9AL, 01844 208244.
51.7751, -0.9915 ⊞

CAMP AND STAY

38 NORTH HILL FARM

Camping plus tree-house, yurt or shepherd's hut accommodation. Views over the Chess Valley in an area of brown trout, kingfishers and orchids. Farm B&B available.
→ North Hill Farm, Chorleywood, Rickmansworth WD3 6HA, 01923 287040.
51.6644, -0.5108 ⊞

39 ASHRIDGE CAMPING & BUNKHOUSE

Help out with habitat conservation on a working holiday, staying in a wooded area with fallow deer. Daily jobs include scrub clearance and grassland management. Weekends or midweek in autumn/winter preferred.
→ Main entrance and visitor centre off the B4506 between Berkhamsted and Dagnall (HP4 1LT). Exact location given on booking, contact Nationaltrust.org.uk
51.8027, -0.5818

40 LAKESIDE TOWN FARM

Farmhouse at foot of Chilterns, with self-catering, lakeside cabin. Set down a quiet lane with rural views from the cabin's veranda.

→ Brook Street, Kingston Blount, OX39 4RZ, 01844 352152.
51.6903, -0.9365

41 KINGFISHER YURT

Turkomen yurt in a private wildlife garden, visited by kingfishers and herons. Woodburner and antique rugs with adjoining kitchen cabin and dining deck.

→ 0117 204 7830 Canopyandstars.co.uk Church Ln, Wendover, 07809 153590.
51.7583, -0.7393

42 HOME FARM RADNAGE CAMPING

Rural campsite with easy access to Ridgeway and Icknield Way. Great for red kites.

→ Radnage, High Wycombe. HP14 4DW, 01494 484136.
51.6639, -0.8680

43 HILL FARM ORCHARD

Two luxury en-suite wigwams in mature orchards. Near Grand Union Canal towpath, with views of Ivinghoe Hills.

→ Hill Farm & Orchard, Slapton, LU7 9DD, 07761 903628.
51.9086, -0.5980

44 ASHWELL FARM

Very simple camping in basic field on a working farm.

→ Great Missenden HP16 0DZ, 01494 862231.
51.6825, -0.7059

45 TOWN FARM CAMPING

Working farm, which allows small fires, BBQs and fire pit hire. Lovely views.

→ Town Farm, Ivinghoe, LU7 9EL, 07906 265435.
51.8387, -0.6217

46 LOWER BASSIBONES FARM

Beautifully converted barn with exposed beams set in rolling hills on farm at edge of Lee village (shop, pub). Large garden.

→ Lee Common, HP16 9LA, 01494 837798.
51.7280, -0.6814

47 CHILTERN HILLS RURAL B&B

Simple converted dairy, far from shops or pubs. Surrounded by meadows and ancient hedgerows.

→ Approach on foot via The Ridgeway National Trail. Exact location given on booking, via Our-land.co.uk.
51.7718, -0.6995

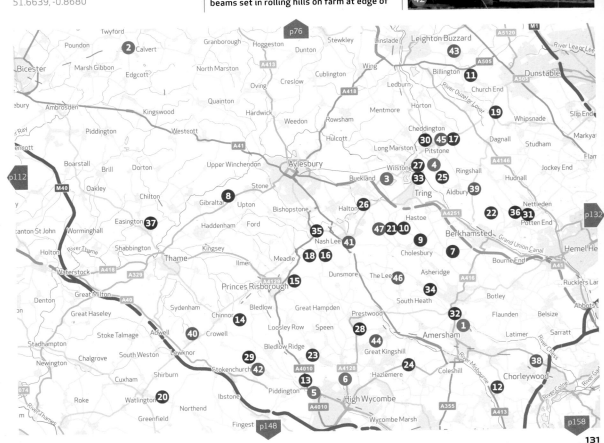

HERTS & LEA VALLEY

Our perfect weekend

→ **Travel** back to the Middle Ages in Hatfield Forest, Europe's greatest medieval woods.

→ **Lick** squashed strawberries from your fingers at Cammas Hall Farm, and scoff freshly baked scones and Victoria sponge in the tea barn.

→ **Canoe** or swim in the river Beane at Bengeo.

→ **Enter** the dense network of trees and bluebells at enchanted Bricket Wood then paddle in the ford or take a drink at the Old Fox.

→ **Ghost-watch** at Minsden Chapel, and discover if the phantom monk really does toll the bells.

→ **Hide** out beside the badger sett in Hoskyns Wood and watch the nocturnal world unfold.

→ **Walk** the Essex Way to find the world's oldest wooden church in Greenstead.

→ **Follow** the Roman road of Ermine Street, sleeping wild beside grand oaks and ancient yews.

→ **Disappear** into the folds of John Bunyan's 'Delectable Mountains' and find his hollow oak.

→ **Discover** the ruins of Cold Christmas Church with its abandoned graveyard.

Here in the very heart of the Home Counties, the rolling Hertfordshire Green Belt merges east with the boulder clays of Essex and west with the chalky Chiltern Hills. Raked fields pan towards the horizon, mysterious ruins sit shrouded by trees, and wooded lanes criss-cross a landscape of villages and pretty valleys.

Perhaps best known for its ancient forests, a wealth of woodland thrives here. Hatfield dates back to medieval times and, in his book *The Last Forest*, botanist Oliver Rackman declared that, in Hatfield 'all the elements of a medieval Forest survive: deer, cattle, coppice woods, pollards, scrub, timber trees, grassland and fen.' 'Hatfield,' he explains, 'is the only place where one can step back into the Middle Ages to see, with only a small effort of the imagination, what a Forest looked like.' Meanwhile, Epping Forest has been continuously wooded since Neolithic times and is home to contorted oaks and iron-age earthworks where Dick Turpin hid out and Boudicca is said to have camped.

So close to London, there are many ancient routes to explore. Ermine Street strikes out to York and can best be found in Broxbourne Wood, while the more ancient Icknield Way tracks east to Norfolk. A more modern route is the circular Hertfordshire Way, which passes the haunted ruin of Minsden Chapel. While they are pleasant for Sunday strolls, the best way to experience these long-distance routes is to fill a rucksack with supplies and set off on a multi-day hike, bivvying out en route.

Further north, into Bedfordshire, are the landscapes that influenced John Bunyan, author of *Pilgrim's Progress*. Bunyan's 79-mile waymarked route trails through his home county of Bedfordshire, passing the illustrious hollow oak from where he once preached. South of here, the dips and dells of the Pegsdon and Barton Hills are thought to have inspired the book's 'Delectable Mountains'. Today, these are perfect places to stake-out on a summers evening and watch for glow-worms, bats and starry night skies. A beautiful spring-fed stream rises beneath Barton Hill while high points like Deacon Hill are magical spots to watch dawn's golden glow highlight the hills and pour into the plains.

For more watery adventures close to London seek out some of the more secluded lakes of the Lea Valley Regional Park, or paddle in the Stort, Beane or Mimram; three of the area's lesser-known but beautiful rivers, perfect places to while away a summer's day and escape from London.

RIVERS & LAKES

1 WATERFORD MARSH, R BEANE

Pretty meadow and young willow-lined river
for paddling and a dip.

→ Waterford is 2 miles N of Hertford on A119.
Take first R (Vicarage Ln) to find footpath on R
after 200m onto common (SG14 2QA).

10 mins, 51.8141, -0.0937

2 BENGEO, R BEANE

River meadow and footbridge with good
swimming spots up or downstream, including
a weir and waterfall.

→ Find St Leonard's Church (SG14 3JW, all the
way down New Rd from Bengeo main street
past Holy Trinity church). Pass through gate
onto Hartham Common 100m to bridge. Close
to Hertford East station (head N via Mill Rd,
across the canal, 500m) or Hertford North
station.

5 mins, 51.8059, -0.0683

3 GLEN FABA, DOBB'S WEIR

One of the most secluded and cleanest lakes
in the Lea Valley area.

→ From Fish and Eels, Dobbs Weir Rd (EN11
0AY, 01992 466073) take footpath upstream

NE and cross the footbridge to R to reach lake
shore after 500m, under pylons. Or from end
of Glen Faba Rd (CM19 5JW).

10 mins, 51.7592, 0.0194

4 NAZEING MEAD LAKES, BROXBOURNE

Three pleasant lakes used for fishing and
sailing, on Cycle route 1 S of Dobb's weir.
Good footpath access to shores.

→ Between Broxbourne and Lower Nazeing,
B194, turn off N on National Cycle Route 1
from B194/Nazeing Rd (up Nursery Rd, EN9
2HU). First lake is after 200m on L. Or access
from Dobbs Weir (see above). Watch for blue-
green algae in late summer.

10 mins, 51.7411, 0.0079

5 SAWBRIDGEWORTH, R STORT

A pretty rural stretch of river for a mile down
to Feakes Lock.

→ Follow the Stort Walkway S from Sheering
Mill Lane (CM21 9LR) in Sawbridgeworth, or via
Pishiobury Park car park, A1184 (CM21 0AL).

15 mins, 51.8035, 0.1538

6 POPLARS GREEN, R MIMRAM

Pretty stretch of stream for kids and
paddling. Further down are several lakes.

→ B1000 E of Welwyn Gdn City (dir Hertford).
Pass turn-off for Tewin Mill, then Archers
Green, to find footpath on L after 400m
(before SG14 2NQ). Or continue on and turn
R after 300m for path (from gatehouse at
51.8024, -0.1438) to several lakes in Mimram
valley dowstream (51.7994, -0.1326).

3 mins, 51.8047, -0.1475

ANCIENT & SACRED

7 MINSDEN CHAPEL RUIN

Apparently haunted by a monk, this roofless
ruin with overgrown, flint walls is rumoured
to have secret tunnels and buried treasure.
Ghostly bells are said to toll at night.

→ Park at the Rusty Gun pub on the B656
(London Rd, SG4 7PG, 01462 432653) and
follow the Hertfordshire Way S for 600m to
the ruin, which sits in trees on the near tip of
small woodland. Return to the pub for a post
ghost-hunting pint.

51.9070, -0.2594 87h

8 THUNDRIDGE CHURCH RUIN

All that remains of Thundridge village, this
15th-century ruin and abandoned graveyard
once stood near a moated manor house.
Known locally as Cold Christmas Church.

8

11

12

→ Take road opposite The Sow & Pigs, Thundridge (SG12 0ST 01920 463281), dir Cold Christmas (signed Cold Christmas Ln). Continue E over A10, park immediately on L and follow signed footpath on L for approx 150m. Take right and go 300m to find ruins among trees on L at bend.
8 mins, 51.8378, -0.0157 ⛪📷🚶

9 OLD GORHAMBURY HOUSE
Ruined Elizabethan mansion with a two-storey porch, chapel and clock tower. Built in 1563–8 by Sir Francis Bacon's father, using bricks from the old abbey in St Albans.
→ From A414 Hemel Hempstead, take A4147 dir St Albans. After two miles, immediately after crossing M1, turn L onto Beechtree Ln. At end of Beechtree Ln, enter Gorhambury House Estate (AL3 6AH) on foot and follow main path for approx ½ mile back to the ruin.
10 mins, 51.7582, -0.3916 📷

10 ST ANDREWS LOG CHURCH
Reputed to be the world's oldest wooden church, with timber planks dating back to 1060. The long distance footpath, the Essex Way, passes by.
→ End of Church Ln, Greensted, Ongar, CM5

9LD. Clearly signed from Chipping Ongar. Essex Way footpath also leads directly past.
1 min, 51.7044, 0.2254 ⛪

11 PRIORY WELL CONDUIT
Hidden in a farmer's field, the ruins of this once-sacred spring have been overtaken by trees. Visit in winter when the field is crop-free. Wear wellies.
→ From The Green Man (SG4 7EU 01438 357217), Great Wymondley, head E dir Graveley. Where road turns S towards Little Wymondley, take L onto Gravely Ln heading E. After 500m, park in verge at 51.9420, -0.2237, walk in between fields. Ruin is hidden 400m S in a clump of trees in field R (marked 'Conduit' on OS maps).
4 mins, 51.9396, -0.2233 📷

12 ERMINE STREET, BROXBOURNE WOODS
This Roman road once ran from London to York. From here, you could follow it to London, bivvying along the way. The woods are enchanting, with oaks, coppiced hornbeams, yews and ancient earthworks. Wildest, wettest sections in the west.
→ Follow Lord St W out of Hoddesdon, passing High Leigh Conference Centre (EN11 8SG) on L before crossing the A10. Continue to small parking area on R between terraced cottages and equestrian centre, by Ermine Street welcome sign.
1 min, 51.7613, -0.0484 🔦

13 LOUGHTON CAMP, EPPING FOREST
Deep in Epping Forest, legend says that Boudicca camped at Loughton (where Dick Turpin later had his hideout) and was defeated at Ambresbury in AD61. Set out to find these camps while exploring the ancient trackways in this 5,600-acre forest.
→ For Loughton (51.6584, 0.0486), follow A104 north of Chingford, over roundabout by The Robin Hood (a mile N of IG10 4AA), to signed park on R. Follow Forest Way path SE for approx 500m to camp. Ambresbury Banks (51.6839, 0.0786) is E of the B1393, in woods opposite the Upshire turn-off.
7 mins, 51.6584, 0.0486 🔦

SUNSET HILLTOPS

14 DEACON HILL & PEGSDON HILLS
John Bunyan found his 'Delectable Mountains' in these steep chalk valleys and hills. Find glow-worms on summer evenings, see rare skipper butterflies, and look for bats at sunset or sunrise. Pretty chalk stream at Barton Hill.

→ From Hexton (Live & Let Live Country Inn, SG5 3JX) head ½ mile E on B655 to parking area on R. Walk SW along the Icknield Way for 600m, to where Deacon Hill rises to the R. Continue for less than a mile to Telegraph Hill or explore the woods and hills of the Pegsdon nature reserve to the R. From Hexton head W to follow stream from end of cemetery at Barton-le-Clay (MK45 4LA) up to Barton Hills (51.9544, -0.4194).
10 mins, 51.9572, -0.3535

15 SHARPENHOE CLAPPERS

This chalk escarpment towers above the Bedfordhire plains. Crowned with beech trees and an Iron Age hillfort, the stunning views are enhanced by wildflowers and butterflies in summer.

→ Large car park on Sharpenhoe Rd, between Streatley and Sharpenhoe, ¾ mile N of The Chequers pub (LU3 3PS, 01582 882072). The Icknield Way and Bunyan Trail passes through.
10 mins, 51.9542, -0.4508

ANCIENT WOODLAND

16 HATFIELD FOREST, TREES & DEER

Britain's most intact example of a medieval hunting forest, Hatfield has everything from rutting deer to huge ancient oaks.

→ From B1256 W of Takeley follow Hatfield Forest signs opp Green Man pub (CM22 6QU) to NT parking area ½ mile. Go through gate and follow access road approx 100m to find 400-year-old oak on L. Turn L to signposted boardwalk for a 400-year-old hornbeam pollard (L) and the coppiced field maple (R). Round Coppice (51.8594, 0.2273) has reliable sightings of the autumn deer rut, when stags lock horns over does.
10 min, 51.8587, 0.2445

17 BUNYAN'S OAK, HARLINGTON

John Bunyan, author of *Pilgrim's Progress*, preached from the natural pulpit of this hollow oak in the 17th century. Still an impressive sight, with footholds inside. The tree sits close to the 79-mile John Bunyan circular walk.

→ Exit Harlington heading E on the Barton Rd towards Barton-le-Cley (LU5 6NU). Immediately after national speed limit signs as you exit Harlington, find footpath (John Bunyan Trail) on L, marked by a blue plaque. After 100m, tree is visible in the field to the N but following for around 400m will bring you closer.
5 mins, 51.9701, -0.4784

16

18 BRICKET WOOD & COLNE VALLEY

Amazingly twisted and spooky ancient woodland with stunning bluebells in spring. The Colne creates an idyllic ford and pool in parkland of Munden House below.

→ Turn R (S) out of Bricket Wood station and follow road 500m to School Ln on L (Bricket Wood Common). Follow one of the trails R into wood off School Ln or continue to the rural Old Fox pub (AL2 3XU, 01923 675354) at the far end of the lane (1½ miles). For the Colne riverside walk turn off School Lane SE onto the bridleway at the blue Munden Estate sign.
1 min, 51.6931, -0.3637

WILDLIFE & MEADOWS

19 HUNSDON MEAD NATURE RESERVE

A 68-acre flooded meadow and wildflower wonderland. Farmed traditionally: grazed by cattle in spring, harvested for hay in July and left to flood in winter. Look for cowslips, cuckoo flowers, ragged robin and dragonflies.

→ From Roydon train station (CM19 5EH), signed footpath follows the River Stort E out of Roydon. After less than a mile, branch L on footpath that leads away from the river, deeper into the meadows.
20 mins, 51.7769, 0.0520

15

16

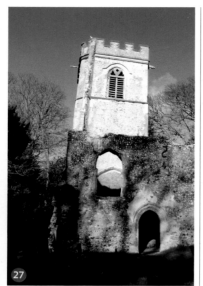

20 BARN OWLS, PIRTON

Local conservationists are encouraging barn owls in this area. Set out at dusk or dawn.
→ Walk E on the Hambridge Way (at SG5 3QS) or W on footpath towards Tingley Wood from near the Motte & Bailey pub (SG5 3QD).
1 min, 51.9727, -0.3313

21 TEWIN ORCHARD & BADGERS

Traditional orchard with 110 apple varieties and a hide to watch the badger cubs from.
→ Upper Green, Tewin, AL6 0LY (find entrance 300m E of Plume of Feathers). Contact Herts & Middlesex Badger Group (07733 051760) to volunteer on this site or use the badger-watching hide.
10 mins, 51.8239, -0.1617

SLOW FOOD

22 THE FOX INN, FINCHINGFIELD

16th-century coaching inn in a pretty village. Menu often features local meats, River Deben mussels and Essex 'huffers' (a local sandwich).
→ The Green, Finchingfield, CM7 4JX, 01371 810151.
51.9686, 0.4504

23 THE SUN AT NORTHAW

A local forager collects samphire, wild mussels and more for the pub kitchen, which uses more than 20 local producers. Local ales, pretty garden.
→ Judges Hill, EN6 4NL, 01707 655507.
51.7050, -0.1516

24 EMILY'S TEA SHOP, WHITWELL

Converted barn and courtyard on a small farm. Serves home-made cakes, jacket potatoes and ploughman's.
→ Water Hall Farm, Whitwell, SG4 8BN, 01438 871928. Signed from B651.
51.8775, -0.2808

25 REDBOURNBURY MILL

Last working watermill on the River Ver, has produced flour for over 1,000 years. Bakery open Saturdays (9am–1pm), baking classes on Mondays. Lovely walks in surrounding water meadows.
→ Redbournbury Lane, AL3 6RS, 01582 792173.
51.7841, -0.3797

26 JOLLY WAGGONER, ARDELEY

Boasts a 'one-mile menu' with meat, veg, fruit and herbs sourced from Church Farm, across the road.

→ The Jolly Waggoner Pub, Ardeley, SG2 7AH, 01438 861350.
51.9276, -0.0965

27 BROCKET ARMS, AYOT SAINT LAWRENCE

14th-century village inn, once a monastic quarters and pit-stop for pilgrims to St Albans Abbey. The village's partially ruined church is impressive and you can also visit George Bernard Shaw's house.
→ Ayot Saint Lawrence, AL6 9BT, 01438 820250.
51.8375, -0.2661

28 GRANNY SMITH'S TEA SHOP

Large shop and tea rooms with dairy. Tea room serves Foxhole's beef, ham, eggs, butter, local ice-cream and more. Busy working farm.
→ London Rd, Hertford, SG13 7NT, 01992 552900.
51.7931, -0.0500

29 THE HOLLY BUSH, POTTERS CROUCH

Cosy, 17th-century pub set in a small hamlet. Timber-framed, with log fire and mature garden.
→ Potters Crouch, AL2 3NN, 01727 851792.
51.7348, -0.3842

30 THE BEEHIVE, EPPING GREEN

Traditional country pub, specialising in fish, with daily deliveries from Billingsgate. Local rambles across open countryside and woods.
→ Epping Green, SG13 8NB, 01707 875959.
51.7460, -0.1241

31 THE VIPER, MILL GREEN

Rustic, unspoilt pub, surrounded by thick woodland. Beautiful cottage garden with hanging baskets. Simple lunches served.
→ Mill Green Rd, Mill Green, CM4 0PT, 01277 352010.
51.6913, 0.3722

32 FORAGING DAY, LAMBOURNE END

Inexperienced foragers could join an afternoon or one-day course to learn how to identify and prepare edible woodland plants and fungi.
→ Forest Foragers, 020 8985 2914. Courses held at Lambourne End Outdoor Centre, Manor Rd, Lambourne End, RM4 1NB.
51.6314, 0.1379

33 CAMMAS HALL PYO AND TEA BARN

PYO table-top (no bending required!) strawberries, raspberries and blackberries, with excellent home-made cakes in the Tea Barn. Picnic meadows free to use, kids very welcome. Sunflowers, sweetcorn, jams and farm honey also sold.

→ Hatfield Broad Oak, CM22 7JT, 01279 718777. Seasonal opening.
51.8136, 0.2687 🍴🦫

CAMP & SLEEP

34 BELLOWS MILL

Log cabin, yurt and cottages set by a Chilterns watermill. Bring a rod to fish in the lakes. Local honey sold.

→ Eaton Bray, LU6 1QZ, 01525 220548.
51.8670, 0.5763 🦫

35 SPRINGFIELD PARK CAMPSITE

Tent-only campsite beside wildlife-rich woodland and a stream. Allocated fire pits, breakfast cooked by the camp chef, archery range. Quiet after 11pm.

→ Old Parkbury Lane, St Albans, AL2 2DQ, 07957 167824.
51.7090, -0.3171 🏕

36 ANSTEY GROVE BARN

Converted barn with open fire, walled garden and herb patio, set in 20 acres of meadow and woodland. B&B or sleeps 12 as an exclusive booking.

→ Anstey, Nr Buntingford, SG9 0BJ, 01763 848828.
51.9776, 0.0559 🦫

37 HARESTREET HOLIDAY BARNS

On a working farm across from Hertfordshire's last remaining windmill (Cromer Mill, 51.9407, -0.1036). Markham bluebell wood one mile SW.

→ Harestreet Farm, Cottered, SG9 9QE, 07734 866382.
51.9399, -0.0958 🦫🐦

38 HIGH TREES FARM, WARE

Barn cottages on a 600-year-old farm operating under the Countryside Stewardship Scheme, with ancient woodland, natural spring and beetle banks.

→ Beggarmans Lane, Ware, SG11 1HB, 01920 438275.
51.8777, -0.0306 🦫🍴

39 CHURCH FARM CAMPSITE, ARDELEY

Tent pitches and secluded cabins on a 175-acre ecological farm. Sells free-range meats, fruit and veg at their shop, and supplies the Jolly Waggoner Inn, opposite. Has badger setts, barn owls and red kites. Compost loos.

→ Ardeley, Stevenage SG2 7AH, 01438 861447.
51.9272, -0.0967

40 RADWELL LAKE CAMPING, BALDOCK

Simple campsite with no electric hook-ups or hot water. Orchard and meadow pitches bordered by poplar trees. The dark skies here can give great stargazing.

→ Radwell Mill, Baldock, SG7 5ET for satnav, 01462 730242.
52.0062, -0.2106 ⛺

41 DEBDEN HOUSE CAMPSITE

Fifty-acre site surrounded by Epping Forest. Fire pits, forest walks, local pubs and a London-line train station within walking distance. Potential for weekend party crowds.

→ Debden Green, Loughton, IG10 2NZ, 020 8508 3008.
51.6656, 0.0798 🏕🚂

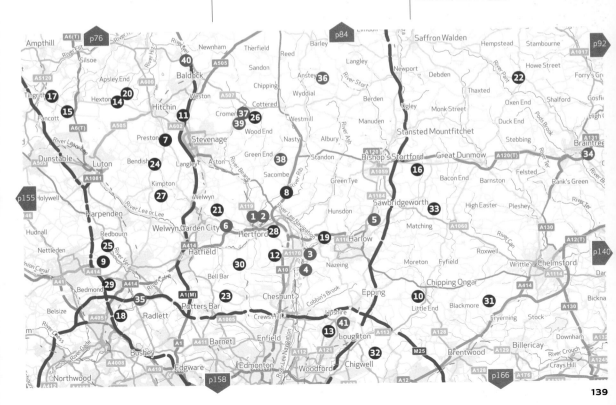

ESSEX COAST & CREEKS

Our perfect weekend

→ **Jump** into the creek at Beaumont Quay, made from the stones of old London Bridge.

→ **Climb** up into Old Knobbley, England's oldest oak.

→ **Canoe** or swim down the river Chelmer past pretty Ulting church.

→ **Hunt** glow-worms in the dusk at Stow Maries Halt and explore the Charity Lane tree tunnel.

→ **Wild** camp on Stone Point beach, arriving by kayak through the creeks of the 'Secret Waters'.

→ **Venture** out to the Dengie Marshes to watch wildfowl and waders, or stargaze until sunrise.

→ **Slurp** oysters in the Company Shed on Mersea Island and wash them down with a bottle of Maldon ale or local wine.

→ **Climb** the Naze Tower for a gull's eye view of the Walton backwaters, then hunt for sharks' teeth in the fossil-stuffed cliffs.

→ **Sleep** in a tented encampment beneath England's tallest Tudor tower.

Along the Essex coast, 350 miles of beaches, mudflats and marshes slide in and out of the sea each day, submerged at high water then exposed as the tide peels back to reveal temporary passages to low-lying islands and lonely landscapes that ache to be explored.

The sky melts to sea, the sea into saltings, and the saltings into shingly shores. The cries and calls of dark-bellied geese, scarlet-legged redshanks and black-tailed godwits echo across grey-brown coastal flats throughout the winter, while in summer, those same flats glow mauve with sea lavender. On the Dengie Peninsula, the solitary church of St Peter on the Wall gazes out towards lonely marshes and a rare spit of cockleshells which attracts terns, oystercatchers and short-eared owls.

Further north, the intertidal world was immortalised by Arthur Ransome in his *Swallows and Amazons* series, in which the islands and inlets of Hamford Water became the setting for a summer of childhood adventures. Sixty years on, Ransome's world remains as he described it, and you can still sail through the Walton Channel to swim with seals, and canoe to Horsey Island or bivvy out on the beach at Stone Point.

In a shoreline riddled with creeks, wide estuaries create the deepest cavities along the Essex coast. Halfway down, Blackwater Estuary (the largest) bathes the fragile islands of Osea and Northey, snaking north around Mersea, where it meets the River Colne. Here, some of the world's finest oysters have been harvested since Roman times and are just as delicious today, slurped straight from the shell, brine and all, with a squeeze of lemon or a tot of Tabasco.

Weaving to the west are rivers and streams rich in wildlife, where the Chelmer has pleasant places to swim or canoe. Farms and vineyards provide delicious local fare to village pubs and, in The Compass Inn at Littley Green, you can try traditional Essex huffers – triangular baps filled with meats from the local butcher. For an authentic taste of Essex farm life, camp out in the orchard at Bouncers Farm, or spend a night on Wicks Manor Farm, and watch for otters in the moat while Mrs Howie cooks the farm's own bacon for breakfast.

East of Chelmsford, the magical landscapes of the Danbury Commons are large enough to get lost in and, adjacent, the oaks and hornbeams of Blake's Wood rise above floods of spring bluebells. A little further north, you could disappear into the birch, ash and alder wood at Layer Marney, then climb England's tallest Tudor tower, or listen for nightingales in Fingrinhoe Wick and visit Stow Maries reserve to see glow-worms twinkle at dusk.

13

HIDDEN BEACHES

1 WRABNESS, HARWICH, R STOUR

Stone/silt estuary beach with huts, close to train station. Swimming platform.

→ On foot follow Black Boy Lane from station entrance to footpath and then sea, approx ½ mile, then bear L.

10 mins, 51.9474, 1.1657

2 BEAUMONT QUAY

1831 quay made from 12th-century stones of old London Bridge. From here barges would take hay to London for the horses and bring back manure and commodities. High tide only.

→ From roundabout in Thorpe-le-Soken head N on B1414 then turn R into farm (CO16 0BB) after 1½ mile. Pass through yard 200m to find Beaumont Quay written on wall R. Walk 50m to quay. Two hours either side of HT.

2 mins, 51.8716, 1.1794

3 KIRBY-LE-SOKEN JETTY

Wooden jetty and pool on creek in fields, passing pretty cottages. High tide only.

→ Park in Kirby-le-Soken village, and near post office (CO13 0DF) turn down Quay Lane opp (CO13 0DS) about 500m to waterside.

Cross bridge to L before quay, cross two fields, 300m, to reach jetty and small beach. HT only.

10 mins, 51.8649, 1.2256

4 THE NAZE, WALTON-ON-THE-NAZE

Remote beach and cliffs. There's also an eight-storey folly tower with views for up to 30 miles. Local art exhibited on six floors; teas served in the tower and on cliff-top lawns with tea room.

→ From promenade follow signs 'The Naze' a mile to parking (before CO14 8LG) by Tower (01255 852519) then bear N. Beach gets wilder and wilder as you head N for up to two miles.

5 mins, 51.8646, 1.2881

5 TOLLESBURY AND SHINGLEHEAD

Lovely tidal swimming pool in harbour village.

→ 10 miles E of Maldon on B1026 then B1023. Take L signed Marina, Woodrolfe Rd (CM9 8TB). Or walk out 2 miles E to Shinglehead Point, where you could bivvy.

1 min, 51.759, 0.8495

6 GOLDHANGER BEACH AND CREEK

Tiny high-tide secret beach and slipway.

→ Just S of Goldhanger village. Go R with Chequers Inn (CM9 8AT) on your R, to end of

Fish St, and take footpath to L for ½ mile.

10 mins, 51.7375, 0.7584

7 OSEA ISLAND, STEEPLE

Shingle beach by sailing club overlooking Osea Island.

→ From Steeple follow single-track Stansgate Road to Marconi Sailing Club (CM0 7NU, 01621 772164). Beach is 200m to L. Or try nearby Ramsey Island.

5 mins, 51.7177, 0.7929

8 FINGRINGHOE WICK BEACH, COLNE

Pretty sand beach behind lakes and nature reserve, with mostly-buried wreck of the barge 'Fly' – the only one of three sister ships to survive their maiden voyage from a Devon shipyard in 1899.

→ Signed Fringringhoe Wick, off B1025 S of Colchester. South Green Road out of Fingringhoe to CO5 7DN. Swimming at high tide only. Strong currents at mid tides.

5 mins, 51.8343, 0.9767

9 MERSEA STONE, EAST MERSEA

Famous oyster island. East beach is made up of oyster-shells. Deep swimming. Also accessible from Brightlingsea.

→ Immediately after crossing onto island (B1025) turn L dir East Mersea. Continue 3 miles to road end and find limited parking (near Ivy House, CO5 8US). Walk E to sea wall, then R to corner, then L to cross to beach. Follow beach around L to tip at mouth of estuary to find steep oyster-shell beach – careful of currents at mid-tide. Also reached by ferry from Brightlingsea (CO7 0AP, 01206 302200). Or try Cudmore Grove County Park beach (previous turning, signed) with easier parking and access, to the S part of the same shore (shallower water).

5 mins, 51.7998, 1.0066 🅰️🏕️♿

SEA KAYAKING

10 STONE POINT WILD CAMP, THE NAZE
'Savages Camp' in Arthur Ransome's *Secret Waters*. Best reached by canoe, though possible on foot from The Naze (Walton) after careful consideration of the tides.
→ A mile's walk N of the Naze (see entry) or launch a canoe from Kirby-le-Soken (see entry) at high tide and head down the Walton Channel. Experienced kayakers only.

30 mins, 51.8829, 1.2635 🚣🏕️🔽🅰️🛶

11 COLNE ESTUARY KAYAKING
Launch near the harbour at Brightlingsea Creek and paddle N up the Colne River to the pub at Wivenhoe. Or paddle S to sea and pitch up on wild Colne Point or St Osyth beach.
→ Experienced kayakers only. Start near the marina (CO7 0GE), or contact Nomadseakayaking.co.uk (0845 872 4868) for guided trips.

60 mins, 51.8055, 1.0232 🚣🏕️🔽🅰️🛶

12 RAY ISLAND NATURE RESERVE
Adventurous souls can canoe around this desolate spit, while Essex Wildlife Trust members can walk the path in season. Explore the shingle foreshore and sheep-grazed grassland, soaking up the silence and looking for finches, waders and water voles.
→ Launch at high tide from the moorings by Coast Rd, Mersea Island, CO5 8PA. Paddle NE up Ray Channel, crossing N to the reserve.

20 mins, 51.7987, 0.9136 🏕️🚣🐾🅰️

RIVER SWIMMING

13 ULTING & HOEMILL BR, R CHELMER
Lovely clean swimming and canoeing, for up to two miles downstream of bridge, or opposite pretty church. Watch out for boats.
→ Signed Nounsley/Ulting off B1019 at S end of Hatfield Peverel. From Ulting (after CM9 6QU) head S to the causeway and lock. Follow the footpath downstream. Limited parking, cycle route 1. Also explore downstream from Boreham Bridge, upstream (51.7485, 0.5596).

5 mins, 51.7485, 0.6081 🚣🏊

14 THORRINGTON TIDE MILL AND POND
This restored water mill (open bank holidays and last Sunday of month April–September) stands by a pretty mill pond and creek.
→ Sign on entrance, L on B1029 one mile N of Brightlingsea (CO7 8JL).

5 mins, 51.8350, 1.0204 📷❓

38

15 ST PETER'S CHURCH RUIN, ALRESFORD

Ruined 14th-century church. Destroyed by fire in 1971, it stands roofless with a pretty graveyard. Easy access.

→ From Alresford station, head S on Station Rd. Stay straight, crossing to Church Rd (CO7 8AB. Follow for around 700m, becoming a lane and passing school fields to reach parking area by stone cross and church on R.

1 min, 51.8465, 0.9969 ✝ ⌖

16 ST PETER ON THE WALL, DENGIE MARSH

One of England's most remote churches, founded by Anglo-Saxon bishop St Cedd (AD654). Wander S along the sea wall for marsh views and stargazing. Head N past the monastic community to find a simple remote mud/sand beach with stakes, and cockles.

→ Drive to end of East End Road, Bradwell-on-Sea from church (CM0 7QL). Follow track to coast and ruin.

5 mins, 51.7353, 0.9399 ⌖ ✝ ⌖ ⌖

17 WOOL STREET, CHALKNEY WOODS

This Roman trackway runs through a wood more than 10,000 years old. Bluebells and anemones in spring, nightingale song early summer. Home to the greatest concentration of small-leaved limes in Essex.

→ From A1124 SE in Earls Colne, turn down Tey Rd (CO6 2LG). After approx ½ mile, at sharp bend, take rough track L signed Chalkney Wood to parking area and entrance. L-hand path leads to Wool St (distinct as a plunging path).

2 mins, 51.9200, 0.7274 ⌖ ⌖

18 CHARITY LANE, STOW MARIES

This medieval trackway lane is a tree-lined tunnel between the local farms. Oak, ash, holly, hawthorn, blackthorn, hornbeam, elm. Fantastic autumn fungi.

→ From Cock Clarks (CM3 6RE), follow Hackmans Lane ½ mile S and find bridleway on R, opp Corporation Farm (CM3 6RH). Walk 200m SW for beginning of wooded trackway. A nicer but more intricate approach is from S end (lane past Charity Farm, near CM3 8RT).

15 mins, 51.6723, 0.6247 ⌖

19 OLD KNOBBLEY, FURZE HILL WOOD

Great for climbing, this contorted 800-year-old oak is thought to be England's oldest and has a girth that measures almost 10m.

16

Hunted witches once hid inside its hollow trunk. More oaks and tree swings here, plus lake.

→ Park at Mistley Football Club (Shrubland Road, CO11 1HS, lane S just at junction with B1352. Walk SW across football pitches (far right hand corner) to find path into wood (to L of split oak), after 100m bear R to see Old Knobbley ahead.

10 mins, 51.9383, 1.0813 ⌖

20 STOUR WOOD, WRABNESS

Essex's best saltmarsh woodland, with a diversity of woodland and watery habitats.

The chestnuts and oaks supplied Harwich shipyards in the 17th century. Arrive by train for views across the Dedham estuary.

→ From Wrabness station, follow Rectory Rd S for 400m, to and along edge of village. Turn L at footpath sign at corner, onto 'Private Rd Leading to Woodcutters Cottages'. Follow footpath to wood. If driving, main carpark is off the B1352 Wrabness Rd at S edge of wood.
5 mins, 51.9381, 1.1855 🅿️🚆

WILDLIFE & MEADOWS

21 BLAKES WOOD, BLUEBELLS

Spring bluebells, colourful wildflowers, clear streams and ancient oaks typify this wood, which fringes Danbury Common. Set beside the Danbury Ridge Reserves, a mosaic of meadows, heathland, woods and streams.

→ Main entrance off Riffhams Chase (on National Cycle Route 1), Little Baddow CM3 4AU, opposite mock-Tudor house.
1 min, 51.7289, 0.5691 🅿️

22 NORTHEY ISLAND

This remote island gives a taste of true wilderness. Site of Britain's best-recorded battle with Viking raiders (The Battle of Maldon, AD991). Each winter 5,000 Brent geese visit. Advanced booking only, so if closed enjoy a walk along the wild saltings shoreline instead.

→ Maldon, CM9 6PP. Call NT on 01621 853142 for a permit.
20 mins, 51.7229, 0.7218 🏞️

23 FINGRINHOE WICK, NIGHTINGALES

Wander through this reserve on an early-summer evening and get treated to a concerto of nightingale song. Varied birdlife (lots of waders). Carry on to beach for a high tide dip in the Colne Estuary.

→ South Green Road, Fingringhoe, CO5 7DN (signed from Fingringhoe). Gates shut to cars at 5pm.
1 min, 51.8345, 0.9709 🐕🚻

24 STOW MARIES, GLOW-WORMS

Small reserve with summer glow-worm displays at dusk.

→ From Prince of Wales (Woodham Rd, CM3 6SA, 01621 828971) head E. After 300m turn R onto Church Ln. Park in layby by reserve entrance just after national speed limit signs. If you have time also explore Charity Lane, N of village (see entry).
1 min, 51.6611, 0.6516 🚶🚻

25 THE WHALEBONE INN

Meadows roll down to the Roman River outside this listed building. Exposed beams, woodburner and stripped floors. Menu prioritises local producers.

→ Chapel Road, Fingringhoe CO5 7BG, 01206 729307. Near Fingringhoe Wick reserve.
51.8447, 0.9440 🍴

26 DEDHAM VALE VINEYARD

Serene and secluded Stour Valley setting. Produces six styles of wine, plus cider. Book ahead for afternoon tea, picnics or BBQs.

→ Green Lane, Boxted, CO4 5TS, 01206 271136.
51.9541, 0.8950 🍴

27 THE COMPASSES, LITTLEY GREEN

Essex ales are pulled fresh from the barrel in this traditional country pub. Local butcher, fishmonger and greengrocer supply the kitchen, which specialises in Essex huffers (triangular baps).

→ Littley Green, CM3 1BU, 01245 362308.
51.8285, 0.4641 🍴🍴

28 LATHCOATS FARM

Black timber barns, specialising in apples but selling a full range of produce. PYO, buy in the shop or eat apple cake in the coffee shed.

→ Beehive Lane, Galley Wood, Chelmsford, CM2 8LX, 01245 352021.
51.7105, 0.4765 🍴

29 THATCHERS ARMS, MOUNT BURES

Everything from meat to ice-cream is sourced locally, with food miles chalked-up alongside producers' names. Rural setting with Stour Valley views.

→ Hall Road, Mount Bures, CO8 5AT, 01787 227460.
51.9520, 0.7714 🍴

30 MERSEA ISLAND VINEYARD & TEAS

Ten-acre vineyard with wines and island beers served in Maria's Vintage Tea Room. Sunday roasts and barn-style accommodation available.

→ Rewsalls Lane, East Mersea, CO5 8SX, 01206 385900.
51.7834, 0.9555 🍴

31 THE COMPANY SHED, WEST MERSEA

Legendary no-frills seafood hut with a BYO

policy. Try brown crab, local lobster, Essex cockles and native oysters. Bring wine from Mersea Vineyard.

→ 129 Coast Rd, West Mersea, CO5 8PA, 01206 382700.
51.7806, 0.8995 🍴

32 THE BELL, PURLEIGH

Hill-top pub with views over the marshes. Local produce includes wines from neighbouring vineyard. Good walks nearby.

→ The Street, Purleigh, CM3 6QJ, 01621 828348.
51.6864, 0.6630 🍴🍺

CAMP & SLEEP

33 MALTING FARM, LANGHAM

Help out with the animals on this family farm, explore the water meadows or try pottery. Stay in a safari-style tent with wooden floor. Indoor and outdoor stoves. No gas or electricity.

→ Langham Ln, Langham, CO4 5NW, 01420 80804. Featherdown.co.uk
51.9438, 0.9301 🏕🏠

34 LAYER MARNEY TOWER

Six safari-style tents set in the wooded grounds of England's tallest Tudor tower–coastal views from top. Expect log stoves and hot tubs.

→ Layer Marney, CO5 9US, 01206 330784, Featherdown.co.uk
51.8229, 0.7972 🏕🔥

35 WICKS MANOR B&B

Moated family farmhouse for an authentic taste of Essex farm life. Look for water voles in the moat. Own pork served at breakfast and supplied to The Chequers pub (CM9 8AS) nearby.

→ Wicks Manor Farm, Witham Road, Tolleshunt Major, CM9 8JU, 01621 860629.
51.7763, 0.7493 🏕🍴

36 THE RAFT AT CHIGBOROUGH FARM

Floating cabin and wood fired hot-tub set on a trout lake. Fish, row and stargaze to your heart's content.

→ Chigborough Road, Heybridge, CM9 4RD. Canopyandstars.co.uk, 0117 204 7830.
51.7385, 0.7188 🏕🔥

37 WOODPECKER YURT

Yurt and bell tent in a walled orchard and veg garden. BBQ, fire-pit, bikes and games.

→ Mount Hall, London Road, Great Horkesley, CO6 4BZ, 01206 271359.
51.9486, 0.8628 🏕🔥

38 BOUNCERS FARM, WICKHAM BISHOPS

Sleep beneath apple trees on this off-grid farm campsite, or stay in a bow-top wagon. Opera in the Orchard often held in July.

→ 0117 204 7830 Canopyandstars.co.uk Bouncers Farm, Wickham Hall lane, CM8 3JJ, 01621 894112. Entrance opposite White House Farm.
51.7725, 0.6591

39 GREEN LANE CAMPING & CARAVANNING

No frills, five-acre camping field set behind the Hunstman & Hounds thatched pub. Water block and basic showers.

→ Althorne, CM3 6BJ, 01621 740387.
51.6700, 0.7550

BERKSHIRE & THAMES

Our perfect weekend

→ **Explore** the fabulous Burnham Beeches, whose ancient trees have featured in *Harry Potter*.

→ **Paddle** along the Thames to Hurley Lock and sleep under the stars on your own private island.

→ **Canoe** from the Three Men in a Boat pub through empty meadows then watch the sunset from the tumulus at Wittenham Clumps.

→ **Disappear** into the deep folds at Bix Bottom to find the wildly overgrown Church of St James.

→ **Glug** local ale at England's oldest freehouse at Royal Standard.

→ **Moonlight** swim down the Thames past Temple Island, from Henley to Aston.

→ **Cycle** on from Reading to Newbury on the river path, swimming in the Kennet along the way.

→ **Dance** around the ramparts of Segsbury Camp hillfort at dawn, where human bones are buried.

→ **Climb** through the glacier-rippled Vale of the White Horse.

The Wild Woods and changing seasons, the gentle pace of river life and the carefree pursuit of 'simply messing about in boats'.

The nostalgia of the Thames Valley was so beautifully evoked in Kenneth Grahame's *Wind in the Willows*. The stretch between Hurley and Marlow, where the Chilterns fold away, was the inspiration for much of his children's classic. This is where Ratty spent so much time swimming with ducks, and Mole trying not to fall in. Grahame's own childhood was spent with his grandparents, rowing out to the little islands near Cookham Dean, a seasonally braided section of the Thames. Today, this stretch is speckled with riverside campsites, remote island pitches and magical swim spots, such as those at Hurley and Cookham locks.

A few miles south, the Ice House in Bisham Woods was the setting for Toad's dungeon. Here, you can wander through the sunken lanes of the Wild Woods that Badger called home, while on the edge of Ashley Hill Forest to the east, the woodland setting of the Dew Drop Inn makes it a magical place for a pint. In a region rich in ancient woods, there are many more enchanting places to discover, such as the twisted trees in Burnham Beeches, which have featured in Hollywood blockbusters such as the *Harry Potter* films and *Robin Hood Prince of Thieves*, while the wizened oaks in Windsor Park are said to be haunted by a Saxon hunter and his hounds.

Where the river travels south of Oxford, billowing hay meadows flank the parish of Clifton Hampden. A bucolic retreat within easy reach of London, this was a 19th-century playground for London society, and a favourite place of Jerome K. Jerome, who wrote *Three Men in a Boat* (1889), a comic manifesto for a simpler way of living – river swimming before breakfast, moonlit chat around the fire, and sleeping lulled by the lapping waters. Near here, the high points of the Wittenham Clumps give stunning panoramas over the countryside, while further west towards the Cotswolds are secluded swimming spots near Lechlade-on-Thames, and the spectacular chalk etching, rippled slopes and ancient barrows of Uffington.

Escaping the pressures of London, neither Grahame nor Jerome wanted to break the spell of this serene Thames Valley world, and it's hardly surprising: "Beyond the Wild Wood comes the Wide World", says Ratty to Mole. " And that's something that doesn't matter, either to you or me. I've never been there, and I'm never going, nor you either, if you've got any sense at all".

2

RIVER THAMES

1 CHOLSEY, R THAMES

A long stretch of rural riverside with no locks and little overhanging vegetation, so great for a longer swim or canoe or a moonlit swim.

→ Head S from Wallingford on A329 and at about 2 miles find Ferry Lane (dead end, OX10 9GZ) on L, opp the South Moreton turning. Continue to boatclub at end. Explore downstream. Beware fast-moving rowing teams. Cholsey train station nearby.

5 mins, 51.5649, -1.1339

2 PANGBOURNE, R THAMES

Popular swimming meadows near station. Walk from Pangbourne to Goring on the NE bank and return by train. About halfway is a pretty wooded section with rope swings.

→ Meadows are downstream of Whitchurch bridge (RG8 7BP, Pangbourne station 5 mins). Continue across bridge and climb hill for ½ mile to find bridleway on L (at 40mph sign). This leads for 1½ mile to Hartslock Wood descending to riverbank. A lovely wild stretch of the Thames. Or access opp bank from Lower Basildon church (RG8 9NH, signed 'Church' off A329 2¼ NW of Pangbourne).

40 mins, 51.5080, -1.1108

3 ASTON FERRY, HENLEY

Open grassy river meadows and quite lanes near a pub – great for family picnics. Or a walk downstream from Henley, past famous Temple Island at Remenham.

→ It's a pretty drive to Aston on lanes from Henley via Remenham. Or signed off A4130 2 miles E of Henley. At Flower Pot Hotel (RG9 3DG, 01491 574721) follow Ferry Lane to small car park at end. Meadow is upstream to L.

3 mins, 51.5540, -0.8666

4 DORNEY, JUBILEE RIVER

A wonderful wide off-shoot of the Thames, lined by open fields, in an otherwise very built-up area by Slough and M4.

→ Head for the bridge just past The Pineapple (SL4 6QS) on B3026/Lake End Rd between Slough (M4 J7) and Eton Wick Park, and find car park. Explore up or downstream. Retire afterward for lunch at Dorney Court Kitchen Garden (SL4 6QP, 01628 669999). Cycle path 61 between Maidenhead or Windsor stations.

5 mins, 51.5056, -0.6566

5 HURLEY ISLAND, THAMES

A historic village with wooded river islands and ancient pub. Several places to swim up or downstream plus riverside campsite.

→ From A404 take A4130 dir Henley. After a mile turn R signed 'Hurley village only'. Continue straight after The Olde Bell (SL6 5LX, 01628 825881) to find small car park opposite churchyard wall. Head down path beside car park to cross footbridge to island and lock, then bear R 200m to find a beach and shallows on far side. Or explore upstream above lock for several miles, past the campsite.

10 min, 51.5522, -0.8061

OTHER RIVERS & LAKES

6 MARSH BENHAM, R KENNET

A large junction pool in the River Kennet.

→ Signed Marsh Benham off A4 2 miles W of Newbury edge. Continue ¾ mile to Hamstead lock (RG20 0JE) and follow the towpath upstream 300m. Cycle route 4 to Newbury. Food at the Red House (RG20 8LY, 01635 582017).

5 mins, 51.4010, -1.3963

7 WOOLHAMPTON LAKES & R KENNET

Secluded and wooded river downstream, secret lake upstream. Pub, station and cycle path. Great canoeing.

→ Head upstream 300m from Rowbarge

Inn (RG7 5SH, 01189 712213), turn L at footbridge to find track leading to lake shore (200m). Follow river downstream for pools and a secret wooded stretch for over a mile beyond footbridge. Perfect for canoes.
10 mins, 51.3934, -1.1844

8 SULHAMSTEAD, R KENNET
Beautiful open meadows and good access up and downstream of lock.
→ Turn off A4 at Spring Inn, 2 miles W of M4 J12 at Reading, and find parking at second bridge (RG7 4BS). Old willows upstream. Pretty swing bridge downstream, leading eventually (20 mins) to Sheffield Bottom Lock Lake (see below). Canoeing. National Cycle Route 4.
10 mins, 51.4186, -1.0999

9 SHEFFIELD BOTTOM LOCK LAKE
This is one of the huge spring-fed lakes that can be seen from the M4 near Reading. The gravel was used to build the new city.
→ From M4 J12 head towards Sheffield Bottom lock picnic area and car park (Hangar Road, Theale, RG7 4AP). Follow the canal downstream and after 300m lake is on R. Keep clear of sailing dinghies. Or walk in from Sulhamstead. National Cycle Route 4.
5 mins, 51.4312, -1.0604

10 HEATH POND, CROWTHORNE
Birch and pine line this little lake in the woods. An island of pine trees beckons you to swim.
→ Turn L from Crowthorne station and head to A321 roundabout (100m). Cross to R (2 o'clock) to find footpath. After 700m at diagonal crossroads by gate, take byway L into Simons Wood to find pond after approx 180m and a crossrods (S of Hollybush Ride, RG40 3QL).
15 mins, 51.3697, -0.8352

11 CHOBHAM COMMON, SUNNINGDALE
Wild lake hidden in stunning heather-filled heathland.
→ About 1¼ miles S of Sunningdale Station/ Broomhall on B383, past SL5 0HY, find car park on L for Victoria Memorial. Cross road and find rough path W to lakes, 500m.
10 mins, 51.3824, -0.6198

12 BOTANY BAY, VIRGINIA WATERS
The evocatively named lake beach overlooks the Roman ruins brought from Leptis Magna in Libya. However, for a discreet swim, the S bank of this huge lake is a bit quieter.
→ A footpath follows the lake around the shore. Easiest entry from the car park by the

15

Wheatsheaf Hotel (GU25 4QF) then bear L. 20 mins walk from Virginia Water station.
15 mins, 51.4112, -0.5965 🚏❓🚻

ANCIENT & SACRED

13 WAYLAND'S SMITHY LONG BARROW

Enter the Neolithic chambered barrow, once inhabited in legend by a Saxon smith-god. High on the Ridgeway with great views.

→ On B4507 between Ashbury and Woolstone, take unnamed turning opposite Knighton and Compton Beauchamp (SN6 8NX) and drive up hill and over top. Turn R onto the restricted byway (the Ridgeway, limited parking) and walk 450m to find the smithy in trees off the track on R.
6 mins, 51.5661, -1.5952 🚻🏞🏔

14 LAMBOURN SEVEN BARROWS

There are actually 26 barrows scattered here, dating to around 2,200BC. Nature reserve.
→ Signed off B4001, N of Lambourne (RG17 8UH). Track on R at bend after a mile.
2 mins, 51.5426, -1.5261 🚻🏞🏔

15 DONNINGTON CASTLE, NEWBURY

Twin-towered gatehouse, once part of a medieval castle which Parliament voted to demolish in 1646 after a Civil War siege.
→ Signed from Donnington village (B4494, RG14 2LE, outskirts of Newbury). English Heritage: free, daylight hours.
2 mins, 51.4197, -1.3385 🚻🅱

16 ST JAMES CHURCH, BIX BOTTOM

Once part of the abandoned village of Bix Brand; ceremonies ceased here in 1874. Wildly overgrown. Warburg Nature Reserve is nearby.
→ Follow signs to Bix Bottom from the B480 at Middle Assendon, heading towards the Warburg reserve. 300m after passing Valley Farm on L (RG9 6BJ, redbrick farm house and buildings), find ruin on L by farm track and green footpath sign. Just visible from road.
1 min, 51.5769, -0.9533 ✝🚻🏔

17 ALFRED'S CASTLE, ASHDOWN PARK

This little Iron Age hillfort is wonderfully remote with great views and walks across the Berkshire Downs. Where King Alfred is said to have defeated the Danes in AD871.
→ Walk here from the Rose and Crown, Ashbury (serves local food, SN6 8NA, 01793 710222), following the footpath that leads S behind the pub and church, and crosses the

13

16

18

20

21

Ridgeway (2 miles to hillfort, also connects to Wayland's Smithy, see above). Alternatively, from Ashdown House and Estate car park (RG17 8RE, signed off B4000 N of Lambourn, National Trust) walk 500m to hillfort.

40 mins, 51.5382, -1.6003 🚶🖼️🏕️✨

SUNSET HILLTOPS

18 WITTENHAM CLUMPS & THE POEM TREE

England's oldest beech trees, planted in the 1740s on a tumulus viewpoint overlooking the Thames. Also Brightwell Barrow and the site of the collapsed 'Poem Tree,' which had words carved into its bark.

→ Footpath access (and further info) at Earth Trust Centre, S of Little Wittenham (OX14 4QZ, 01865 407792). Exit Little Wittenham S and head ½ mile to the Earth Trust parking (on L). Footpaths to clumps are opposite entrance. Continue N through village for swimming in the Thames nr Dorchester.

10 mins, 51.6305, -1.1828 🚶🖼️

19 WALBURY HILLFORT AND INKPEN HILL

The site of an Iron Age hillfort, Walbury Hill is Britain's highest chalk hill and is linked to its twin summit, Inkpen Hill, by a ridge walk.

→ From Crown and Garter, Inkpen (RG17 9QR,

01488 668325) go S and take two lefts, signed Combe. Continue ¾ mile then fork L signed Faccombe and Ashmansworth. After ½ mile find parking area on R by bend (51.3519, -1.4556). Follow the Wayfarers Walk 600m W to the summit of Walbury, then continue W along the ridge for 1¼ miles, crossing a minor road, to reach Inkpen Hill. Good café, bakery and restaurant in Inkpen.

7 mins, 51.3519, -1.4556 🖼️✨

20 UFFINGTON HILLFORT & WHITE HORSE

Oxfordshire's highest point, with views of six counties and a huge stylised horse etched into its upper slopes.

→ Signed off B4507, 2 miles S of Uffington, on Dragon Hill Rd (near SN7 7QJ). 500m NW is The Manger, fluted slopes left by the last Ice Age. The Ridgeway route above connects to Wayland's Smithy and Alfred's Castle, see above.

10 mins, 51.5775, -1.5664 🖼️🅱️

21 SEGSBURY CAMP, LETCOMBE REGIS

Iron Age hillfort on the northern face of Berkshire Downs, with extensive ditch, ramparts and four gateways. Views over the Vale of the White Horse.

→ Leave Letcombe Regis S on Warborough Rd

15

Wheatsheaf Hotel (GU25 4QF) then bear L. 20 mins walk from Virginia Water station.
15 mins, 51.4112, -0.5965 🚩❓📷

ANCIENT & SACRED

13 WAYLAND'S SMITHY LONG BARROW

Enter the Neolithic chambered barrow, once inhabited in legend by a Saxon smith-god. High on the Ridgeway with great views.

→ On B4507 between Ashbury and Woolstone, take unnamed turning opposite Knighton and Compton Beauchamp (SN6 8NX) and drive up hill and over top. Turn R onto the restricted byway (the Ridgeway, limited parking) and walk 450m to find the smithy in trees off the track on R.
6 mins, 51.5661, -1.5952 📷🖼🏔

14 LAMBOURN SEVEN BARROWS

There are actually 26 barrows scattered here, dating to around 2,200BC. Nature reserve.
→ Signed off B4001, N of Lambourne (RG17 8UH). Track on R at bend after a mile.
2 mins, 51.5426, -1.5261 📷🖼🏔

15 DONNINGTON CASTLE, NEWBURY

Twin-towered gatehouse, once part of a medieval castle which Parliament voted to demolish in 1646 after a Civil War siege.
→ Signed from Donnington village (B4494, RG14 2LE, outskirts of Newbury). English Heritage: free, daylight hours.
2 mins, 51.4197, -1.3385 📷 B

16 ST JAMES CHURCH, BIX BOTTOM

Once part of the abandoned village of Bix Brand; ceremonies ceased here in 1874. Wildly overgrown. Warburg Nature Reserve is nearby.
→ Follow signs to Bix Bottom from the B480 at Middle Assendon, heading towards the Warburg reserve. 300m after passing Valley Farm on L (RG9 6BJ), redbrick farm house and buildings), find ruin on L by farm track and green footpath sign. Just visible from road.
1 min, 51.5769, -0.9533 ✝📷🏔

17 ALFRED'S CASTLE, ASHDOWN PARK

This little Iron Age hillfort is wonderfully remote with great views and walks across the Berkshire Downs. Where King Alfred is said to have defeated the Danes in AD871.
→ Walk here from the Rose and Crown, Ashbury (serves local food, SN6 8NA, 01793 710222), following the footpath that leads S behind the pub and church, and crosses the

13

16

18

20

21

Ridgeway (2 miles to hillfort, also connects to Wayland's Smithy, see above). Alternatively, from Ashdown House and Estate car park (RG17 8RE, signed off B4000 N of Lambourn, National Trust) walk 500m to hillfort.

40 mins, 51.5382, -1.6003 🚶📷🖼️📷

SUNSET HILLTOPS

18 WITTENHAM CLUMPS & THE POEM TREE

England's oldest beech trees, planted in the 1740s on a tumulus viewpoint overlooking the Thames. Also Brightwell Barrow and the site of the collapsed 'Poem Tree,' which had words carved into its bark.

→ Footpath access (and further info) at Earth Trust Centre, S of Little Wittenham (OX14 4QZ, 01865 407792). Exit Little Wittenham S and head ½ mile to the Earth Trust parking (on L). Footpaths to clumps are opposite entrance. Continue N through village for swimming in the Thames nr Dorchester.

10 mins, 51.6305, -1.1828 🚶📷

19 WALBURY HILLFORT AND INKPEN HILL

The site of an Iron Age hillfort, Walbury Hill is Britain's highest chalk hill and is linked to its twin summit, Inkpen Hill, by a ridge walk.

→ From Crown and Garter, Inkpen (RG17 9QR,

01488 668325) go S and take two lefts, signed Combe. Continue ¾ mile then fork L signed Faccombe and Ashmansworth. After ½ mile find parking area on R by bend (51.3519, -1.4556). Follow the Wayfarers Walk 600m W to the summit of Walbury, then continue W along the ridge for 1¼ miles, crossing a minor road, to reach Inkpen Hill. Good café, bakery and restaurant in Inkpen.

7 mins, 51.3519, -1.4556 📷📷

20 UFFINGTON HILLFORT & WHITE HORSE

Oxfordshire's highest point, with views of six counties and a huge stylised horse etched into its upper slopes.

→ Signed off B4507, 2 miles S of Uffington, on Dragon Hill Rd (near SN7 7QJ). 500m NW is The Manger, fluted slopes left by the last Ice Age. The Ridgeway route above connects to Wayland's Smithy and Alfred's Castle, see above.

10 mins, 51.5775, -1.5664 📷 B

21 SEGSBURY CAMP, LETCOMBE REGIS

Iron Age hillfort on the northern face of Berkshire Downs, with extensive ditch, ramparts and four gateways. Views over the Vale of the White Horse.

→ Leave Letcombe Regis S on Warborough Rd

(OX12 9LD), climbing up onto and along the dirt track. Park by the wooden gates and stile in the centre of the fort.

1 min, 51.5574, -1.4470 🚶

ANCIENT FOREST

22 BISHAM 'WILD WOOD'

The inspiration for the Wild Wood in *The Wind in the Willows*, this is a place of beeches, bluebells and sunken lanes.

→ Along Quarry Wood Rd for about ½ mile between Cookham Dean and Marlow bridge. There's a small but convenient place to park at the Cookham end (SL6 9TZ). Several footpaths lead off the two hairpin bends.

1 min, 51.5625, -0.7563 🅿🚶🚲

23 WINDSOR GREAT PARK, OAKS

4,800-acre park with Europe's largest collection of ancient oaks, several over 1,000 years old.

→ The ancient oaks are widely spread but the Cranbourne Gate, 3 miles SW of Windsor on A332 with parking, is a good place to start (SL4 2BT). One huge oak is at 51.4516, -0.6137, a mile NE from the gate, in the SW corner of the spinney beside Prince of Wales pond, or 300m W of Long Walk. This is also

approx ¾ mile SW after entering the park on foot from Windsor at SL4 2RA.

20 mins, 51.4453, -0.6380 📷

24 DRUIDS OAK, BURNHAM BEECHES

The contorted trees of Burnham Beeches featured in *Harry Potter*. Seek out the 800-year-old Druids Oak. Nearby is Seven Ways hillfort.

→ Burnham Beeches is clearly signed off the A355 in Farnham Common. Druids Oak is located just SE of Lord Mayor's Drive. Access from car park on Hawthorn Lane by red postbox (SL2 3TF) on S side of woods and follow the Drive NE for 300m past the hillfort on L to Druids on R. Or follow the Drive W from the main car park and café (near SL2 3PS), about a mile.

6 mins, 51.5523, -0.6346 🅿🚶🚲

25 NORTH GROVE WOOD, NR WOODCOTE

Beautiful beech trees twist skywards, with bluebells in spring and red kites in summer.

→ Leave Woodcote N on the B471 to reach the A4074 (RG8 0PA). Turn R (dir Reading) then immediately L (Rushmore Ln). After 100m, take the Chiltern Way through metal gate on L.

1 min, 51.5405, -1.0720 📷

WILDLIFE WONDERS

26 CHURCH WOOD, WOODPECKERS

Listen for great spotted woodpeckers drumming on deadwood in spring, and hear the laughter of green woodpeckers. Jays, nuthatches and buzzards also here.

→ Follow signed footpath to the S of The White Horse pub, Hedgerley (SL2 3UY). Path leads behind the pub.

5 mins, 51.5757, -0.5994

27 WARBURG NATURE RESERVE

The early summer dawn chorus is spectacular in this twisting, dry valley of grassland and woods. Tranquil spot, high in the Chilterns, with spring bluebells, anemones and orchids, and summer butterflies.

→ Follow signs to Bix Bottom from the B480 at Middle Assendon (RG9 6AT), and then signs for the reserve (RG9 6BL).

1 min, 51.5849, -0.9618

28 GREENHAM COMMON OLD AIRBASE

Cycle around this famous former nuclear airbase and runway, now decaying and returned to nature. Skylarks, nightingales and the rare Dartford warbler.

→ Signed Greenham Common/Retail Park from A339 roundabout S of Newbury (RG14 7EY). After a mile, just after fourth roundabout (leisure centre sign, before RG19 8SL) find car park.

1 min, 51.3777, -1.2788

LOCAL FOOD

29 THE SWAN, INKPEN

Traditional country pub with farm shop, selling and serving their own organic beef, sloe gin and more. Surrounding footpaths through the North Wessex Downs.

→ Craven Road, Inkpen, RG17 9DX, 01488 668326.

51.3763, -1.4849

30 REBELLION BEER COMPANY

Independent brewery with on-site shop and informal tours of the brew house. Taste and buy award-winning beers alongside local produce. Open Mon-Sat, 8am-7pm.

→ Bencombe Farm, Marlow Bottom, SL7 3LT, 01628 476594.

51.5868, -0.7688

31 DORNEY COURT KITCHEN GARDENS

Everything is locally sourced or grown within the historic kitchen gardens. A lovely spot for lunch or tea.

→ Court Lane, Dorney, SL4 6QP, 01628 669999.

51.5021, -0.6658

32 THE BELL INN, ALDWORTH

Simple, old-fashioned village pub with woodburner and traditional pub games. No mobile phones or credit cards. Closed Mondays.

→ Aldworth, RG8 9SE, 01635 578272.

51.5131, -1.2005

33 LACEY'S FAMILY FARM

With a pedigree herd of Guernsey cows, Lacey's specialises in milk, ice-cream and fresh cream. Visitors encouraged to explore the farm footpaths. Open 7am-6pm daily.

→ Bolter End Farm, Lane End, HP14 3LP, 01494 881979.

51.6210, -0.8461

34 THE WHITE HORSE, HEDGERLEY

Whitewashed pub with gas lamps, low beams and beers drawn direct from cask. Simple meals such as ploughman's and local pheasant. Lovely garden with woodland feel.

→ Village Lane, Hedgerley, Slough, SL2 3UY, 01753 643225.

51.5772, -0.6021

35 Q GARDENS FARM SHOP

Large range of seasonal PYO fruits. Farm shop stocks own juices, bread, meats and more. Tea room open daily.

→ Milton Hill, Steventon, OX13 6AB, 01235 820988.

51.6139, -1.3141

36 THE CROOKED BILLET, STOKE ROW

Local farms supply produce for the daily-changing menu, while locals trade home-grown veg for lunch credits. Homespun interior. Overlooks fields near Henley.

→ Newlands Lane, Stoke Row, RG9 5PU, 01491 681048.

51.5538, -1.0140

37 THE POT KILN, FRILSHAM

Wild venison and other game are a focus of the menu in this very rural country pub. Beautiful views, sunny garden, option to go deer stalking with the owner.

→ Frilsham, RG18 0XX, 01635 201366.

51.4537, -1.2063

38 ROYAL STANDARD, FORTY GREEN

Dating back to 1213, this apparently haunted country pub is said to be England's oldest freehouse. Uneven floors, open fireplace, low beams, wonderfully atmospheric.

→ Forty Green Road, HP9 1XS, 01494 673382.
51.6187, -0.6685 🍺

39 THE DEW DROP, HURLEY

Flint-and-brick pub hidden in the woods. Food served, with plans to develop a more self-sufficient kitchen. Allegedly visited by Dick Turpin.

→ Honey Lane, SL6 6RB, 01628 315662.
51.5262, -0.8145 🍺

40 SONNING TEA ROOM

Take tea hidden in the trees on this Thames island, beside Sonning Lock. Spectacular setting. Walk here along the river.

→ Sonning Lock, Sonning-on-Thames, RG4 0UR.
51.4758, -0.9144

CAMP & STAY

41 COOKHAM LOCK CAMPING

Sheltered, lock-side campsite with fabulous birdlife. Simple facilities and snack hut. Not accessible by car.

→ Odney Lane, Cookham, SL6 9SR, 01628 520752.
51.5615, -0.6983 ⛺

42 JORDANS YOUTH HOSTEL

Rustic hostel near the historic Friends Meeting House and Jordans village, of Quaker heritage. Patio, fire pit and BBQ. Small camping area.

→ Welders Lane, Jordans, Beaconsfield, HP9 2SN, 0845 371 9523.
51.6098, -0.5938 🛏️

43 HURLEY RIVERSIDE CAMPING

Thames-side site in rolling farmland. Holds a Gold David Bellamy award for its sustainability commitment. Arrive by canoe and pull into the slipway.

→ Shepherds Lane, Hurley, SL6 5NE, 01628 824493.
51.5486, -0.8169 🛶

44 HURLEY LOCK

Seasonal lock campsite, set on a private Thames island with 10 tents max. Quiet village with pub (Olde Bell SL6 5LX) and walks nearby. Access by boat or foot.

→ Hurley, SL6 5ND, 01628 824334.
51.5511, -0.8103 ⛺

45 BRITCHCOMBE FARM

Rural site beneath the Uffington White Horse. Cream teas served in the Teapot Tearoom, firewood provided for campfires.

→ Uffington, SN7 7QJ, 01367 821022.
51.5829, -1.5572 🔥

46 BIG HAT BUSHCAMP, CHERTSEY

Tranquil lakeside spot offering woodland bushcraft courses for families – learn to cook squirrel and build bivvies. Pitches have wild settings.

→ Hardwick Lane, Lyne, Chertsey, KT16 0AF, 07957 184341.
51.3878, -0.5275 ⛺🔥

47 FARMER GOW'S CAMPING, LONGCOT

24-pitch site with fire pits, farm shop and kids' farm park.

→ Fernham Road, Longcot, nr Faringdon, SN7 7PR, 01793 780555.
51.6187, -1.5937 🔥

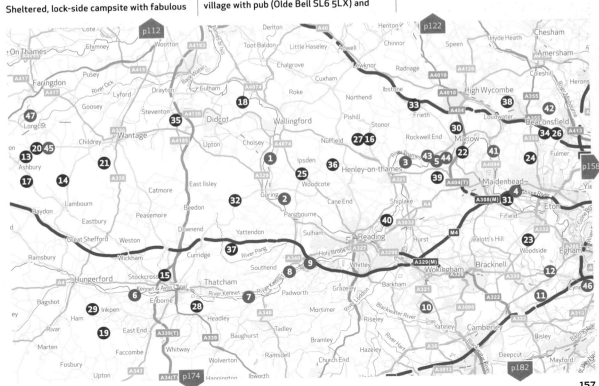

LONDON

Our perfect weekend

→ **Marvel** at the wildlife-rich ruins of bombed-out medieval St Dunstan in the East.

→ **Swim** the River Thames at Runnymede then find the 2,000-year-old Ankerwycke Yew and explore the ruins of St Mary's Priory.

→ **Tuck** into delicious, sustainably sourced food at the Castle Café after climbing in the Castle Climbing Centre.

→ **Scramble** down to your own little low-tide Thameside beach and enjoy a private picnic.

→ **Wander** through the rambling, overgrown grandeur of Highgate or Abney Park Cemetery.

→ **Sample** the great selection of real ales at The Boater's Inn, while watching the river pass by.

→ **Snuggle** down in the Rudyard Kipling houseboat on the River Thames and breakfast in the sunshine on the large outdoor deck.

→ **Lose** yourself following deer in Richmond Park and find the ancient Royal Oak.

→ **Plunge** into Hampstead lakes at dawn, then find the tumulus or the hollow beech tree.

Think of London, and wild spaces don't usually come to mind. Yet within London's great concrete sprawl there are a surprising number of hidden green oases of all shapes and sizes, from community gardens to huge parks and commons, from ruined churches to rambling cemeteries.

Green space in London comes in both large and small packets, from the great tracts of common land, such as Hampstead Heath and Farthing Down, to the tiny community gardens like The Phoenix Garden in the West End. The eight Royal Parks across London are former royal hunting grounds, and cover nearly 5,000 acres all together. Today there is increasing interest in not only preserving green space in the city but recreating it from industrial and derelict spaces. St Dunstan in the East is a medieval church bombed during the Blitz, which has become a beautiful little garden park, and Camley Street Natural Park was created from an old coalyard in 1984 to become a wildlife oasis.

Some of the best wild spaces in London are the sprawling old cemeteries. Perhaps most famous are the 'Magnificent Seven' – large 19th-century cemeteries established to alleviate overcrowding in existing burial grounds, which have since become wildlife havens, many with guided walks and activities. Kensal Green, West Norwood, Highgate, Abney Park, Nunhead, Brompton and Tower Hamlets all have different characteristics, but are all great escapes from the busy streets.

The three Hampstead Heath swimming ponds, dating back to the endW of the 17th century, are probably the best known of central London's wild swimming spots — a painting by Constable depicts people bathing at Hampstead as early as 1829. Gravel pits offer further opportunities for swimming near London and many have become SSSIs, providing nationally important wetland habitats for wintering wildfowl. The six-mile bike path from Rickmansworth to Denham Country Park passes more than 20 gravel lakes, and close to Staines there are even more. The banks are fringed with alder and the water shelves deeply into the chalky green depths, as pure and clean as you could want.

More and more attention is being paid to wild and local food across London – and being in the middle of a city is certainly not a hurdle: cafés such as the Castle Café in Stoke Newington grow organic produce in their own gardens; city farms supply their own cafés (Stepney City Farm); pubs like The Boater's Inn support local microbreweries and foraging is on the up across the city. Increasingly popular, city foraging can be as simple as collecting blackberries and nettles, but there are numerous walks and courses across London if you'd like to learn more. Join a wild food walk with Jason of Forage Wild Food (foragewildfood.com), or John of Forage London (foragelondon.co.uk).

RIVERS & LAKES

1 HAMPSTEAD PONDS, THE HEATH

Three beautiful woodland swimming lakes set in the rolling hills of the heath. Deep, dark and green. Changing areas and lifeguards. Close to train and tube.

→ From Hampstead tube turn R down High St, then L after 500m down Downshire Hill (NW3 1PA). Cross onto Heath, bear L to pass first then second pond (both non-swimming). Mixed pond is next one up. Men's pond and Ladies' pond (beautiful and enclosed by trees) are ½ mile away, on opposite side of Heath, or via Millfield Lane off Highgate West Hill (N6 6JB).

15 mins, 51.5608, -0.1655

2 SERPENTINE LAKE, HYDE PARK

40-acre lake in central London fed by underground springs.

→ Extends between Lancaster Gate and Knightsbridge tube stations. On S side of lake, to E of bridge, with changing rooms. Lido Café Bar (W2 2UH, 020 7706 7098).

10 mins, 51.505, -0.1692

3 RUISLIP LIDO LAKE

Sandy beach and traditional swimming lake, with campaign to formally allow swimming again. Nearby is Mad Bess Wood (Mad Bess was an old woman who prowled the woods at night looking for poachers – or alternatively a headless horsewoman).

→ Reservoir Rd (HA4 7TT), signed off Ducks Hill Rd, Ruislip (A4180). Or by tube to Northwood Hills or Ruislip and enter park from Fore St (HA5 2NQ). Carry on up A4180 ½ mile to find Mad Bess Wood on L (HA6 2SS)

10 mins, 51.5886, -0.4302

4 RICKMANSWORTH LAKES

Bury Lake was once a famous swimming lake, though now the authorities prefer other watersports instead. To the W are three wilder lakes: Stockers, Springwell and Inns, where we sometimes dip.

→ Turn L off Uxbridge Rd (A412) on Drayton Ford/Springwell Ln, and find small car park on R after 300m (by WD3 8UR). Small wild fishing lakes are on either side of road. Or continue another 300m to find path on L along Colne stream (not the canal) NE to the shores of Stocker's Lake (with Bury Lake/ Rickmansworth Aquadrome beyond). Be discreet. Rickmansworth tube is ½ mile (WD3 1FL). Also visit the relaxed Café in the Park (WD3 1NB, 01923 711131)

10 mins, 51.6288, -0.4964

5 WRAYSBURY/HORTON LAKES

Vast area of wild gravel lakes a short walk from Wraysbury train station.

→ Turn L out of Wraysbury station (W) and R after ½ mile down Douglas Lane (TW19 5NF). Find lake shore on L or continue on 200m, across railway line to find Kingsmead Lake to L. Path leads on to Horton (Park Lane, SL3 9PT) also an alternative entry point. Great sunsets.

30 min, 51.4652, -0.5475

6 HYTHE END LAKE/RUNNYMEDE THAMES

Take a secret dip at this fishing lake or head for the popular banks of the R Thames.

→ From M25/J13 head for Wraysbury/ B376. Entrance is opposite Bell Weir Garage (TW19 6HE) – people pull off R beyond, next to Spice Lounge restaurant (TW19 5AJ). The Runnymede Pleasure Ground banks of the Thames are close by too, with good parking and facilities (Windsor Road/A308, TW20 0AE).

5 mins, 51.4445, -0.5369

7 DENHAM LAKES AND WOODS

Four beautiful lakes alongside the Colne Valley way. Sometimes used for fishing. Country Park and nature reserves. All close to the train stations.

16

→ Park at Uxbridge golf club (with public bar and basic carvery, UB10 8AQ, 01895 272457, off Harvil Rd, Hillingdon) and follow footpath bearing L to lakes. Or access from Denham station on W side, 30 mins. From Platform 2 drop down and head SE across golf course on tree-lined footpath. Bear R at Buckinghamshire Golf Club house (upmarket bar and food, UB9 5PG misleading, 01895 835777), L across canal to lakes.
5 mins, 51.5695, -0.4782 ⬛⬛⬛

8 CHERTSEY BRIDGE, R THAMES
Large area of open park and river bank with several beaches downstream of bridge. Dumsey Meadow – a large area of undeveloped meadow – is opposite.
→ Find small car park 200m E of bridge on S side of Chertsey Bridge Rd (KT16 8LF).
5 mins, 51.3879, -0.4817 ⬛

9 BATTERSEA BEACH, R THAMES
Enjoy a picnic on your own private low-tide beach in the middle of London.
→ Near Albert Bridge (SW11 4NJ). Check over the wall to find your own little beach to scramble down to. Take care! Battersea Park station.
20 mins, 51.4814, -0.1651 ⬛⬛⬛

SACRED & ANCIENT

10 HIGHGATE CEMETERY
The best known of London's 'Magnificent Seven' cemeteries, Highgate contains the tomb of Karl Marx. With fabulous Victorian graves, the W section is the oldest but can only be visited by guided tour, while the E section is open to the public.
→ Top of Swain's Lane, N6 6PJ (020 8340 1834). Archway tube station is ¾ mile SE, across Waterlow Park and along Highgate Hill/ B519. 11am to 3.30pm daily, £4.
20 mins, 51.5670, -0.1466 ⬛

11 TOWER HAMLETS CEMETERY
Known locally as Bow Cemetery, this is also the largest area of woodland in East London. A designated nature reserve, it feels wonderfully wild and overgrown. Open dawn-dusk.
→ 200m SE of Mile End tube. R out of station, R down Southern Grove (E3 4PX).
5 min, 51.5235, -0.0306 ⬛⬛⬛⬛

12 ABNEY PARK CEMETERY
Opened in 1840 as a non-denominational cemetery and arboretum combined. At its height it held 2,500 different species

of trees and plants – more than the Royal Park at Kew. Intricate paths weave past overgrown tombs, including those of William Booth, founder of the Salvation Army and the Chartist leader Patrick Bronterre O'Brien. Open 8am-dusk.
→ Abney Park, Stoke Newington High Street, London N16 0LH, 0207 275 7557. 200m S of Stoke Newington train station.
5 mins, 51.5634, -0.0732 ⬛⬛⬛

13 CHISLEHURST CAVES
Huge labyrinth of man-made tunnels, 30m beneath woodland. During the air raids of the Blitz, over 15,000 people sheltered here.
→ Caveside Close, Old Hill, Chislehurst, BR7 5NL, 020 8467 3264. 200m N of Chislehurst station. Open Wed–Sun, bank holidays and daily during school holidays. Entry ~£6.
5 mins, 51.4069, 0.0568 ⬛⬛

14 ST DUNSTAN IN THE EAST
Ruins of a medieval church and Wren Tower, bombed in the Blitz and turned into an imaginative and biodiverse public garden. Virginia creeper and ornamental vines adorn the ruined walls and the Japanese snowball near the fountain blossoms in late spring.
→ St Dunstan's Hill, off Lower Thames Street,

19

EC3R 8DX. Open 8am-7pm or dusk (whichever is earlier). Between Monument (via Eastcheap) and Tower Hill (via Gt Tower St, Tower Hill) tube stations, also close to Bank and Aldgate on other lines.

5 mins, 51.5096, -0.0824 🚆🅱🚇

15 LESNES ABBEY, BELVEDERE

Founded in 1178, this ruin now lies surrounded by ancient woodland, contrasting with the skyscrapers of London Docklands in the background. In the grounds is a rare black mulberry tree, said to have been planted by King James I.

→ From Abbey Wood station head S on Wilton Road past the Abbey Arms. After 100m turn L onto the B213 Abbey Road and head E for 300m. At the footbridge turn R into park and head 100m S to the ruin (DA17 5RE).

10 mins, 51.4885, 0.1284 🚆

SUNSET HILLTOPS

16 HAMPSTEAD HEATH TUMULUS

Nearly 800 acres of heath, meadow and ancient woodland, formally protected by Act of Parliament in 1871. Find the hollow beech that you can climb into, or the ruined rose pergola walk. The old

Duelling Ground in South Wood is exactly 40 paces wide, and was one of London's most notorious duelling sites in the 18th and 19th centuries.

→ The tumulus is at the heart of the Heath, with good views and long meadow grass in summer. From Millfield Lane (N6 6JD, off Highgate West Hill) follow the cycle path across the Heath with the tumulus R, into the woods, turning R and following path NW to find the famous hollow beech about 50m before the mock Tudor loos. The entrance to the ruins of the rose pergola walk are found behind Jack Straw's castle. Best sunsets are from Parliament Hill.

15 mins, 51.5629, -0.1637 🚵♿🚻🚶

17 FARTHING DOWNS AND NEW HILL

Expansive area of chalk grassland, with pockets of ancient woodland, old hedgerows and rare herbs and wildflowers.

→ From Coulston South station, cross the railway tracks via footbridge to path, turn L on Reddown Rd and walk N to Memorial ground. Turn R onto B276 then immediately R up Downs Rd (CR5 1AA) and fork L onto byway through the parkland.

10 mins, 51.3066, -0.1361 📷🐕♿🚶

15

ANCIENT TREES & WOODS

18 'OLD LIONS', KEW GARDENS

Dotted around these famous botanic gardens are the five 'Old Lions', the oldest trees dating back to 1762. The most impressive is the huge oriental plane. Don't miss the treetop walkway in the arboretum, which offers splendid views across the trees and gardens of Kew.

→ Royal Botanic Gardens, Kew, Richmond, Surrey, TW9 3AB, 020 8332 5655. The oriental plane stands opposite the Orangery, at the northern end of the Broad Walk, 300m

12

from the Elizabeth Gate entrance (800m S of Kew Bridge Station) or past the Palm House and up the Broad Walk from the Victoria Gate (500m from Kew Gardens tube station). Open daily from 9.30am. Entry fee.
10 mins, 51.4833, -0.2936 🅱🅡🅠

19 RICHMOND PARK OAKS AND DEER

Pollarded oaks, gnarled and hollowed. The 750-year-old Richmond Royal Oak is the most impressive. Around 630 red and fallow deer have roamed here since 1529 and can be heard clashing antlers during the autumn rut (Oct–Nov), when males compete for females.

→ Park in the Pembroke Lodge car park on Queens Road, 500m S of Richmond Gate (TW10 5HX, 0208 940 8207). The Richmond Royal Oak is on the path between Sidmouth Wood and Queen Elizabeth's Plantation, 300m S of Sawyer's Hill road. Opens 7am in summer and 7.30am in winter.
15 mins, 51.4456, -0.2812 🐾🐦🚶

20 ANKERWYCKE YEW & ST MARY'S

Surrounded by fields, near the ruins of St Mary's Benedictine Priory, stands a 2,000-year-old yew that was mentioned in the Domesday Book. Said to have witnessed the signing of the Magna Carta in 1215, this is also where Henry VIII may have met Anne Boleyn in the 1530s.

→ Park in the NT Ankerwycke car park, Magna Carta Lane, off the Staines Rd/B376 (TW19 5AD). Head down track to St Mary's Priory to find the yew 200m further S (head through the woods along the track).
20 mins, 51.4447, -0.5562 🏞✝🚗🅿

21

WILDLIFE WONDERS

21 LONDON WETLAND CENTRE, BARNES

Rare snake's-head fritillaries in spring, water birds and otters in their wetland homes. Café and play areas.

→ Queen Elizabeth Walk, Barnes, SW13 9WT, 020 8409 4400. Barnes Bridge railway station is 1 mile away. Entry fee. Open 9.30am–5pm daily.
20 mins, 51.4771, -0.2351 🅿🐦

10

22 WOODLANDS FARM TRUST, WELLING

Rambling, 89-acre working city farm, a fragment of countryside within sight of Canary Wharf. Great fun for kids (lambing is especially popular).

→ 331 Shooters Hill, Welling, DA16 3RP, 020 8319 8900. A mile W of Welling station. Open 9.30am–4.30pm, Tues – Sun.
20 mins, 51.4672, 0.0791 🐄🅿

38

23 THE PHOENIX GARDEN

Tiny, volunteer-managed, community wildlife garden in the West End – popular for picnic lunches.

→ St Giles Passage, WC2H 8DG. Off the N of Shaftesbury Avenue, 200m from NE end. Tottenham Court Road, Leicester Square, or Covent Garden tube.
5 mins, 51.5144, -0.1284 🅿🅑

24 CAMLEY STREET NATURAL PARK

Behind St Pancras International lie two acres of wild nature reserve on the banks of Regent's Canal. Created from an old coalyard in 1984, the area is rich in birds and butterflies.

→ 12 Camley Street, N1C 4PW, 020 7833 2311. 100m N of St Pancras International. Up the E side of Kings Cross St Pancras, N on Pancras Rd (A5202) onto Camley St. Entrance on R through red gates. Open 10am–4pm/5pm.
3 mins, 51.5354, -0.1281

SLOW FOOD

25 BRIXTON FARMERS' MARKET

Producers' market run by London Farmers' Markets every Sunday 10am–2pm.

→ Brixton Station Rd, SW9 8PD, 020 7833 0338.
51.4625, -0.1132 🍴🅿

26 SERPENTINE BAR & KITCHEN

With fabulous views across the Serpentine in Hyde Park, this is an especially good breakfast or lunch spot. Wood-fired pizza, seasonal salads and freshly made smoothies.

→ Serpentine Road, Hyde Park, W2 2UH, 020 7706 8114.
51.5051, -0.1598 🅿

27 THE BOATER'S INN, KINGSTON

Riverside pub that backs onto a park. Great selection of real ales from local and national microbreweries, and a seasonally changing menu. Laid-back and dog-friendly.

→ Canbury Gardens, Lower Ham Road, KT2 5AU, 0208 541 4672.
51.4186, -0.3058 🅿

28 THE WHITE SWAN, TWICKENHAM

Charming little pub on the banks of the Thames with cosy log fires indoors. Selection of real ales updated regularly.

→ Riverside, Twickenham, TW1 3DN, 020 8744 2951.
51.4470, -0.3213 🍴🅿

29 THE CASTLE CAFÉ, STOKE NEWINGTON

Great little café in a Victorian water-pumping-station-turned-climbing centre. Food sourced from its own organic garden.

→ The Castle Climbing Centre, Green Lanes, N4 2HA, 020 8211 7000.
51.5652, -0.0922

30 THE SHED, NOTTING HILL

Run by two brothers, who forage or source most of their ingredients from the family farm in Sussex. Daily-changing menu with a focus on using the whole animal (nose to tail).

→ 122 Palace Gardens Terrace, W8 4RT, 0207 229 4024. Their sister restaurant, Rabbit, is also worth a visit (172 Kings Road, Chelsea, SW3 4UP, 020 3750 0172).
51.5091, -0.1938

31 STEPNEY CITY FARM CAFÉ

Award-winning café on a thriving city farm. Ingredients are sourced from the farm, and include everything from sausages to edible flowers. Also visit the farm, shop and Saturday farmers' market. Open Wed–Sun.

→ Stepney Way, E1 3DG, 020 7790 8204.
51.5170, -0.0434

32 THE DOVE, HAMMERSMITH

Historic riverside pub, where Charles II is said to have romanced his mistress Nell Gwyn in the 17th century.

→ 19 Upper Mall, W6 9TA, 020 8748 9474.
51.4905, -0.2348

33 THE OLD SHIP W6, HAMMERSMITH

Watch rowers and ducks passing by on the Thames as you sit with beer in hand at this popular 18th-century watering hole. Serves hearty pub grub.

→ 25 Upper Mall, W6 9TD, 020 8748 2593.
51.4900, -0.2401

34 WILD FOOD CAFE, COVENT GARDEN

Raw-centric restaurant focusing on wild, fresh and foraged vegan and vegetarian food. Funky and colourful interior.

→ 1st Floor, 14 Neal's Yard, Covent Garden, WC2H 9DP, 020 7419 2014.
51.5145, -0.1263

35 DUKE OF CAMBRIDGE, ISLINGTON

100% organic pub, now teamed up with Riverford after the two founders married!

→ 30 St Peter's Street, N1 8JT. Islington tube. 020 7359 3066.
51.5348, -0.0988

CAMP & STAY

36 RIPPLE RIVERSIDE BOATHOUSE

Glass-fronted boathouse on the Thames. Light and bright with eaved ceiling, wooden floors and a child-safe garden on the river bank.

→ Eel Pie Island, Twickenham, 07946 331793.
51.4456, -0.3228

37 RUDYARD KIPLING HOUSEBOAT

Bright and spacious houseboat with a large outdoor deck and gorgeous river views on the Chelsea Embankment.

→ Cheyne Walkk, Airbnb.com
51.4831, -0.1676

38 CAMPING SKIFFS, WALTON

Hire one of these beautiful camping punts for the weekend and sleep out on the water.

→ Carlton Road, KT12 2DG, 01932 232433 skiffhire.com
51.3900, -0.4233

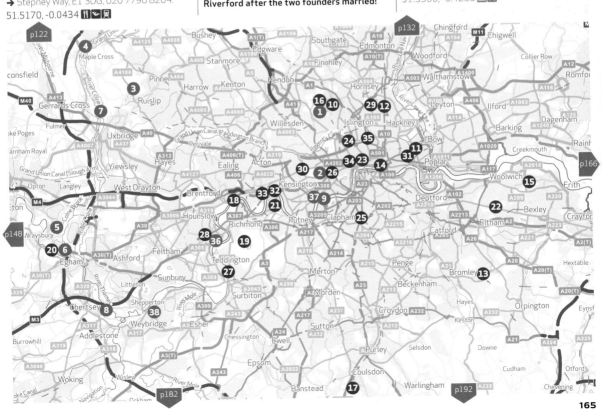

THAMES ESTUARY

Our perfect weekend

→ **Sail** out to and explore the Maunsell Forts – a cluster of abandoned steel forts on legs, towering above the sea.

→ **Shiver** as you gaze out across the rotting bones of a ships' graveyard at Bedlams Bottom.

→ **Wake** up on gorgeous Elmley Nature Reserve after a night in a luxurious shepherd's hut.

→ **Venture** a short way out onto the ancient Broomway, a perilous tidal causeway.

→ **Discover** Leigh-on-Sea cockle sheds – tasting the fresh sea bounty as you go.

→ **Walk** along the sea wall from Whitstable to The Sportsman for a swim and some fantastic food.

→ **Pitch** your tent in 30-acre Badgells Wood and join a bushcraft lesson.

→ **Swim** in the vast blue lagoons at Cliffe, then explore the fort ruins and Dickensian graveyard.

→ **Splash** in the Darent chalk stream ford at Eynsford, and explore two castles and a Roman villa.

Windswept, bleak and strangely beautiful, these marshlands and islands are a far cry from the bucolic landscape of the Kent Downs to the south, or the rolling Essex hills to the north. Part industrial wasteland, these marshes and watery lands also teem with incredible bird life and a wonderful sense of the wild.

The Thames Estuary is bordered on both sides by low-lying mudflats, salt marshes and open beaches. Writer Joseph Conrad lived in Stanford-Le-Hope close to the Essex marshes, and the opening pages of *Heart of Darkness* give a vivid description of this area: "… the sea and the sky were welded together without a joint … a haze rested on the low shore that ran out to sea in the vanishing flatness." The Thames here has been a great artery of industry through the centuries and the bleak, wild landscape is rich with history. The traditional Thames sailing barges that used to adorn the estuary have been replaced by large oil tankers and container ships. Bedlam's Bottom, the ships' graveyard at Iwade, is now the best place to see what is left of the historic ruined hulks. You can still ride aboard an old working Thames barge, however, on a visit to the three-legged Maunsell Forts, which stand guard over the sea in the estuary off the coast from Whitstable.

Testament to how much this coastline has shifted over the years and created huge swathes of marshland out of the sea is the Saxon Shore Way, which follows a line from Gravesend all the way around the coast to Hastings in East Sussex. There are many other old ways too, including the Broomway to the north, which leads to Foulness Island and has been described as the most perilous byway in England. Once traced by a line of markers resembling brooms, it is now revealed only at low tide, and covered again when the waves sweep in. Near the start of the Saxon Shore Way, the area around Higham Marshes was made famous by Charles Dickens, who used it as the setting for Pip's first meeting with the convict Magwitch in *Great Expectations*. Pip's "dark flat wilderness" could just as easily be describing the marshes of North Kent today. In fact, Oare Marshes Nature Reserve – a bird reserve of international importance – was used as the setting for Mike Newell's 2012 film adaptation of the novel. The Shipwright Arms at Hollowshore nearby is a perfect point to pause for a pint of local ale on a longer walk.

The island marshes of Kent and the Thames Estuary have long yielded delicious oysters. Once consumed only by the poor, oysters are now considered a luxury, and this fashionable shellfish has been central to the resurgence of nearby Whitstable, which has beach huts for rent as well as hip Art Deco oyster bars. The steep, shingle harbour beach is perfect for a refreshing morning plunge or a midnight dip. Or for a really wild weekend, set out to Elmley Marsh Nature Reserve and camp in a gypsy caravan, with only the sky, birds and sea for company.

LAKES & STREAMS

1 HIGHAM CHURCH & CLIFFE CLAY PITS

Remote and adventurous clay pits on estuary shore, reached from the pretty chuch at Higham which helped inspire *Great Expectations*.

→ From Higham station in Lower Higham follow Church St a mile up to St Mary's church (ME3 7LS). Take footpath through field gate, towards pylons, and across railway tracks. Head along L shore of first lake (with crane) for second lake, by sea wall. Sides can be steep. A somewhat industrial feel!

20 mins, 51.4530, 0.4641 🚣🏊⛪🏞🎣

2 HALLING SECRET LAKE

Hidden behind high hedges, in a huge crater, is this glimmering blue oasis. Often closed.

→ Locals climb down on steep rough banks, sometimes accessible from opposite (and W of) the pumping station on Vicarage Rd, Upper Halling. There is also a more easily reached secret lake (51.3310, 0.4215) behind St Benedict's Church (see below). Or pay for a swim at Holoborough Quarry (Nemes Dive Academy, ME6 5GN, 0750 762 4911).

15 mins, 51.35318, 0.43501 ❓🅥

3 EYNSFORD, DARENT

Clear, clean, shallow ford and stream with pub and ruined Eynsford Castle across the road. Great fun for kids. You can also walk upstream to the Roman Villa (EH) and Lullingstone Castle with modern botanical garden and large lovely-looking lake.

→ Eynsford station or from M25/J3 follow 'Farningham A225', then A225 to Eynsford, then signed Lullingstone Castle from the village shop. The stream is by The Plough (DA4 0AE, 01322 862281) or continue on lane to villa and Lullington Castle. Eynsford Castle is free (10am-4pm) and accessed from the main road.

3 mins, 51.3680, 0.2092 🚂🍺ℹ️🚻🏰

BEACHES & CREEKS

4 SHELLNESS, ISLE OF SHEPPEY

Spend a leisurely afternoon searching for shells on the beach at the aptly named Shellness. Also a naturist beach.

→ Follow Shellness Road S from Leysdown-on-Sea for 1½ miles, past the 'no through road' sign and ¾ mile down very bumpy track (ME12 4RJ). Continue on foot for about 800m past beach houses and old boats until you get to the huge shell-covered beach.

15 mins, 51.3670, 0.9444 🐚🦆🏖🚮

5 UPLEES MARSHES DISUSED DOCK

Ruins of Second World War piers and slipway, used for boat building and launching. Muddy, with swimming at HT only. An isolated place to bivvy down and watch the stars with the tides.

→ Continue beyond Oare Marshes (ME13 0QD, see below) upstream W along the shore line on the Saxon Shore Way. After ¾ mile find the first slipway, continue for ½ mile for a second jetty.

20 mins, 51.3542, 0.8744 🏚🏊🏞⛺

RUINS & FOLLIES

6 CLIFFE FORT, CLIFFE

Huge 1860s fort built to protect the Thames. Casemates, gun rails and gun carriages, plus wire-guided torpedo system from the 1890s.

→ Just to the N of Cliffe lakes or W from Cliffe (ME3 7QD), on the Saxon Shore Way.

20 mins, 51.4637, 0.4562 ❓🅥

7 BEDLAMS BOTTOM, IWADE

A bleak ships' graveyard - the rotting shells of at least ten Thames barges show above the mudflats. Gnarled hawthorn bushes lean with the winds and old Kingsnorth Power Station looms across the Medway.

5

17

10

→ 2½ miles E of Lower Halstow (ME9 7DY) along Raspberry Hill Ln (dir Sheerness). Find footpath and metal kissing gate on L.
5 mins, 51.3879, 0.7192

8 HADLEIGH CASTLE, BENFLEET

Ruined castle tower and earthworks standing high above the Essex marshes.

→ Park at the end of Castle Lane in Hadleigh, by Salvation Army Hadleigh Farm (SS7 2AP). Ruin very obvious through gate.
1 min, 51.5445, 0.6092

9 MAUNSELL FORTS, THAMES ESTUARY

Eight miles offshore in the Thames Estuary, six steel Second World War forts on huge legs rise above the sea. Decommissioned in the 1950s and squatted by pirate radio broadcasters. Visible from the shore around Herne Bay, one of the best ways to see them up close is a trip in the historic 'Greta', a 120-year-old sailing barge that assisted in the 1940 evacuation of Dunkirk.

→ 'Greta' boat trips depart from Whitstable Harbour during the summer (6 hours, £48, 07711 657919). To actually land, contact X-Pilot and Project Redsand (groups of 12, £50 per head, 07952 784311).
1 min, 51.4477, 1.0961

SACRED & ANCIENT

10 BROOMWAY, WAKERING STAIRS

Notoriously dangerous and only passable at low tide, this historic byway heads 300m out onto Maplin Sands then two miles parallel to the shore up to Foulness Island. In use since Roman times, but now quicksands fringe the route and the incoming tide returns faster than you can run.

→ As for Foulness Island (below), but from the gates take the byway to Wakering Stairs, a mile. Access Sundays and some Saturdays (call 01702 383211 to check). Guided walks and tractor safaris an option from Wildlifetrips. org.uk. But if you're still keen to walk, study the tide times (South End), take a compass and phone, and only explore out a few hundred metres, on a falling tide. It is impossible to walk to Foulness and back within the LT window.
10 mins, 51.5483, 0.8399

11 ST BENEDICT'S CHURCH

Next to a farmyard, on the Pilgrims' Way, this 900-year-old chapel was used as a barn for 250 years. There is a lovely secret lake behind.

38

→ Take Paddlesworth Road a mile W of Snodding to find the chapel on the roadside by the farm (ME6 5DR). Return back down the lane 500m and enter the field on the R, before the woods, to find the lake 200m beyond.
1 min, 51.3331, 0.4170

12 COLDRUM LONG BARROW

This 3,000-year-old burial chamber is Kent's most intact megalithic long barrow. Visit at sunrise on 1st May to see the Hartley Morris Men 'singing up the sun'.
→ Park at Coldrum Long Barrow Parking (off Pinesfield Lane, Trottiscliffe, ME19 5EL), and follow the signs.
3 mins, 51.3215, 0.3727

13 ST BARTHOLOMEW'S CHURCH

Tiny Norman church, exposed on a knoll next to 15th-century farm buildings, surrounded by hop fields.
→ Goodnestone Court, Goodnestone, ME13 9BZ, a mile NE from the M2 J7. Or a pleasant 2-mile walk through fields and surburbs, from Faversham station via Whitstable Road.
2 mins, 51.3165, 0.9322

14 THE STREET, WHITSTABLE

Walk ½ mile out to sea on this long, low-tide shingle strip. Be wary of incoming tides, which can cut you off if you linger too long.
→ Looking out to sea from the Hotel Continental on Beach Walk (CT5 2BP), turn R and walk 70m along the seafront at low tide.
10 mins, 51.3669, 1.0350

WILDLIFE WONDERS

15 FOSSIL-HUNT AT WARDEN CLIFFS

Bring your wellies and prepare to get muddy as you search for fossils in these 'London Clay' cliffs. Kent lay beneath a shallow, warm sea around 52 million years ago, so you may even find ancient sharks' teeth here. Best at low tide.
→ North coast, Isle of Sheppey. Car park at the end of Imperial Drive in Warden (ME12 4SD). Facing the sea, turn L and walk along the sea shore for 500m.
5 mins, 51.4163, 0.9015

16 FOULNESS ISLAND BIRDLIFE

Notoriously difficult to get to, but internationally famous for wildlife, England's fourth-largest island has a population of just 200 people and is flat and lonely. Its name derives from the Old English 'fulga-naess', meaning 'wild bird's nest'.
→ Owned by the MOD, public access only possible when the Heritage Centre is open (12-4pm, first Sunday of the month April– October). From Great Wakering, drive to the end of New Road to the roundabout behind large 'QinetiQ' gates (SS3 0DH). Explain you are visiting the Heritage Centre.
5 mins, 51.5530, 0.8240

17 CAPEL FLEET RAPTOR VIEWPOINT

Bird of prey viewpoint on elevated ground. Experience marsh harriers gathering at dusk for communal roosting.
→ Two miles down the Harty Ferry Road from the B2231, towards the Ferry House Inn. (ME12 4BQ, 01795 510214). Well signposted.
1 min, 51.3765, 0.9048

18 OARE MARSHES

Marshland and mudflats of international importance for migratory birds. Windswept, and riddled with dykes and saltmarsh.
→ Park near the sea wall at the end of the Church Road, Oare, ME13 0QD. You are in the middle of the marshes.
1 min, 51.3459, 0.8893

8

32

26

38

19 FERRY HOUSE INN, SHEPPEY

Gorgeous little pub serving local food, including game shot at the local estate. Site of ferry that once linked to the mainland.

→ Harty Ferry Road (ME12 4BQ, 01795 510214).

51.3549, 0.8911 ▣

20 BLUEY'S FISH STALL, OARE

Wet fish stall run by Barry (known locally as Bluey) and his daughter. Sells the catch from Bluey's own boat, 'Louise'. Arrive early on Fridays and Saturdays.

→ On the road into Oare from Faversham, turn R down the dirt track immediately before The Castle Inn (ME13 0PY) and then take first L. 07970 896143.

51.3298, 0.8799 ▣

21 FLYNN'S BEE FARM TEA ROOM

Rambling place with grassy garden and a pond. Taste an array of honeys in the little shop, hear tales of how the farm began, and enjoy a honey cream tea.

→ Double J Farm, Elmley Road, Sheppey, ME12 3SS (well signposted past a garage, down a very bumpy road), 01795 874935.

51.4074, 0.8156 ▣

22 LEIGH-ON-SEA COCKLE SHEDS

Try everything from freshly landed cockles and shrimp, to oysters and smoked fish from these 19th-century seafront shacks. Buy a pint from the Crooked Billet (opposite) and eat by the water – or mud, depending on the tides.

→ High Street, Leigh-on-Sea, SS9 2ER.

51.5408, 0.6481 ▣ B

23 MONKSHILL FARM SHOP & CAFÉ

Perched atop a hill by a field of geese. Shop sells local foods, including Monkshill's own meat. Café is basic, with lovely views out to sea. Run by the Royal School for Deaf Children.

→ Monkshill Road, Waterham, ME13 9EH, 01227 750211.

51.3264, 0.9661 ▣ ▣

24 THE ALMA, PAINTER'S FORSTAL

Traditional rural pub with meat locally sourced from Brogdale Butchers. Good selection of real ales. Garden plays host to Bat and Trap interpub games on Sunday evenings.

→ ME13 0DU, 01795 533835.

51.2947, 0.8556 ▣ ▣

25 THE THREE TUNS, LOWER HALSTOW

Award-winning, traditional village pub with a constantly changing seasonal menu, serving a great selection of real ale from local microbreweries.

→ The Street, Lower Halstow, ME9 7DY, 01795 842840.

51.3739, 0.6697 ▣ ▣

26 THE OLD NEPTUNE, WHITSTABLE

Right on the beach, the Old Neptune retains a wonderful sense of the seafaring past and is the perfect place to watch the sunset. Rebuilt from reclaimed timbers after a storm in 1897, it was the setting for the film *Venus*, which earned Peter O'Toole his last Oscar nomination.

→ Island Wall, Marine Terrace, CT5 1EJ, 01227 272262.

51.3589, 1.0201 ▣ ▣

27 THE BELL, HORNDON

Proper 'pubby' pub with wide range of ales.

→ High Road, Horndon-on-the-Hill, SS17 8LD, 01375 642463.

51.5235, 0.4061 ▣

28 THE DOVE, DARGATE

Bright, cosy country pub with a changing menu that reflects the seasons and local fare.

→ Plumpudding Lane, ME13 9HB, 01227 751360.

51.3150, 0.9842 ▣ ▣

29 THE HONEY POT, SHOREHAM

Sweet little village cafe. Very popular, so service can be a bit slow, but the cakes are well worth the wait.

→ 4 High Street, TN14 7TD.

51.3336, 0.1778 ▣ B

30 THE SHIP INN, CONYER

Warm up by the fire in winter, or gaze across Conyer Creek to the marshes from the garden in summer. Own-baked bread and food from local suppliers. Set on the Saxon Shore Way, near National Cycle Route 1.

→ The Quay, ME9 9HR, 01795 520881.

51.3481, 0.8151 ▣ ▣ ▣

31 SHIPWRIGHT'S ARMS, HOLLOWSHORE

Historic pub on the Saxon Shore Way, adjacent to a working boatyard, serving local fish and real ales. Apparently haunted by the ghosts of smugglers, pirates, sailors and fishermen – the corner seat by the small fire may feel cold, even on a hot summer's day...

→ Nr Faversham, ME13 7TU, 01795 590088. For a lovely walk, arrive across the marshes from Faversham, following signs along the Saxon Shore Way.
51.3357, 0.8949 🚶🏃

32 THE SPORTSMAN, SEASALTER

Outstanding if slightly pricey food, in a bright pub behind the sea wall. Real focus on local produce, including Whitstable oysters. The beach here is great for a remote swim, but be prepared for the mudflats! To really work up an appetite, walk here from Whitstable along the sea wall (80 mins).
→ Faversham Road, CT5 4BP, 01227 273370.
51.3439, 0.9591 🦪🍴⛱🏃

CAMP & STAY

33 BADGELL'S WOOD CAMPING, MEOPHAM

Spacious, off-grid woodland camping in an AONB. Free range hens, farm shop, optional bushcraft lessons and 30-acre woodland full of wildlife make this a perfect campsite for campers of all ages.

→ Badgell's Wood, Whitehorse Road, DA13 0UF, 07528 609324.
51.3350, 0.3845 🔥🏕

34 OLD STABLE BUNK BARN, BOUGHTON

Hostel-style barn accommodation in a converted Georgian stable building surrounded by orchards. Bring a sleeping bag. B&B also available.
→ Brenley Farm, Brenley Lane, ME13 9LY, 01227 751203.
51.2938, 0.9215 🏕

35 KITS COTY GLAMPING, AYLESFORD

Family-run glamping site with themed bell tents and a shepherd's hut.
→ 84 Collingwood Road, Kit's Coty Estate, ME20 7ER, 01634 685862.
51.3239, 0.5002 🏕

36 MOCKETTS FARM COTTAGES, HARTY

Self-catering cottages overlooking remote marshlands, minutes from the Ferry House Inn.

→ Harty Ferry Road, Sheppey, ME12 4BQ, 01795 510214. Well signposted from Harty Ferry Road, near the end.
51.3621, 0.8909 🏕

37 UPLEES FARM, OARE

Renovated 16th-century farmhouse on a small sheep farm in the Kentish countryside, with chickens, ducks and a goat. Self-catering.
→ Uplees Road, ME13 0QR, 01795 532133.
51.3438, 0.8691 🏕

38 ELMLEY SHEPHERDS' HUTS

The only place in the UK where you can spend the night within a National Nature Reserve. The luxury huts look across the reserve, ideal for birdwatching, photography or getting away from it all beneath the huge Sheppey skies.
→ Kingshill Farm, Sheerness, ME12 3RW, 0117 204 7830 Canopyandstars.co.uk
51.3772, 0.7841 🏕

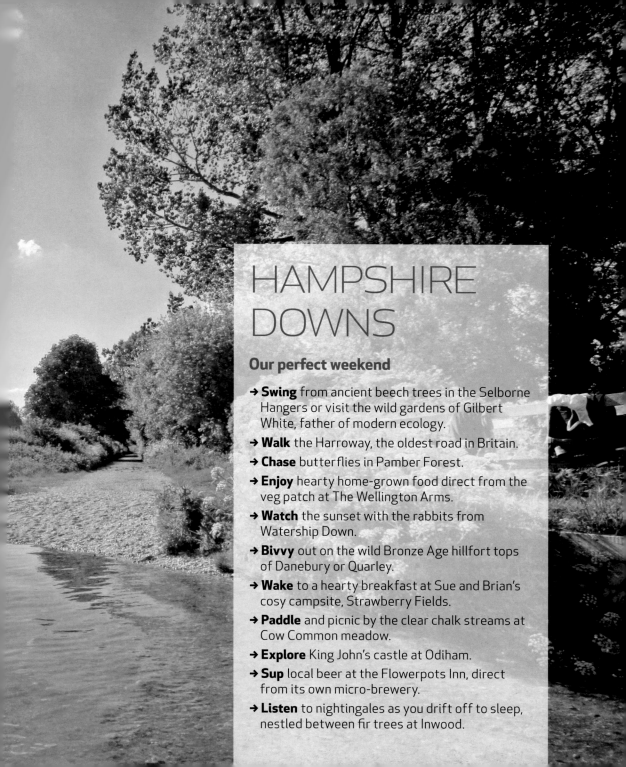

HAMPSHIRE DOWNS

Our perfect weekend

→ **Swing** from ancient beech trees in the Selborne Hangers or visit the wild gardens of Gilbert White, father of modern ecology.

→ **Walk** the Harroway, the oldest road in Britain.

→ **Chase** butterflies in Pamber Forest.

→ **Enjoy** hearty home-grown food direct from the veg patch at The Wellington Arms.

→ **Watch** the sunset with the rabbits from Watership Down.

→ **Bivvy** out on the wild Bronze Age hillfort tops of Danebury or Quarley.

→ **Wake** to a hearty breakfast at Sue and Brian's cosy campsite, Strawberry Fields.

→ **Paddle** and picnic by the clear chalk streams at Cow Common meadow.

→ **Explore** King John's castle at Odiham.

→ **Sup** local beer at the Flowerpots Inn, direct from its own micro-brewery.

→ **Listen** to nightingales as you drift off to sleep, nestled between fir trees at Inwood.

Dotted with ancient hillforts, this undulating green downland boasts silky chalk streams, dramatic woodlands and the oldest road in Britain.

The wide braids of the River Test run through some of the least developed parts of the South East. Wily and fast, the stream picks its way through the most tranquil parts of Hampshire as it heads for the sea from its headwater on Watership Down, that chalk downland immortalised by Richard Adams. These were the hills down which Pipkin and Hazel fled, first from the bulldozers, then from Efrafan rabbit soldiers, before jumping onto a punt moored on the river at Laverstoke. Public access to the bankside is rare, but at Chilbolton Cow Common, near Cherwell Priory, there has been open access since ancient times.

As well as Watership Down, North Hampshire has some fantastic hillforts to climb and on which to bivvy down at sunset to watch the stars come out. Within the fortification on Beacon Hill is the grave of the fifth Earl of Carnarvon, part of the expedition that discovered Tutankhamun's tomb, and on St Catherine's Hill is the site of a 13th-century chapel and a 17th-century mizmaze.

The dramatic Hampshire Hangers at Ashford and Selborne have intriguing associations as well as being exciting to explore in themselves. The poet Edward Thomas lived within the Ashford Hangers before his death in the First World War, and the 'parson-naturalist' Gilbert White famously lived on the edge of the Selborne Hangers. His house is now a museum, and well worth a visit after a walk in the woods. There are beautiful meadows and his barrel 'wine pipe' seat.

At Houghton a white shingle bay of the Test opens out onto a large shallow pool under a bridge where you can swim against the current. The river course has changed much in the last 300 years. Channels have been cut for the creation of 'floating' water meadows, and it's now difficult to know which is the original river course and which an old irrigation path. Running through nearby Winchester, the Itchen is another famous chalk stream that has been much altered by man. Deepened for barge navigation in the 18th century, most of it has returned to shallows, though there is still a deep pool under the little waterfall at Twyford. Both the Itchen and the Test are mainly shallow, exceptionally clear and pure, but also very cold. They are also very valuable fishing rivers, so if you do decide to take a dip, be discreet and make sure no fishermen are watching you!

6

RIVERS & STREAMS

1 CHILBOLTON COW COMMON, R TEST
Ancient rural common with paddling in crystal-clear pools by footbridge.

➜ Turn off the A3057 at the pretty riverside Mayfly pub (SO20 6AX, 01264 860283) and after a mile turn L down Joy's Lane. Park at end and head to footbridge (200m). Also similar paddling and deep spots downstream at Stockbridge on Marsh Common (SO20 6JA, 51.1067, -1.4968).
20 mins, 51.1591, -1.4442

2 HOUGHTON, R TEST
A wide, white chalk bay and wooden footbridge at the end of bridleway in beautiful countryside. Crowsfoot and water buttercup in spring.

➜ Entering Houghton (SO20 6LU) from Stockbridge, find footpath at end of village on L, signed Clarendon Way, and follow it to bridge.
2 mins, 51.0843, -1.5119

3 LONGPARISH WALK, R TEST
Exquisite stretch of the young Test alongside a tiny lane. Lots of grassy bank and open access, perfect for picnics.

➜ From the Cricketers Inn in Longparish (SP11 6PZ, 01264 720335) turn R and R again across water meadow to arrive at millhouse (10 mins, small pool) then bear R on lane to find ½ mile of grassy banks, for paddling only.
30 mins, 51.2005, -1.3710

4 OVINGTON, R ITCHEN
Lovely riverside pub with footbridge and riverside walk. Idyllic but no swimming.

➜ Bush Inn (SO24 0RE, 01962 732764) NE of Winchester. Shallow but paddling by footbridge.
5 mins, 51.0831, -1.2003

5 EASTON/MARTYR WORTHY, R ITCHEN
Lush meadows praised by William Cobbett as 'one of the prettiest places in the country'. Paddling, picnics and tree climbing, also ½ mile upstream at 51.0896, -1.2545. Or to explore the lakes of Avington House country park, stop on lane another mile further up.

➜ Head E out of Easton (past gastropub Chestnut Horse, SO21 1EG, 01962 779257), find footpath to river signed on L after 200m. Or walk down from Martyr Worthy (with fine church) on other bank. There's another footpath ½ mile further along, to Chilland.
5 mins, 51.0897, -1.2636

6 ST CROSS WINCHESTER, R ITCHEN
Water meadows and deepish pools behind this wonderful ancient almshouse.

➜ Heading into Winchester from S, turn down by the Bell Inn (SO23 9RE, 01962 865284).
5 mins, 51.0477, -1.3197

7 TWYFORD, R ITCHEN
Once an old lock, this is now one of the few deep pools on the Itchen. Footbridge and waterfall chute, partly lined with concrete. Clear and cold! Some people like to jump.

➜ ½ mile walk from Shawford station. Or M3/J11 to Twyford, turn R into Berry Lane (SO21 1NS) and continue from church over footbridge, 500m along fence boundary to pool. Tumbling Bay sluices ½ mile upstream.
10 mins, 51.0272, -1.3221

8 MOTTISFONT, R DUNN
Exquisite and secluded stream tributary of the Test, near lovely Mottisfont House and water gardens. The fishermen here might not smile upon you if you go swimming.

➜ Walk down Church Lane from Mottisfont village (SO51 0LP). Continue on Test Way ½ mile to meet river and footbridge.
10 mins, 51.0325, -1.5372

19

18

15

9 TUNDRY POND, DOGMERSFIELD
Exposed parkland lake with picnic tables.
→ Head S from Domersfield and 500m past the church find footpath on R, through white garden gates of Double Bridge Fm (RG27 8TB). Or E of Basingstocke Canal.
10 mins, 51.2656, -0.8900

10 SHERFIELD-ON-LODDON
Mill pool in meadows behind pub.
→ Accessible from The Longbridge Mill pub (RG27 0DL, 01256 883483) or the road bridge.
5 mins, 51.3189, -1.0199

RUINS & ANCIENT WAYS

11 ODIHAM RUINED CASTLE
One of three castles built by King John in the early 13th century. Pleasant walk along the canal to get there. Crystal-clear spring waters emerge from the old tunnel with ethereal hues. Very clean and good for swimming, but cold.
→ ¾ mile walk NE along the Basingstoke Canal from the Fox & Goose, Greywell (RG29 1BY, 01256 702062).
15 mins, 51.2613, -0.9616

12 SILCHESTER ROMAN CITY
Originally the site of an important Iron Age settlement, Silchester was later taken over by the Romans and remains one of the best-preserved Roman towns in Britain.
→ Head S from the Red Lion in Mortimer West End (RG7 2HU) for ½ mile and look for signpost for Silchester on L (English Heritage, free). Short signposted walk from car park (closes 7pm in summer).
2 mins, 51.3579, -1.0828

13 THE HARROWAY AT 'EFRAFA'
The oldest road in Britain, this 6,000-year-old Neolithic trackway runs from Dorset to Surrey. A crossing of paths at this North Hampshire point is said to be the inspiration for Efrafa, the fictional barracks of the militaristic warren run by the dictator rabbit General Woundwort, in Richard Adams' *Watership Down*.
→ Crosses B3051/Kingsclere road ½ mile N from Overton train station (RG25 3JG). Or from Whitchurch train station take the Newbury Road N and then first R. Then 2nd R after a mile to find the trackway.
15 mins, 51.2543, -1.2877

SUNSET HILLFORTS

14 ST CATHERINE'S HILL, WINCHESTER

The site of a 13th-century chapel, a 17th-century mizmaze and huge ramparts from an Iron Age hillfort. Overlooks Winchester and M3.

→ Exit M3 at J10 (exit for N bound cars only, otherwise J9 and head S on A31) and head W following signs for Winchester/St Catherine's Hill. After 500m park in public car park L between Tun Bridge and river (SO23 9PA). Take footpath S, 300m up hill.

10 mins, 51.0463, -1.3109 🚶🏞✝

15 DANEBURY HILLFORT

A forested Iron Age hillfort in use for almost 500 years from the 6th century BC.

→ Head NE out of Middle Wallop on the A343 and turn R after passing the army aviation centre, following the signs to Danebury Hillfort (on R before turning to SO20 6HZ).

5 mins, 51.1383, -1.5309 🏞

16 QUARLEY HILL HILLFORT

Iron Age hillfort with fantastic views across the countryside. Four Bronze Age ditches radiate outwards, thought to be part of a Bronze Age farming settlement.

→ From Grateley railway station take the B3084 (SP11 8SH) NW. After about ½ mile take footpath R across fields towards visible hill.

15 mins, 51.1795, -1.6261 🏞🚉

17 BEACON HILL, BURGHCLERE

Iron Age hillfort and site of Hampshire's most famous beacon. Within the fortification lies the grave of the fifth Earl of Carnarvon, who was part of the expedition that discovered Tutankhamun's tomb.

→ Take the A34 N from Whitchurch and after around 6 miles take the exit signposted for Kingsclere and Burghclere. Turn L, and follow the small road round to the L to park in second wider parking space overlooking slip road. Follow footpath for 500m, away from road.

10 mins, 51.3126, -1.3445 🏞🚶

18 WATERSHIP DOWN

Beautiful views from the setting of Richard Adams' 1972 novel about rabbits.

→ Travel E out of Sydmonton (dir Kingsclere). After ½ mile, take R turn for Ashely Warren and continue for 500m to top of steep hill. Take marked footpath L up hill, opposite large metal gate.

5 mins, 51.3059, -1.2959 🏞🚶

28

22

35

25

19 ASHFORD HANGERS

Dramatic ancient woodlands clinging to steep slopes near the edge of the Hampshire Downs. The poet Edward Thomas lived here with his wife Helen up to his death in the First World War.

→ 1 mile E of High Cross. From The Trooper Inn (Trooper Bottom, GU32 1BD, 01730 827293) go 50m S to crossroads, turn L onto Honeycritch Ln and go ¾ mile, staying R onto Old Litten Ln where road splits. 50m after Cockshott Ln joins from R take footpath on R and follow S into woods.

5 mins, 51.0361, -0.9486 🚶

20 PAMBER FOREST BUTTERFLIES

During summer the sunlit clearings of this forest are spectacular for their abundance of butterflies. This is a remnant of the Royal Forest of Windsor, which was set up as a hunting ground in Norman times.

→ Park at the end of Forest Lane (off Winston Avenue), Tadley, RG26 3NX. Follow footpath E into forest.

10 mins, 51.3438, -1.1191 🐾

21 SELBORNE HANGERS

Steep beech woodland near the old house of Gilbert White, the pioneering English parson-naturalist, father of modern ecology and author of *The Natural History of Selborne*, continuously in print since 1789. Wonderful meadows and lookout house.

→ Heading S through Selborne, pass Gilbert White's house on R (GU34 3JH, open to visitors, enjoy the meadows and the barrel lookout called the 'wine pipe') and find car park on R after 100m, behind the Selborne Arms (GU34 3JR, 01420 511247). Path leads to the Zig-Zag path into woods.

5 mins, 51.0955, -0.9515 📍

22 GREAT PLANE TREE, MOTTISFONT

UK's largest plane tree, in the grounds of a 12th-century Augustinian priory. The grounds are also home to ancient oak, sweet chestnut, hornbeam and beech, as well as a beautiful river and well. From here you can walk to the River Dunn (see listing).

→ Mottisfont Abbey is well signposted from the A3057 at Mottisfont (SO51 0LP).

5 mins, 51.0407, -1.5347 📍

23 KIMBRIDGE FARM SHOP, ROMSEY

Traditional butchers and local farm shop in a beautiful rural setting. Pork, beef and lamb is all sourced locally. There is also a restaurant on site.

→ Kimbridge Farm Shop, Kimbridge, SO51 0LE, 01794 341681

51.0286, -1.5337 🍴

24 THE FLOWERPOTS INN, CHERITON

Cosy log fire in winter, gorgeous orchard in summer. Flowerpots Brewery is on the same site, and supplies beer to the pub.

→ Brandy Mount, Alresford, SO24 0QQ, 01962 771318.

51.0508, -1.1726 🛏🍴

25 THE HARROW INN, STEEP

Award-winning family-run pub with delicious home-cooked food and a great range of ales. Authentic and unspoilt with two traditional bar areas (no children inside).

→ Steep, GU32 2DA, 01730 262685

51.0204, -0.9302 🛏

26 THE HAWKLEY INN, PETERSFIELD

A traditional South Downs village pub down a secluded lane. Great choice of real ales. Hikers and horseriders very welcome.

→ Pococks Lane, Hawkley, Nr Liss, GU33 6NE, 01730 827205.

51.0574, -0.9358 🛏🍴

27 THE HODDINGTON ARMS, UPTON GREY

Country pub in a small rural village serving locally sourced food. Log fires and wood beams, with an outdoor cabana and fire pit.

→ Bidden Road, RG25 2RL, 01256 862371.

51.2293, -0.9988 🍴🛏

28 THE WELLINGTON ARMS, BAUGHURST

Award-winning pub using home-grown, free-range and local produce. Own veg patch and strong commitment to recycling. Rustic accommodation available.

→ Baughurst Road, RG26 5LP, 0118 982 0110.

51.3400, -1.1627 🍴

29 THE WOOLPACK INN, TOTFORD

Lovely country pub in the beautiful Candover Valley. Head chef Paul is a keen forager, and game comes from local estates.

→ Totford, nr Northington, SO24 9TJ, 01962 734184.

51.1379, -1.1851 🍴

30 ABBOTSTONE WOOD CAMPING

Woodland camping with compost toilets and woodland showers. Campfires are encouraged and bushcraft sessions are offered on weekends.

→ Basingstoke Road/B3046, Abbotstone Down, SO24 9TQ. Postcode takes you roughly one mile NW of entrance on the B3046. Continue dir Old Alresford, and the site is well signposted before Abbotstone Down hillfort. Abbotstonewoodcamping@gmail.com
51.1229, -1.1747 🔥🛶

31 MELLOW FARM CAMPSITES

Family-friendly camping with on-site assault course, canoeing and archery. The Front Meadow is suitable for wheelchairs.

→ Mellow Farm, Dockenfield, GU10 4HH, 01428 717815.
51.1427, -0.8264 🔥🛶

32 INWOOD CAMPING, FARLEIGH WALLOP

Grassy meadows, woodland camping, compost toilets and campfires - this is eco-camping at its best. Fall asleep nestled between the fir trees of the 'Gothic' camping area as you listen to the song of nightingales.

→ Farleigh Road, Basingstoke, RG25 2HP. Postcode takes you to B3046 S of Farliegh Wallop. Continue S approx 600m looking for signs into woods R.
Inwoodcamping@gmail.com
51.2119, -1.1283 🔥

33 STRAWBERRY FIELDS, ROMSEY

Simple campsite at the end of a long narrow lane with lots of space for each pitch. Sue and Brian's main focus is their B&B next door, and campers can also take advantage of a home-cooked breakfast delivered to their tent.

→ The Prophets, Newtown, SO51 0GJ, 01794 342400.
51.0117, -1.5659

34 TWO HOOTS CAMPSITE, ALRESFORD

Glamping and caravans. Quiet, adult-only site with lovely views and a secluded bluebell wood. The wooden, carbon-neutral Eco Pods are available year-round.

→ Sutton Wood Lane, Bighton, SO24 9SG, 01962 772242.
51.0930, -1.1011 🛶

35 ADHURST YURTS

Four individually designed yurts with wood burners and comfy beds, all set within a 100-acre woodland full of dens, rope swings and footpaths.

→ Near Petersfield, GU31 5AD, 07789 954476.
51.0165, -0.9082 🛶🛶

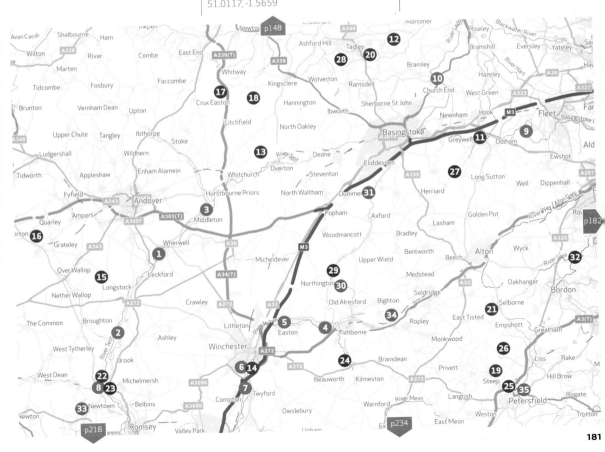

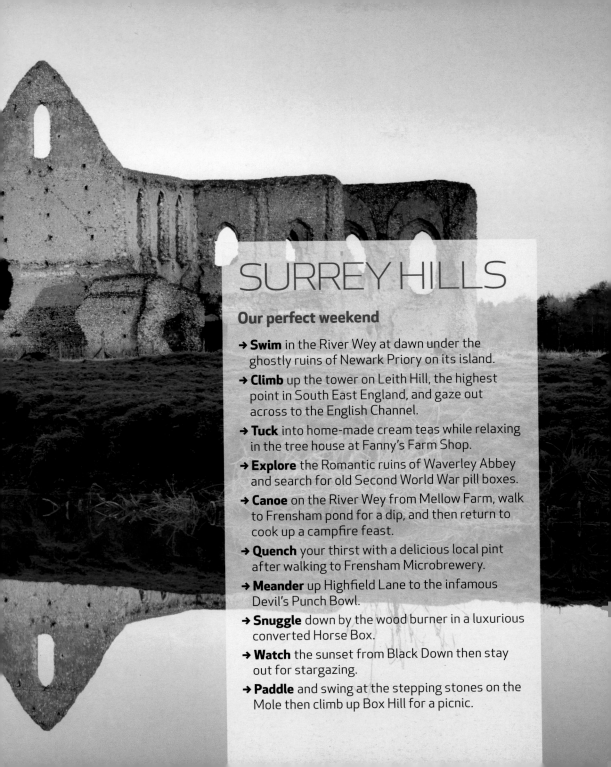

SURREY HILLS

Our perfect weekend

→ **Swim** in the River Wey at dawn under the ghostly ruins of Newark Priory on its island.

→ **Climb** up the tower on Leith Hill, the highest point in South East England, and gaze out across to the English Channel.

→ **Tuck** into home-made cream teas while relaxing in the tree house at Fanny's Farm Shop.

→ **Explore** the Romantic ruins of Waverley Abbey and search for old Second World War pill boxes.

→ **Canoe** on the River Wey from Mellow Farm, walk to Frensham pond for a dip, and then return to cook up a campfire feast.

→ **Quench** your thirst with a delicious local pint after walking to Frensham Microbrewery.

→ **Meander** up Highfield Lane to the infamous Devil's Punch Bowl.

→ **Snuggle** down by the wood burner in a luxurious converted Horse Box.

→ **Watch** the sunset from Black Down then stay out for stargazing.

→ **Paddle** and swing at the stepping stones on the Mole then climb up Box Hill for a picnic.

Tucked up close to London, the Surrey Hills remain a land of glorious woodlands and open heathlands. The chalky ridge of the North Downs sweeps through the middle of Surrey, and the North Downs Way meanders eastward from Farnham.

Perhaps surprisingly, this is the most wooded county in England, with over a fifth of the area covered by woodland. Head to Ashtead Common to walk between thousands of veteran pollarded oak trees, or go to Druid's Grove in Norbury Park to see the ancient yew trees mentioned in the Domesday Book. To sleep in a cosy shepherd's hut within a secluded six-acre woodland, try The Green Escape near Leith Hill.

The North Downs are bursting with highpoints and views. Leith Hill, the highest point in South East England, offers dramatic views as far as the English Channel and has a tower that you can climb. Nearby Box Hill, with its similarly fantastic views, trees and wild flowers, has been selected by the National Trust as one of the top 10 places in the UK to picnic. The famously disastrous picnic there in Jane Austen's *Emma* has obviously not had too much of a negative effect! Black Down, a lesser-visited, wooded high point, is one of the top stargazing spots in the country.

There are many swimming places, from rivers to ancient lakes. Frensham Great Pond was built as a fish pond by the Bishop of Winchester in 1246 and was drained every five years to grow barley and cleanse it. The last time it was emptied, however, was in 1942, during the Second World War, as it had become a great moonlit landmark for the German bombers. It is shallow and warmish, and has two bays with natural sandy beaches marked out for swimming. Near Frensham Ponds is a fantastic independent microbrewery, which can only be reached on foot, and during the summer has been known to slake the thirst of many a walker who has stopped on the footpath to buy a pint from the brewers themselves.

The River Wey is the main river of the region, perfect for canoeing and swimming, with good bathing on the Pilgrim's Way at sandy St Catherine's Hill, and the beautiful meadows at Thundry. There are also several riverside ruins along the Wey, such as the abbey at Waverley. Newark Priory sits upon a remote island – which the brave can swim across to – and is particularly evocative at sunset or dawn.

RIVERS & LAKES

1 FRENSHAM GREAT POND, FARNHAM

Sandy lake with beaches and buoyed-off swimming area. Set within forest and open heathland. Parking, café and small museum. Popular with families.

→ Approx 3½ miles S of Farnham centre on A287, signed Frensham Pond Hotel on R, then first L after ½ mile into carpark. Frensham Little Pond is signed on L approx 3 miles S of Farnham centre. This is more beautiful, but has 'no swimming' signs. Behind is a bridleway which leads down to a ford on the young River Wey.

5 mins, 51.1575, -0.7919 🍴⛺🏞️🏊

2 TILFORD GREEN/STOCKBRIDGE POND

Popular village green and pub. Paddling and pools just downstream of the bridge, though the parish council have recently put up 'no paddling' notices. Also try nearby Stockbridge Pond and the River Wey.

→ 3 miles SE of Farnham off B3001. Parking opposite Barley Mow pub (GU10 2BU, 01252 792205). For the pond, head S (dir Rushmoor) and after 200m find track byway on L which lead to pond (500m, 51.1793, -0.7419). If fishermen here head on 300m, bearing L into

Yagden Heath, to find the R Wey with tree and rope swings on L (51.1797, -0.7353).

10 mins, 51.182, -0.7499 🛶🍴🏊

3 THUNDRY MEADOW ELSTEAD, R WEY

Tranquil meadow-side swimming near famous mill pub.

→ Heading from Elstead to Charleshill on B3001 pass the Mill (GU8 6LE, 01252 703333 – a great riverside location with working wheel). After 600m, just after turning for Seale on R, find layby, gate and footpath to meadows on L.

5 mins, 51.1873, -0.7149 🐾🏞️🏊

4 GODALMING, R WEY

Meadow, ancient oaks and deep water.

→ From Manor Inn/Beefeater pub garden (A3100/Guildford Rd, GU7 3BX, 01483 427134) follow river path downstream to open fields and meadow (300m).

10 min, 51.1984, -0.5862 🍴🏊🏞️🏊

5 ST CATHERINE'S HILL, R WEY

Sandy beach, ruined chapel and bridge for jumping from, on the old Pilgrims' Way. Or explore upstream to Shalford.

→ Walk 20 mins from Shalford station on

cycle path opposite water fountain near GU4 8LE, across railway, then L down to river, crossing over at St Catherine's lock. Or a mile S of Guildford on the A3100 Goldalming Rd, find tiny Ferry Lane on L near Ye Olde Ship Inn, GU2 4EB, 01483 575731).

20 mins, 51.2243, -0.5772 🚶🏞️🏊🚴🏊

6 OLD WOKING/BROADMEAD, R WEY

Remote meaders of the Wey run deep along meadow land and commons. Look out for the aircraft bunker ruins nearby.

→ Between Send and Old Woking. S from London House pub at roundabout (GU22 9JN), over bridge and find track on L onto common at end of houses after 100m. River is to L, bunker ruins to R.

10 mins, 51.2989, -0.5348 🏊🏞️

7 NEWARK PRIORY, R WEY

Romantic, inaccessible ruins of Augustinian priory stand silent on an island on the Wey.

→ Not open to the public, but you can view from the river, or swim across. E of Woking, between Ripley and Pyrford (B367). At the bridge and traffic lights take the tow path downstream 300m, across the lock, to see island on L.

5 mins, 51.3089, -0.5068 ❓🏞️

8 STEPPING STONES, RIVER MOLE

Famous stepping stones on the River Mole at Box Hill Country Park. Deeper section in the meadows downstream.

→ Drop down from the main viewpoint and car park for Box Hill, following the North Downs Way. Or walk down the A24 for 5 mins from the Stepping Stones pub (RH5 6BS, 01306 889932) to find footpath on L. Box Hill & Westhumble train station.

10 mins, 51.2488, -0.3216

9 BOLDER MERE, OCKHAM COMMON

Just off the M25 near RHS Wisley, a nature reserve but a popular spot for a discreet dip.

→ From the sliproad joining the A3 heading S from M25 junction, then signed before joining the main carriageway just after lorry parking, so be ready. Car parks on L before KT11 1NA.

5 mins, 51.3135, -0.4570

10 BOURLEY BOTTOM, ALDERSHOT

Series of old reservoir lakes in pine forest on MOD training land. Popular in summer.

→ Leave B3013 at S edge of Fleet, L onto Bourley Rd just S of GU52 8UJ. After about a mile, find a large gravel car park on L. 200m further S, a gated track leads 300m up to first

lake, with another to the R and one beyond.

15 mins, 51.2488, -0.8117

11 FRIDAY STREET, LEITH HILL

Mill pool and inn among thick-wooded hills.

→ Signed Abinger Common from A25, approx 2 miles W of Dorking edge, then signed Friday St on R after 1½ miles. Best entry is far wooded bank. Stephan Langton pub is just up lane (RH5 6JR, 01306 730775). Or take dead end lane 1¼ miles S of A25 to remote Broadmoor to find waterfall and series of idyllic private lakes (51.2016, -0.3757).

3 mins, 51.1999, -0.3865

RUINS & CAVES

12 WAVERLEY ABBEY, FARNHAM

Romantic ruins of England's first Cistercian Abbey. Picnic in the monks' refectory, and marvel at the twisted roots of a huge ancient yew tree behind the high altar. Search the precincts for Second World War relics, from pillboxes to anti-tank ditches. Swim in the young river Wey, which runs alongside.

→ Waverley Lane, Farnham, GU9 8EP. Well signposted.

3 mins, 51.2015, -0.7564

20

13 REIGATE CAVES

Extensive network of old sand-mine tunnels
beneath Reigate, cared for by a small charity.

→ Tunnel Road, off High Street, Reigate, RH2
9AA. Open some Saturdays in summer only,
10am - 4pm, £5, check ahead at wcms.org.uk.
Private tours are also possible.

1 min, 51.2382, -0.2058 🚗🚽

SUNSET HILLTOPS

14 BLACK DOWN, HASLEMERE

This is a fantastic spot for stargazing –
not the darkest, but still among the most
atmospheric. The view by day is also
stunning, and is said to have inspired Alfred
Lord Tennyson. Head for Temple of Winds for
best lookout.

→ Take the B2131 E out of Haslemere, and
500m after the roundabout with a building in
the middle take steep R up Haste Hill. After
300m keep L and then cross into Tennyson's
Lane. After a mile look for car park R (before
bends and GU27 3BJ). Park and follow
footpath S, all the way up to the summit. Or
this car park (Fernden Lane, 51.0537, -0.6849)
takes you straight to the lookout.

20 mins, 51.0584, -0.6900 📷🚶

15 BOX HILL, DORKING

Known for centuries as a perfect picnic spot,
Box Hill boasts the oldest untouched area of
natural woodland in the UK. Can be busy, but
well worth a visit.

→ Follow signs for Box Hill from the A24 a mile
N of Dorking (KT20 7LB).

1 min, 51.2490, -0.3131 🅱️🍴🚶🚽

16 DEVIL'S PUNCH BOWL, HINDHEAD

Much wilder since the A3 was buried beneath
the ground, with grazing Highland cattle
and Exmoor ponies. Nearby Gibbet Hill is
the second-highest point in Surrey, with
fantastic views across the Weald, and takes
its name from a triple hanging that followed
the murder of a sailor. Go early or late in the
day to avoid crowds.

→ Head S along the A3 through the tunnel
and take the first exit (A333) signposted to
Hindhead and then Devil's Punch Bowl. At the
lights (GU26 6AB) carry straight on to car park L.

5 mins, 51.1172, -0.7273 📷🚶🅱️

17 HOLMBURY HILL

Iron Age hillfort two miles west of Leith Hill.
Popular for walking and mountain biking.

13

17

→ From The Hurtwood Inn (GU5 9RR), Peaslake, head S on Radnor Road (L at the red phone box by the memorial) and after a mile look out for car park, L, up a dusty track. Take footpath E up hill for 500m.

5 mins, 51.1769, -0.4209 ▣

18 LEITH HILL & TOWER

The highest point in southern England, with sweeping views across the English Channel. Lovely picnic spot, amid woodland and open heathland. The Greensand Way (long-distance walking path from Haslemere in to Hamstreet in Kent) crosses this spot. The 250-year-old tower near the summit serves tea and home-made cake from a quirky hatch.

→ Heading W on Abinger Road from Coldharbour, look for the car park R after ¾ mile (RH5 6LX). Follow the signed footpath up the hill. Non-NT members can go to the top of the tower for a reasonable £1. On a clear day it is said that 14 counties and the south coast can be seen from the summit.

5 mins, 51.1771, -0.3724 ▣ B

19 DRUIDS GROVE, NORBURY PARK

Some of the most ancient trees in Great

Britain, at 2,000 years old. Mentioned in the Domesday Book, legend has it that this grove of yews was used by druids for ritual and ceremony.

→ From Box Hill & Westhumble station, head NW on Westhumble St. At the stone arch, fork R onto Crabtree Ln (dead-end road). Follow NW out of Westhumble and look out for Norbury Park car park on R after about ¾ mile (after RH5 6BQ). Footpath leads N from here – follow for just over ½ mile.

15 mins, 51.2667, -0.3426 ▣ ▣

20 GLOVER'S WOOD, CHARLWOOD

Small woodland with fantastic bluebell display in spring. Picturesque Lowfield Heath Windmill is often surrounded by sheep on nearby Rectory Lane, 500m SW.

→ Take public footpath at the end of Glovers Rd (RH6 0EH, dead end). Pass historic aircraft in field L and follow footpath through tree avenue.

5 mins, 51.1548, -0.2420 B ▣

21 KING OAK, ASHTEAD COMMON

A rambling wild space with a veteran pollarded oak tree by an earthwork, one of over 2,300 ancient pollarded oaks on the common. There is also the site of an old Roman villa to be explored to the NE.

36

→ From Epsom take the B280 W, cross two mini-roundabouts, and about a mile after the second park in car park L, before KT18 7TR. Following the bridleway 1½ miles along edge of woods and then looking for a L into woods will bring you to the earthwork. Or follow the footpath to the pond, turn R, pass two crossroads, and take the second path L (pass two benches from the second crossroads), continue for about 50m. Best bring a map, many paths.

20 mins, 51.3267, -0.3147 ◻◻◻

22 SLAUGHAM YEW, ST MARY'S CHURCH

Huge ancient churchyard yew, surviving from William the Conqueror's reign. Explore beyond to find romantic remains of 17th century manor house with gardens and a quite lake.

→ Staplefield Road, RH17 6AQ, just off A23. Follow the footpath from the church SE 10 mins for the ruins. Or follow the S footpath 10 mins to find lake on the R.

1 min, 51.0382, -0.2076 ◻◻◻◻

WILDLIFE & MEADOWS

23 HYDON'S BALL AND HEATH

Heath and woodland with fantastic views across Surrey towards the Sussex border. Listen for nightingales and nightjars in spring.

→ From Hydestile crossroads, take Salt Lane towards Hascombe/Dunsfold. After ½ mile (past GU8 4BB) take sometimes muddy track into parking area R, immediately after sign for Godalming L.

1 min, 51.1527, -0.6017 ◻

24 WOOLBEDING COMMON

Heather-clad heathland with lots of space to get lost. Listen out for the rattle of nightjars.

→ From Woolbeding village (GU29 9RR) take single-track Brambling Ln for Liphook. After 1½ miles take R fork signed Oder Hill. Follow road ¾ mile to Access sign, and turn R to park in Woolbeding Common NT car park. Follow the footpath to explore the common.

15 mins, 51.0255, -0.7585 ◻

25

25

34

42

40

39

25 F CONISBEE & SON, EAST HORSLEY

Traditional family butchers since 1760. All meat is locally sourced and there is a good selection of game.

→ Park Corner, Ockham Road S, KT24 6RZ, 01483 282073.
51.2690, -0.4325 🍴

26 FANNY'S FARM SHOP, MERTSHAM

Delicious local food and cream teas. Book in advance and take your afternoon tea up in the tree house.

→ Markedge Lane, Mertsham, RH1 3AW, 01737 554444.
51.2746, -0.1704 🍴

27 THE ABINGER HATCH PUB

Quintessential English country pub with good selection of cask ales. Garden bar & BBQ.

→ Abinger Lane, Abinger Common, RH5 6HZ, 01306 730737.
51.2019, -0.4042 🍺

28 THE PLOUGH INN, COLDHARBOUR

17th-century coaching house nestled in the Surrey Hills. Home-cooked food and ale brewed on site in the pub's own microbrewery. Comfortable B&B also available.

→ Coldharbour, RH5 6HD, 01306 711793.
51.1843, -0.3539 🍴

29 THE SURREY OAKS, NEWDIGATE

Award-winning real-ale pub with rustic local food and a wood-burning stove.

→ Parkgate Road, Newdigate, RH5 5DZ, 01306 631200.
51.1790, -0.2773 🍺🍴

30 THE WILLIAM IV, ALBURY

Roaring fires and home-cooked, unpretentious food, including free-range pork raised by the owner. Choice of beers from local microbreweries.

→ Little London, Albury, Guildford, GU5 9DG, 01483 202685.
51.2097, -0.4759 🍺🍴

31 FRENSHAM BREWERY

Independent microbrewery, producing hand-crafted cask ale using locally sourced ingredients. Only accessible by foot – Miles and Emily can serve you a refreshing pint directly on the footpath. Opening hours are limited.

→ The Old Dairy, Pierrepont Home Farm, The Reeds, GU10 3BS, 01252 793956. Park in Frensham Little Pond NT car park on Priory Lane (GU10 3BT), and take footpath N across the River Wey until you reach the farm buildings after 500m.
51.1733, -0.7725 🍴

32 THE WINDMILL, EWHURST

Tuck into seasonal, locally sourced food at this gorgeous gastropub, while enjoying some of the the best pub views in the South of England.

→ Pitch Hill, Cranleigh, GU6 7NN, 01483 548389.
51.1706, -0.4565 🛏️🍴

33 THE DUKE OF CUMBERLAND

Historic, hill-top pub with fantastic views and award-winning locally sourced food.

→ Henley, Fernhurst, West Sussex, GU27 3HQ, 01428 652280
51.0243, -0.7262 🍴

34 ETHERLEY FARM CAMPING, DORKING

Relaxed family camping on a working farm. Home-made marmalade, hand-reared meat and free-range eggs all available to buy for breakfast.

→ Leith Hill Lane, Ockley, RH5 5PA, 01306 621423.
51.1625, -0.3858

35 'GES' THE CONVERTED HORSE BOX

Adventure and luxury are combined in this beautifully converted 1975 horse box. Picnic outside by day and snuggle up with retro quilts and crocheted blankets by night.

→ Chiddingford, GU8 4XR, Canopyandstars. co.uk, 0117 2047830.
51.1145, -0.6528 🏕️

36 GLAMPING HOLIDAY, ALFOLD

Enjoy a bit of luxury away from it all in a beautifully decorated, shabby-chic bell tent. Everything you could possibly need is supplied, including pots, pans, firewood and firelighters. You can even order cooked meals and afternoon teas.

→ Sprinbok Farm Estate, Alfold, GU6 8EX, 07925 571461.
51.1035, -0.5277

37 HENMAN BUNKHOUSE, LEITH HILL

National Trust self-catering bunkhouse amid footpaths and bridleways.

→ Leith Hill Ln, nr Coldharbour, Surrey RH5 6JZ, 01306 712711. Nationaltrust.org.uk
51.1962, -0.3719

38 LONG COPSE B&B, CRANLEIGH
Beautiful Arts and Crafts house in an AONB. Views sweep down over the Weald as far as the South Downs, and behind the house the Surrey Hills rise up, providing wonderful walks. Mouth-watering home baking.
→ Pitch Hill, GU6 7NN, 01483 277458.
51.1674, -0.4549

39 SHEPHERD'S HUT, SHERE
This cosy shepherd's hut sits in a field on top of a hill, and is hand-built in a traditional style. Wood burner inside, and farmhouse breakfast delivered to your door each morning.
→ Lockhurst Hatch Farm, Shere, GU5 9JN, 01483 202689.
51.1938, -0.4753

40 PUTTENHAM ECO CAMPING BARN
Set beside the North Downs Way and Sustrans Route 22, with communal sleeping areas. Rainwater harvesting, solar electricity and solar hot water. Receive a discount if arriving by foot, bicycle or public transport. Open April–October, booking essential.
→ The Street, Puttenham, GU3 1AR, 01629 592700. No parking at the barn.
51.2227, -0.6658

41 THE GREEN ESCAPE, LEITH HILL
Secluded six-acre woodland, reserved for group bookings. Fire pits, shepherd's huts, compost toilets and a flock of sheep.
→ RH5 6HG. Exact location revealed upon booking, 01306 711053.
51.1661, -0.3805

42 YHA HINDHEAD
Hidden in a secluded valley at the bottom of the Devil's Punch Bowl. Low beams and a wood burning stove make this a cosy place.
→ Devil's Punch Bowl, Portsmouth Rd, Thursley, Godalming, GU8 6NS, 0845 3719022.
51.1239, -0.7261

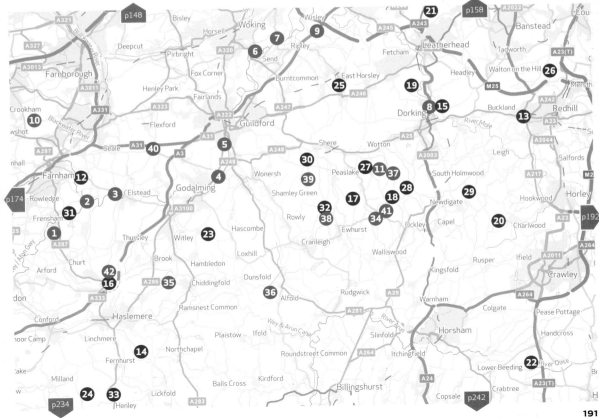

HIGH WEALD

Our perfect weekend

→ **Peer** through the door in the tree at the ancient Crowhurst Yew and wonder who built it there.

→ **Canoe** and swim along the rural Medway near Golden Green.

→ **Boulder** and scramble at Harrison's Rocks, and explore the rock formations at Eridge.

→ **Light** a campfire, paddle in the stream, and listen to local musicians at Bedgebury Camping.

→ **Sleep** in a restored gypsy wagon from 1904, by ancient cobnut trees at Nut Plat retreat.

→ **Enjoy** gorgeous local food at The Vine and relax in the idyllic surroundings.

→ **Play** Poohsticks at Hartfield Bridge and paddle in the stream.

→ **Swim** in a secret 'furnace' hammer pond, once used to power the Wealden iron industry.

→ **Discover** the ruins and twisted tree roots at Bayham Old Abbey.

→ **Climb** through the trees to Oldbury Hillfort and watch the sunset.

→ **Sunset** paddle and dip at one of many secret coves on Bewl Water.

Between the parallel chalk escarpments of the North and South Downs, the High Weald is a high sandstone ridge, formed millions of years ago, and an area of ancient heathland forest.

At the heart of the High Weald is Ashdown Forest, a deer-hunting forest in Norman times; two thirds of its 6,500 acres are open heathland, with sweeping views over the Kent and Sussex countryside. Famously home to Winnie-the-Pooh, many places can be located from A.A. Milne's Pooh stories and E.H. Shepard's illustrations, including the Six Pine Trees by the Heffalump trap, Piglet's house in the middle of the beech tree and, of course, the original Poohsticks Bridge. For more on these, visit Pooh Corner in Hartfield.

The High Weald forests are home to some of the most ancient and best-known trees in the country, including the Tandridge Yew, the Sidney Oak at Penshurst, the Seven Sisters Chestnut (the largest-girthed tree in Britain) and the Crowhurst Yew (possibly the oldest tree in Britain, at 4,000 years). These ancient trees are fascinating and mysterious, and to this day no one is sure who really created the door in the Crowhurst Yew.

Jutting high out of the landscape, the craggy outcrops of the sandstone ridge are impressive and unexpected. Popular with climbers, some of these twisted shapes – such as Eridge Rocks – are also a Site of Special Scientific Interest where rare plants grow. These Wealden bedrocks have also yielded minerals, and the iron industry thrived in the Weald of Kent and Sussex from pre-Roman times until the industrial revolution, using iron ore from the Cretaceous rocks and charcoal from the abundant woodlands. The remains of the industry can still be seen in the many 'hammer ponds' in the area, created to harness water power for the local iron industry. These now make clean and beautiful places to swim, if you are not chased away by anglers. The coming of coal (not charcoal) saw the demise of the industry in the area, but in its heyday the 16-acre lake at Horsmonden powered the giant hammer of John Browne's forge, the flames of which could be seen about the country at 10 miles distance. The cannons made in Horsmonden and other parts of the Weald can be found all over the world.

There are also many beautiful reservoir lakes, where a blind eye is often turned to swimming, and the river Medway, where there is swimming and canoeing galore. The banks of the river slope steeply into rich, clean and weed-free water. The water may appear a little dark and foreboding, but the peaty smell and brownish hue are flavoured by the woodlands above, and to swim is to be infused with an elixir of leaf litter and pine cones.

RIVERS, LAKES & STREAMS

1 THE POOHSTICKS BRIDGE, HARTFIELD

Popular, but worth it for the excitement of playing Poohsticks on Pooh Bear's 'real' Poohsticks bridge, and maybe going paddling too. There are lots of other 'Pooh' places in the area - visit Pooh Corner in Hartfield to find out more.

→ Follow the B2026 S from Pooh Corner (Hartfield, TN7 4AE) for just over a mile, and take the R turn signed Marsh Green and Newbridge. The car park is first on the R. From here, follow the path for 'Pooh Bridge'. To refuel, visit Piglet's Tearoom at Pooh Corner for a 'little smackerel of something' in the sunny garden.

15 mins, 51.0854, 0.0978 🏊🍴

2 POUNDSBRIDGE, R EDEN

In remote fields, a bridge and deep pools under red earth banks. Popular for jumps!

→ From opposite Enterprise Centre sign (TN11 8BG), near Penshurst Bridge, take footpath upstream along Eden, crossing once on footbridge after ½ mile, to reach the bridge. Or quicker via bridleway from Poundsbridge.

30 mins, 51.1580, 0.1914 🍴🏊🚣

3 ENSFIELD BRIDGE, R MEDWAY

Open, sunny stretch of river by lane with river paths in both directions. Steep banks but good for a longer swim. Also on Regional Cycle Route 12 upstream to Penshurst Place, or downstream to lakes.

→ W of Tonbridge, a mile S of Leigh station on lanes (near TN11 8RZ).

2 mins, 51.1857, 0.2133 🏊🚴🚣🚻

4 FORD GREEN BRIDGE, R MEDWAY

This long stretch of the river Medway E of Tonbridge is perfect for canoeing and swimming in summer, if you are careful to avoid the bigger boats and locks. There are open meadows and mainly easy banks into deep water. Large network of gravel lakes on S shore too.

→ ½ mile E of Golden Green (The Bell Inn, TN11 0BD, 01732 851748) is Barnes Street hamlet. Take the Wealdway footpath S (opposite the postbox in the wall) and continue ¾ mile. Upstream W a mile leads through open river and fields past East Lock to Hartlake road bridge, S of Golden Green (a good canoe launching location). Downstream E leads past Oak Weir lock to Stilstead Bridge, with lakes to the R.

15 mins, 51.2010, 0.3560 🏊🚶🚣🚻

5 HORSTED KEYNES

Large area of many hammer ponds – large and small – in beautiful woodland setting.

→ Signed off A275, 2 miles N of Sheffield Park. Park at the church then continue N down track/road 300m to reach main lake on R. Smaller grassy ponds for picnics further on, or more lakes to the E. Avoid fishermen.

10 mins, 51.0447, -0.0269 ❓

6 WADHURST PARK LAKE, BATTS WOOD

A remote lake with a private deer park to N, bordered by a secret wooded shores to the S.

→ 200m E of Bivelham Farm (TN20 6RS) is a track / drive and gate. This is a bridleway that becomes a footpath, heading W then N, down into Batt's Wood and the lake shore.

25 mins, 51.0274, 0.3274 ❓⛰🚶

7 BOUGH BEECH LAKE

This location is rather hidden – and is a nature reserve – so be peaceful.

→ From The Wheatsheaf in Bough Beech (TN8 7NU, 01732 700100) cross railway bridge and turn immediate R. After a mile, and 200m N of Hilders Farm, find footpath on R, leading down to shore (100m).

5 mins, 51.2186, 0.1354 ❓⛰🚶

8 GRAVETYE LAKE, KINGSCOTE

Lovely Forestry Commission lake, hidden in deep woods, though can get weedy later in season.

→ 1½ mile's walk S from Kingscote station on wooded footpaths via Hastings Wood (bring map). Or quicker from Gravetye Manor hotel (amazing food, RH19 4LJ, 01342 810567). Follow signs almost up to house, to find footpath on L (High Weald Landscape Trail) and descend through fields to lake at bottom, on L.
10 mins, 51.0902, -0.0503

9 FURNACE POND, HORSMONDEN

A relic of the Weald's ancient iron industry, once used to make canons.

→ Follow Furnace Lane from Horsmonden village (signed Methodist Church) then continue ½ mile to the lake on L (TN12 8LZ).
3 mins, 51.1449, 0.4217

10 ARDINGLY LAKE, BALCOMBE

A beautiful two-pronged reservoir near Balcombe train station. Good path along N shore. Avoid fishermen and be discreet.

→ From Balcombe follow Mill Lane (signed Ardingly) from mini roundabout/postbox. Pick up footpath from parking layby at bottom, beyond bridge. Or from Ardingly follow Balcombe Lane. Park after a mile in layby R, at top of lane. Take first footpath on L, along E shore to bench (300m). Both paths connect.
15 mins, 51.0489, -0.0991

11 BALCOMBE LAKE, BALCOMBE

One of the many 'hammer ponds' that were created in the Weald of Sussex some 350 years ago, now a haven for wildlife.

→ From Balcombe take the Ardingley road. Turn L at the corner after 500m (Woodward Farm) to find the kissing gate by the lake.
5 mins, 51.0631, -0.1237

12 BEWL WATER

The South East's largest water body, surrounded by orchards and no end of secret beaches to dip from discreetly.

→ There is footpath access around the entire perimeter and a 12-mile mountain bike route. From the main visitor centre head W along the N shore to Bramble Bay. Or try Rosemary Lane off the A21 (51.06300, 0.42055) at the E end. Our favourite is from Three Leg Cross (51.0613, 0.3948) – from the Bull Inn (TN5 7HH) head down Boarders Ln, then turn R at crossroads, downhill to car park and dead end. Camp at Cedar Gables off A21, Flimwell (TN5

13

7QA, 01892 890566). The footpath behind leads down to a sunset-facing wooded cove (20 mins, 51.0675, 0.4097). Scotney Castle is also close by.
5 mins, 51.0613, 0.3948 🐾🏕️♿❓

ANCIENT AND SACRED

13 BAYHAM OLD ABBEY, LITTLE BAYHAM
Despite the entrance charge, this impressive ruin is well worth a visit. Founded in the early 13th century, this crumbling ancient abbey is remote, atmospheric, and surrounded by overgrown trees.
→ 1¾ miles W of Lamberhurst, off B2169 past the Elephants Head pub (TN3 8LJ). Well signposted.
2 min, 51.1033, 0.3555 🏛️

14 OLDBURY HILL, IGHTHAM
The remains of a powerful, two-mile-long, Iron Age hillfort lie buried at the summit of Oldbury Hill, beneath ancient woodland.
→ Car park (TN15 0ET) off Styants Bottom Road is signed from the A25, between Borough Green and Sevenoaks. Find an information board in the car park, with the fort at the hill summit.
5 mins, 51.2786, 0.26216

15 MOOR WOOD SUNKEN LANE
Very impressive old holloway with deep walls of rocks and roots.
→ On Eden Valley Walk footpath ½ mile W out of Hill Hoath towards Hever.
10 mins, 51.1807, 0.1379

16 ST LEONARD'S TOWER, WEST MALLING
Decaying Norman tower in peaceful location near lake.
→ Stands just off roadside, signed on R, 1 mile S of West Malling on St Leonard's St (ME19 6PD). Opposite is path to Manor Park lake. Prettiest approach is from Offham Rd (ME19 6RF).
1 min, 51.2881, 0.4020

NOBLE TREES

17 THE SIDNEY OAK, PENSHURST
An ancient oak, about 1,000 years old. Sir Philip Sidney used to sit beneath this oak to write poetry.
→ 100m N of Lancup Wells lake in Penshurst Place parkland. 300m behind the café and car park (if visiting), or ½-mile walk from the church on public footpaths (TN11 8DG).
5 mins, 51.1815, 0.1848 🅱️

15

18

18 TANDRIDGE CHURCH YEW
This ancient hollow yew is said to be the second largest in the UK, with a girth of over 10 metres.

→ Heading N through Tandridge, the church is on the R just after Jackass Lane on L (RH8 9NJ).

1 min, 51.2430, -0.0320

19 THE CROWHURST YEW
Ancient yew tree full of intriguing holes and shapes - even a door! The history of this noble tree is mysterious and extensive, and there were once benches within the tree itself. Reputed to be 4,000 years old.

→ St George's Church, Crowhurst, RH7 6LR

2 mins, 51.2094, -0.0103 🅿

20 THE SEVEN SISTERS CHESTNUT
Britain's largest tree? Six trunks grow in a circle, surrounding a rocky mound.

→ S from Pensurst on B2188. Turn R signed Chiddingstone. After ¾ mile find and follow track on L, signed PORC (great off-road mountain bike tracks). Tree is up track to R, on hill brow, after 100m.

2 mins, 51.1623, 0.1623 🚶

NATURAL WONDERS

21 ASHDOWN FOREST HORSE RIDING
A network of bridlepaths weave through 6,500 acres of unspoilt woodland and heathland. The Ashdown Forest Riding Centre, at the heart of the forest, is well placed for hiring or lessons.

→ Ashdown Forest Riding Centre, King Standing Farm, Black Hill Road, Crowborough, TN6 1XE, 07818 093880

1 min, 51.0531, 0.1003 🐴🏞

22 ERIDGE ROCKS
Evocative and unexpected, these gigantic sandstone boulders played host to elaborate theatrical dinner parties during the 19th century. Fantastic climbing in some sections for the more experienced (sandstone can be crumbly), although much of the area is an SSSI due to the abundance of native plants.

→ From Tunbridge Wells, travel S on the A26 (dir Crowborough) for 4 miles. In Eridge Green, turn R 100m after the Nevill Crest and Gun (TN3 9JR, 01892 864209) by the church and a wooden bus shelter. Continue up private track to small car park at the base of the rocks.

1 min, 51.0980, 0.2192 🅱🏞

41

23 HARRISON'S ROCKS, ERIDGE
A huge sandstone crag. The largest of the cluster of local outcrops often referred to as Southern Sandstone by local climbers.
➔ Heading NW from Park Corner towards Groombridge on Eridge Road, look for car park L (TN3 9NH).
2 mins, 51.1064, 0.1889 **V B**

SLOW FOOD

24 THE CASTLE INN, CHIDDINGSTONE
This is a gorgeous little pub in a picturesque National Trust-preserved village. Great selection of wines and real ales, famous Sunday lunch, and pretty outdoor space.
➔ Chiddingstone, TN8 7AH, 01892 870247
51.1859, 0.1456 **Y**

25 THE GEORGE AND DRAGON, CHIPSTEAD
Well-liked 16th-century village pub with excellent local, seasonal food.
➔ 39 High Street, TN13 2RW, 01732 779 019
51.2846, 0.1535 **Y Y**

26 THE PLOUGH, IVY HATCH
Country pub popular with cyclists and walkers. The excellent food is local and

seasonal, with some meals sourced from the pub's own pigs and chickens.
➔ High Cross Road, TN15 0NL, 01732 810100
51.2667, 0.2740 **Y Y**

27 THE HATCH INN, COLEMANS HATCH
Popular, weatherboarded pub dating from 1430, set in the heart of the Ashdown Forest. Serves locally sourced food.
➔ TN7 4EJ, 01342 822363
51.0815, 0.0722 **Y**

28 THE ROCK INN, CHIDDINGSTONE HOATH
Historic country pub which has retained the best bits of its past, including one of the few remaining sets of the traditional pub game 'Ring the Bull'. Real ale selection includes brews from the local microbrewery, less than two miles away.
➔ Hoath Corner, TN8 7BS, 01892 870296
51.1675, 0.1399 **Y**

29 PLAW HATCH BIODYNAMIC FARM
Buy biodynamic breads, yoghurts and vegetables straight from this co-operative.
➔ Plawhatch Lane, Sharpthorne, East Grinstead, RH19 4JL, 01342 810201
51.0748, -0.0093

40

30 THE VINE, GOUDHURST
Idyllic village pub serving fantastic locally sourced food, as well as local wines and beers. Dogs and wellies welcomed!
➔ High Street, TN17 1AG, 01580 211753
51.1132, 0.4592 **Y Y**

31 FORAGE IN THE ASHDOWN FOREST
Try one of the many foraging courses run by Ashdown Forage, such as Hedgerow Brewing and Game Preparation.
➔ Courses are held throughout Ashdown Forest, call Iona on 07956 751914 to book.
51.0754, 0.1147 **[]**

32 PENSHURST FARMERS' MARKET

Bustling farmers' market with a focus on local food, in the beautiful setting of Penshurst Place stately home and garden. First Saturday of the month, 9.30–noon.

→ Penshurst Place car park, Penshurst, Tonbridge, TN11 8DG.
51.1746, 0.1836

CAMP & STAY

33 BEDGEBURY CAMPING, GOUDHURST

Paddle in the stream that runs through the campsite, light a fire with skills learnt on the campsite bushcraft course and listen to local musicians play around the crackling logs, then enjoy the peace and quiet after 10pm. This tranquil campsite on a family farm only opens for 28 days during the summer.

→ Pattenden Farm, Bedgebury Road, Goudhurst, TN17 2QX, 01580 213487.
51.1016, 0.4504

34 CHAFFORD PARK, ASHURST

Laid-back campsite with simple facilities and lots of space. Surrounded by golden corn fields, with bluebell wood nearby.

→ Tunbridge Wells, TN3 9UR, 01892 740222.
51.1338, 0.1654

35 EVERGREEN FARM WOODLAND

Small woodland campsite with a wonderfully peaceful feel.

→ West Hoathly Road, East Grinstead, RH19 4NE, 07910 993622. Follow signs to Standen National Trust.
51.1035, -0.0158

36 FORGEWOOD CAMPING, DANEGATE

Good old-fashioned camping in woods and fields. Choose your spot, light your fire and send the kids off to play hide-and-seek or build dens in the woods.

→ Forgewood Barn, Sham Farm Road, TN3 9JA, 07854 901337, 01892 750006.
51.0835, 0.2256

37 HOLE COTTAGE, COWDEN

The surviving wing of a medieval timber-framed house. Grand open fire to warm up next to after exploring the woodland and stream outside.

→ Cowden (exact address given on booking), 01628 825925. Landmarktrust.org.uk
51.1570, 0.1114

38 HOOK FARM, WEST HOATHLY

Back-to-basics campsite on a former dairy farm. Space for 10 tents and basic facilities make this a fantastic spot for unfussy campers who enjoy simple pleasures, tranquility and nature.

→ Hook Lane, RH19 4PT, 01342 811113.
51.0726, -0.0570

39 ST IVES FARM, HARTFIELD

Small camping area with 20 pitches beside a fishing lake. This is a popular site, so book early!

→ Butcherfield Lane, TN7 4JX, 01892 770213.
51.1088, 0.0844

40 THE NUT PLAT RETREAT, DUNKS GREEN

Restored 1904 'living van' or showman's wagon, set on a quiet site of ancient cob nut trees. Dark, unpolluted night skies.

→ 0117 204 7830 Canopyandstars.co.uk From the Kentish Rifleman Pub on the corner of Dunk's Green Road and Roughway Lane (TN11 9RU), follow Roughway Lane to the L-hand bend, where the sign and gateway are on your R. 01732 810975.
51.2496, 0.3118

41 WILD BOAR WOOD CAMPSITE

Stylish bell tents and communal shelter in a five-acre bluebell wood.

→ Horsted Keynes (exact location revealed on booking), 07936 381376.
51.0380, -0.0313

42 FOREST GARDEN, SHOVELSTRODE

This forest garden is based on permaculture principles and encourages a wonderfully diverse ecosystem. Charles and Lisa offer courses, which range from foraging to pole-lathe turning. Accommodation in luxurious yurts or wilder camping area.

→ Shovelstrode Lane, East Grinstead, RH19 3PH, 07957 621672.
51.1276, 0.0306

43 OCTAVIA HILL BUNKHOUSE

National Trust bunkhouse for up to 14 people in a secluded valley surrounded by sheep and oast houses.

→ Park in small lay-by opposite Brasted Chart & Toys Hill cricket ground at the end of Pipers Green Lane (51.2590, 0.0965). Facing cricket ground, turn L and walk 10 mins to the end of the lane. 01732 750169.
51.2529, 0.0959

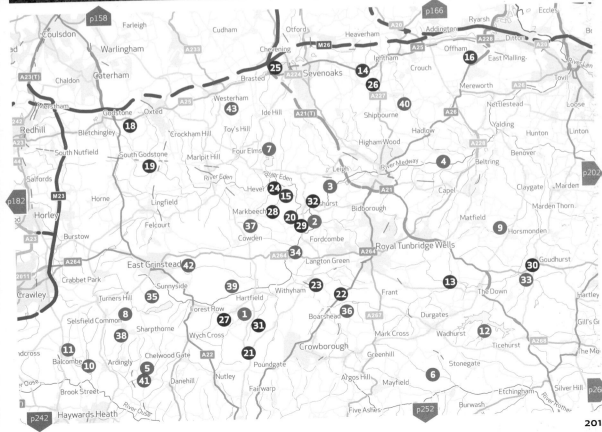

KENT DOWNS

Our perfect weekend

→ **Walk** the Pilgrims' Way through bluebells in the ancient Kings Wood and visit Bigbury Camp.

→ **Climb** the Pulpit in Perry Woods at sunset, then head down to the Rose and Crown for a pint.

→ **Explore** the chapel ruins of St Mary's Church at Eastwell by dusk, find the hidden tomb of an illegitimate king and swim in the lake.

→ **Commune** with sacred yews at Eastling and Ulcombe churches.

→ **Camp** in the glorious wildflower meadow at the Sunny Field, or by the orchard at Welsummer Camping.

→ **Pick** your favourite apples right off the trees at No Man's Community Orchard and settle down for a picnic.

→ **Sing** along at the Five Bells Inn for one of the regular acoustic nights, and taste their fantastic seasonal food.

→ **Swing** into the pretty Great Stour river at Chartham Hatch from the rope swing.

→ **Enjoy** spectacular sunsets from Thurnham Castle's hilltop location.

Apple orchards, hop fields, and cosy pubs remind you that this is the very heart of the Garden of England. Rich with history, you'll also find the ancient Pilgrim's Way on its final approach to Canterbury, a reminder of all the feet that have trodden this part of England.

By the end of the 14th century, two hundred years after the murder of St Thomas Becket, Canterbury Cathedral was welcoming thousands of pilgrims, and only Rome and Jerusalem were more popular. Several sacred and ancient sites dot this area, including two different ruined St Mary's churches - one at Eastwell and one at Little Chart.

Traditionally, medieval pilgrims would have had their first sight of Canterbury from Harbledown, shortly after passing by the even more ancient Roman camp at Bigbury. The track here is mossy and well worn from centuries of use. Chaucer's unfinished *Canterbury Tales* highlights the social as well as religious aspects of pilgrimage at the time, and travelling in larger groups was also necessary for protection against highwaymen and other dangers. The huge, 1,500-acre forest of King's Wood was one of the areas of particular risk, and anyone not already in a large group would wait on the edge until they had formed a larger band and felt safe to pass through. The North Downs Way now follows much of the old Pilgrims' Way, and if you follow the route through King's Wood in the gathering gloom of dusk is it easy to imagine the dangers faced by pilgrims.

The "miles of pink apple orchards" that H E Bates describes in *The Darling Buds of May* still do their part to shape the countryside. No Man's Community Orchard, between Chartham Hatch and Canterbury, is a glorious place for a picnic and some simple foraging, particularly in September when the apples are just waiting to be eaten. For something a bit more substantial, the Kent Downs seems to specialise in lovely little country pubs. Try The Plough Inn in Stalisfield, The Rose and Crown in Selling, or The Five Bells Inn in Brabourne – snuggle up next to the cosy fires or head outside to soak up the surrounding green fields and woodland. Neals Place Farm Camping and Welsummer Camping are both set amid orchards, and it's even possible to stay in a converted apple shed at Bethersden.

Gorgeous in the summer sun, the Great Stour river wends its way from Lenham, through the Downs and further east via Canterbury to the North Sea. There is also paddling to be had at Wye, and swimming downstream at Chartham in cool, deep pools with rope swings.

RIVER & LAKE SWIMS

1 CHARTHAM, R GREAT STOUR
Popular stream pool with rope swing and hidden lake beyond. Kids' canoeing.

➔ Park at Chartham village hall and follow the path 300m down along the stream to find small weir, deep pool beneath and rope swing. Continue on 300m to find lake on L. Chartham has a train station or is 3 miles SW of Canterbury on A28. NCN 18.

5 mins, 51.2562, 1.0215 🚉🏊🚴🚶🅿🍴⛱

2 OLANTIGH, R WYE
Pretty stretch of the young Stour by footbridge, for picnic and paddling.

➔ 1½ miles N of Wye, find footpath on L by junction, 100m after gates for Olantigh House (TN25 5EW). River down below in the meadows.

5 mins, 51.2017, 0.9479 🚉🚶

SACRED & ANCIENT

3 ST MARY'S TOWER, LITTLE CHART
Ivy-clad ruined medieval church, destroyed by a flying bomb in 1944.

➔ The ruin can just be seen from Pluckley Rd by Chart Court Farm (TN27 0QH). But, much better, is the pretty 20-minute walk through orchards that starts at the bend on Swan Lane next to the Swan Inn at Little Chart (TN27 0QB, 01233 840702).

20 mins, 51.1866, 0.7670 📷✝🚻

4 THURNHAM CASTLE
Overgrown 12th-century castle on a hill with spectacular views across the North Downs. The site may have been used as a watchtower even earlier, during the Roman occupation.

➔ From the crossroads at the Black Horse Inn in Thurnham (ME14 3LD, 01622 737185), drive up dead-end Castle Hill Rd opposite the pub. Follow the road round the hairpin bend until you emerge from the trees and see a long lay-by on the R just after a wooden-fenced path R. The castle is just along that path.

3 mins, 51.2941, 0.5905 📷

5 BIGBURY CAMP, CHARTHAM HATCH
Iron Age settlement where Julius Caesar won his first decisive victory against locals in 54 BC. The Pilgrims' Way passes the site at the foot of the slope. There is some noise from traffic, but the views are fantastic and the woodland lush.

➔ Follow Bigbury Road E from Chartham Hatch for just under a mile and look for a footpath sign pointing L. If you get to the fork in the road (CT2 9BJ), you have gone slightly too far. 100m down the footpath, Bigbury Camp is on your R. Continue to the track at the bottom of the hill to look up at the Camp from the Pilgrims' Way. Better yet, walk the North Downs Way from Chartham Hatch (which runs along the Pilgrims' Way route at this point).

5 mins, 51.2787, 1.0313 📷

6 ST MARY'S CHURCH, EASTWELL
Find the tombstone of Richard Plantagenet, illegitimate heir to the throne, and explore the ruined church and graveyard. Birds flap and flutter inside the ivy-clad tower, and the lake stretches away from beneath the trees. Also look for the ancient yew.

➔ Turn L up an unsigned dead-end lane, 1.3 miles E of Westwell, to find church at end (TN25 4JT). Also on the Pilgrims' Way footpath.

2 mins, 51.1899, 0.8747 📷📷✝

SUNSET HILLTOPS

7 DEVIL'S KNEADING TROUGH, WYE
Dramatic valley with views across Romney Marsh and out to the Channel. Popular for

kite flying. Nearby, the Wye Crown chalk etching (51.1813, 0.9622) is a great spot for watching the sunset. It was carved into the chalk by students in 1902, commemorating Edward VII's coronation.

→ From Wye dir Hastingleigh, pass the Devil's Kneading Trough restaurant (TN25 5HE, 01233 813212) and after 150m look for public car park in lay-by L. Cross the road and head through the wooden gates.

2 mins, 51.1688, 0.9721 🖼🚶

8 THE PULPIT, PERRY WOOD, SELLING

Wooden viewing tower built in the 1800s, with views across the Thames Estuary, North Downs and Isle of Thanet. The surrounding woodland is beautiful, and there are usually rope swings hanging from many of the trees. Visit The Rose and Crown afterwards for refreshment.

→ From The Rose and Crown (ME13 9RY, 01227 752214) go 500m dir Selling and turn R at the crossroads, signed 'Perry Wood Car Park'. Car park is 60m on your L. Cross back over the road to the footpath directly opposite, and keep on this path through the woods and up onto the hill for ¾ mile. Continue along the ridge to reach The Pulpit.

20 mins, 51.2553, 0.9276 🖼🖼🚻🚶

9 ULCOMBE CHURCH ANCIENT YEW

A twisted yew thought to be over 2,000 years old. The Eastling yew is close listing 29.

→ All Saints Church, Ulcombe Hill, ME17 1DN. Eastling yew is at ME13 0BA, 10 miles E.

1 min, 51.2169, 0.6425

WOODLAND & WILDLIFE

10 BLUEBELLS, KINGS WOOD

For fantastic bluebells, follow the ancient Pilgrims' Way through this wood in spring. Once a dangerous route for pilgrims on their way to Canterbury, who tended to travel in groups for protection from highwaymen. Today, it is a peaceful place, although still dark and gloomy when the sun sets.

→ Leave the A251 S out of Challock at end of village (after TN25 4AR), signposted Stour Valley Area and Wye. Car park is 500m on L with open paths into the woods.

30 mins, 51.219, 0.9192 🚻🚶🍴🚗

11 BONSAI BANK ORCHIDS, DENGE WOOD

Countless lady orchids grow in this small reserve, set within Denge Wood. It's worth exploring more of this ancient semi-natural woodland via the interlinking footpaths. Lots of great climbing trees.

12

→ From The Compasses Inn, Sole Street (CT4 7ES, 01227 700300) exit the village E. At crossroads, turn L for Chartham/Canterbury NCN 18. After ¾ mile, car park on R. Follow the footpath into the woods on the R, and turn R at the second small crossroads.
20 mins, 51.2200, 1.0095 ⚐🚶🏊

SLOW FOOD

12 NO MAN'S COMMUNITY ORCHARD
Organic community orchard on the North Downs Way, planted in 1947. There are 10 acres with around 150 mature Bramley apple trees and 45 pollinators. Perfect picnic stop-off on a long walk.
→ On North Downs Way between Canterbury and Chartham, signposted from Bigbury Road in Chartham Hatch (CT4 7ND). Turn E into Bigbury Road from Howfield Ln or Denstead Ln, follow footpath L after 120m through the recreation ground and woodland for 10 minutes, then out into the orchard.
51.2751, 1.0197 🚶

13 THE CHAPTER ARMS, CHARTHAM HATCH
Lovely rural pub, three miles outside Canterbury. Known for its £12.95 3-course Pilgrims' Menu, from 12-2:30pm (an extravagant but hearty lunch for those who forgot to pack one).
→ New Town Street, CT4 7LT, 01227 738340
51.2686, 1.0139

14 THE BLACK HORSE INN, THURNHAM
Family-run gastropub on the Pilgrims' Way in rural Kent. Local and homegrown produce.
→ Pilgrims' Way, ME14 3LD, 01622 737185
51.2913, 0.5894 🍺🍴

15 THE DIRTY HABIT, HOLLINGBOURNE
Expect low beams, Georgian wall panelling, and crackling fires in this lovely rest stop by the Pilgrims' Way. Daily-changing menu reflects the seasons.
→ The Pilgrims' Way, Upper Street, ME17 1UW, 01622 880880
51.2672, 0.6429 🍺

16 THE FIVE BELLS INN, BRABOURNE
Quirky village pub with fantastic seasonal food and varied menu. Drop in for one of the regular acoustic nights, farmers' markets, or craft fairs.
→ The Street, East Brabourne, TN25 5LP, 01303 813334
51.1382, 1.0008 🍺🍴

9

21

17 THE MILK HOUSE, SISSINGHURST

Picturesque village gastro-pub with Tudor fireplace and wood-fired pizza oven.

→ The Street, TN17 2JG, 01580 720200.
51.1090, 0.5623

18 THE PEPPERBOX INN, HARRIETSHAM

Welcoming pub for walkers and riders on the Greensand Way, with spectacular views. Seasonal food and inglenook fireplaces.

→ Windmill Hill, ME17 1LP, 01622 842558.
51.2197, 0.6601

19 THE PLOUGH INN, STALISFIELD

Remote pub set back from the road amid fields. Great local food and cosy log fires.

→ Stalisfield Road, ME13 0HY,
01795 890256.
51.2422, 0.7985

20 THE ROSE AND CROWN, PERRY WOOD

Pretty country pub surrounded by woodland, with a focus on Kentish food.

→ Selling, ME13 9RY, 01227 752214.
51.2597, 0.9251

21 THE THREE CHIMNEYS, BIDDENDEN

This lovely country pub has a real Kentish feel about it. Expect beams, hops, and an open fire.

→ Hareplain Road, TN27 8LW, 01580 291472.
51.1190, 0.6080

22 WILD FOOD AND FORAGING COURSES

Learn how to forage for your own wild food with expert Michael White. Courses run in spring and autumn.

→ Brightside, Goudhurst Road, Cranbrook, TN17 2PT. Book in advance: 01580 712490.
51.1105, 0.5411

23 WYE FARMERS' MARKET

Established farmers' market in a lovely village nestled at the foot of the North Downs. Wide choice of local and seasonal food. Every 1st and 3rd Saturday of the month, 9am–12.

→ TN25 5AH, 07804 652156. On the Green by the Post Office in Wye, just off the A28 between Ashford and Canterbury.
51.1835, 0.9382

CAMP & STAY

24 NEALS PLACE FARM, CANTERBURY

Family-run campsite close to Canterbury with orchard pitching.

Neals Place Road, CT2 8HX, 01227 765632. From the A290, turn into Neals Place Rd beside the white water tower. Follow road to the end, with a meadow on your L. The road sweeps R into the entrance. Continue to a large yard area for parking.
51.2910, 1.0561 🚆

25 THORPE FARM SHEPHERD'S HUT

Luxurious hut in the middle of fields on a family smallholding. Gaze at the stars on the short walk back from The Plough Inn nearby. Snuggle up next to the wood burner and wake up to farmyard sounds.
→ Derbies Court, Stalisfield Road, ME13 0HN, 01795 890616.
51.2531, 0.8065 🏕

26 GODWIN OAST HOUSE B&B, CRANBROOK

Immerse yourself in the Kentish experience in this lovely refurbished 16th-century Oast House, which is the oldest in England. Cooked breakfast of local produce served in the Tudor Morning Room, with a view across meadows.
→ Tenterden Road, TN17 3PA, 01580 714880.
51.1000, 0.5693 🏕

27 PALACE FARM, DODDINGTON

Quiet campsite in a grassy field. Foraging, plum orchard, and honesty shop with fresh veg from the farm. Also has a hostel and B&B accommodation.
→ Down Court Road, ME9 0AU, 01795 886200.
51.2860, 0.7742 🔥

28 THE OLD APPLE SHED, BETHERSDEN

Converted apple shed, originally part of a working orchard. With a wood burning stove and lovely meadow, this is a fabulously romantic spot.
→ Cherry Trees, Norton Lane, TN26 3AL, 0785 452 2296.
51.1314, 0.7520 🏕

29 THE PROSPECT TOWER, FAVERSHAM

This Landmark Trust Property is a great treat for two people. Approach the small circular tower by an avenue of walnut trees, and enjoy spectacular views across rural Kent from a cosy seat by the open fire.
→ Belmont Park. Exact location confirmed upon booking. 01628 825925.
51.2744, 0.8460 🏕

30 THE SUNNY FIELD, STELLING MINNIS

Simple family campsite by a wildflower meadow in the heart of the Kent Downs. Hot showers are free but a bit of a walk away, in the main house down the road.
→ Little Pett Bottom Place, Maxted Street, Canterbury (CT4 6DH), 01233 750024.
51.1600, 1.0331 🔥

31 WELSUMMER CAMPING, HARRIETSHAM

Meadow and woodland camping on a smallholding with chickens and bees. There is a small orchard with English apples. Campfires are encouraged. Bell tents also available.
→ Chalk House, Lenham Road, ME17 1NQ, 01622 843051.
51.2229, 0.6738 🔥

32 BLOOMSBURYS GLAMPING, BIDDENDEN

Luxury glamping with turfs and tipis. Therapies and treatments available to book on site.
→ Sissinghurst Road, Ashford, TN27 8DQ, 01580 292992.
51.1148, 0.6271 🏕

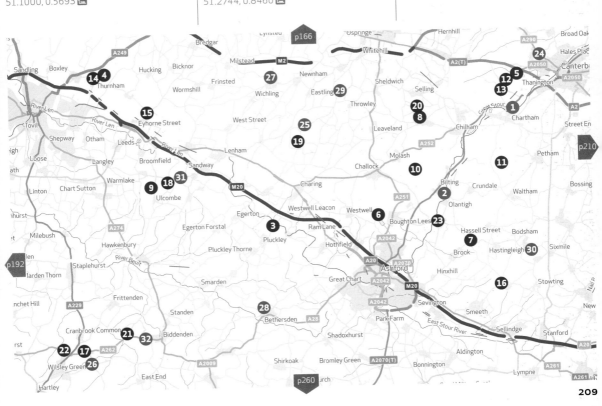

EAST KENT

Our perfect weekend

- → **Climb** into the smuggler's caves carved into the cliffs on the secret beach next to Botany Bay.
- → **Taste** exquisite fresh dishes at the Goods Shed and browse the local food stalls.
- → **Find** ancient trees and Britain's largest oak at Fredville Park.
- → **Discover** a ruined Martello Tower on the beach, half tumbled into the sea.
- → **Camp** among trees at Nethergong Nurseries.
- → **Cycle** through ancient woodland and springtime anemones on the Crab and Winkle Way.
- → **Gaze** out to France from a cosy lighthouse keeper's cottage high on the White Cliffs.
- → **Swim** or canoe in the Stour at Upstreet.
- → **Imagine** Roman life at Richborough Roman Fort or watch the sunrise from its lesser-known ruined amphitheatre.
- → **Forage** with Fergus the Forager and then cook up a feast on the beach, or forage for sea beet on the long wild beach at Sandwich.
- → **Paddle** in the Little Stour stream pool and return for supper at the Rose Inn.

Like scars across the landscape the forts, castles and ruined towers of East Kent are a reminder of an often violent past. Once a wild frontier, the area retains some fantastic beaches and coastline.

East Kent (and particularly Dover) is often seen as the gateway to England, yet this proximity to the continent also made it susceptible to the threat of invasion over the years. In Roman times the eastern tip of Kent was a remote island – the Isle of Thanet – separated from the mainland by the Wantsum channel, which is likely the site of the Roman invasion of Britain. Richborough Roman Fort at one end of the Wantsum, and Reculver at the other were both important sites during the Roman invasion and later Viking invasions. They are now evocative ruins, a reminder of the violent struggles of empires. On the south coast the Martello towers were built to protect against later invasion during the Napoleonic Wars in the early 19th century. There are numerous Martello towers left, in varying states of upkeep and decay.

Shingle predominates as the coast curves around to the south of Kent through the desolate open flats of Sandwich before reaching the famous white cliffs of Dover. Here you can explore one of Britain's newest landforms, Samphire Hoe. The foreshore here was once a no man's land, home to those on the fringes of society, housed in ramshackle shelters and living on fish and chalky spring water below the cliffs. The construction of the Channel Tunnel brought radical change as the tailings removed from the tunnel were dumped on this shore, to create this new country park. The area still manages to retain its air of wild, frontier territory and you can find several miles of beach at Lydden Spout.

To the north are the best beaches. Margate has a long history of sea bathing – the Royal Sea Bathing Infirmary was built in 1791 – and although it still thrives as a resort, the real treasures for the wild swimmer are the sands at Botany, Kingsgate and Joss bays. There are no facilities at Botany except the delightful café that Alison, a local resident, sets up in her cliffside garden every summer. Below, white sand stretches out beneath low chalk cliffs and, in the next bay to the right, which you can only access at low tide or by wading, you can try to climb into the cliff chambers where smugglers once hid their booty.

5

WILD BEACHES

1 ABBOT'S CLIFF, FOLKESTONE
Isolated rock and sand beach beneath the verdant cliffs and woods of The Warren. Partly naturist. Connects to Lydden Spout.
→ Park in Helena Road (Capel-le-Ferne) for the Clifftop Café (CT18 7HT, 01303 255588). Follow path down through cliffs and over railway (footbridge). Turn L and walk 200m to the stairs down to the seawall, then L for 15 mins to beach. Walk on for Lydden Spout.
30 mins, 51.1007, 1.2446

2 LYDDEN SPOUT, DOVER
Remote undercliff next to Samphire Hoe. Climb into the lookout tower on the way.
→ Leave Dover W on A20. After 1 mile Samphire Hoe is signed to the L after last roundabout. Continue down through tunnel to car park. Walk 15 mins to W end of park to find beach extending 800m to cabin and Abbot's Cliff. Shingle at HT, deep rock pools and sand at low tide. Avoid sea wall area.
20 mins, 51.1022, 1.2594

3 ST MARGARET'S AT CLIFFE, DOVER
Popular shingle bay with pub, under the white cliffs and Pines Garden.

→ From A258 head straight through St Margaret's down Bay Hill to beach and the Coastguard pub (CT15 6DY, 01304 853176).
2 mins, 51.1499, 1.3847

4 CHEQUERS, NORTH DEAL
Desolate shingle strand with sea kale.
→ From N Deal follow dead-end Golf Rd a mile N from Ethelbert Rd, past golf club to park at Chequers Inn (CT14 6RG, 01304 362288). Path to beach is after inn on R, via golf course.
5 mins, 51.2525, 1.3971

5 BOTANY BAY, BROADSTAIRS
Sandy bay with white cliffs and a secret beach with smugglers' caves to explore.
→ From Broadstairs follow B2052 N past Joss Bay (surfing) then R after a mile, Botany Road. Park at bottom (lovely Botany Bay Tea Gardens CT10 3SD, 01843 867662). Bear R at low tide to second bay and smugglers' caves.
3 mins, 51.3893, 1.4352

6 KINGSGATE BAY
Perfect sand, with caves and even a sea arch.
→ Just below Captain Digby pub at (CT10 3QH, 01843 867764). Between Joss and Botany.
3 mins, 51.3850, 1.4411

RIVERS & LAKES

7 FORDWICH, R GREAT STOUR
Flowing through England's smallest town, the river is first open and sunny, then becomes wooded and secretive, leading to a wild lake. Great canoeing, good swimming too.
→ Off A28 2 miles NE of Canterbury (Sturry train station). Follow the river's L bank from the bridge to an easy entry point after ½ mile or continue another ½ mile to find a wooded glade on R (51.3001,1.1513). Leads to Westbere Marshes lake, accessible to L, though best reached from N shore.
40 mins, 51.2962, 1.1253

8 WESTBERE MARSHES LAKES
Large, wild unfrequented gravel lakes with south facing bays.
→ From Westbere village, cross the railway and bear R along the N shore, to the first bay. Or continue straight to reach the Stour.
10 mins, 51.3047, 1.1479

9 UPSTREET, R GREAT STOUR
Upstream is clean and silky after four miles meandering through the Stodmarsh nature reserve, or canoe downstream for miles.

9

14

11

→ Opposite Grove Ferry Inn (CT3 4BZ, 01227 860302) signed off A28, find NNR/Stodmarsh gate and river path. Swim upstream from path, or canoe.

5 mins, 51.3226, 1.2029 🏊🛶ℹ️🚴

10 WICKHAMBREAUX, R LITTLE STOUR

Pretty stream and shallow weir pool, near this picturesque village. River walk.

→ 4 miles E of Canterbury, off A257, to Wickhambreaux. Then turn at the 16th-century Rose Inn (CT3 1RQ, 01227 721763) then first R after school down Seaton Rd. After 300m find footpath on L. Cross field to find stream and pool after 500m. Or follow riverside path 1½ miles down the Newnham Valley to Blue Bridge.

10 mins, 51.286, 1.1961 🏊ℹ️🚶

RUINS & CASTLES

11 MARTELLO TOWER 19, WEST HYTHE

One of several small, round, defensive forts built during the Napoleonic Wars to protect the coast. 'Number 19' lies mostly in ruins on the shoreline and is only accessible when the beach is not being used for MOD firing practice.

→ Walk NE along the beach from the Sandy

Bay Caravan Park on Dymchurch Road (A259, CT21 4NF) and look for tower after ¾ mile. Always check that red flags are not being flown. Check foreshore information for range-firing times on hythe-tourism.com. Often accessible weekends or evenings. At the E end of the Hythe ranges (Range Road, Hythe, CT21 6HQ) are the more intact Martello towers: No 14 (51.0622, 1.0701) and 15 (51.0634, 1.0742).

20 mins 51.0557, 1.0510 ❓🚗

12 WELL CHAPEL, BEKESBOURNE

Ruined medieval chapel, originally part of a manor house that once stood nearby. Although near a road, this ruin feels remote and exciting, particularly at dawn and dusk.

→ Exit Bekesbourne station, turn L at end of Station Approach and head beneath bridge. After ¾ mile take the first R down a small unsigned road by a lone letter box. Take the first footpath R, opposite a large farm building. Follow the footpath, with the trees on your L, for 100m.

5 mins, 51.2648, 1.1522 🚉🚗

13 RECULVER TOWERS

Standing tall above the sea are the twin 12th-century towers of a ruined church, all that is

13

left of a once-thriving medieval town. Lovely views out to sea if you ignore the caravan parks behind. The beach below is also worth the scramble down.

→ Signposted at the end of Reculver Lane, a mile NE of Hillborough (CT6 6SU). The towers are clearly visible above the cliff.
3 mins, 51.3794, 1.1994 🅱🖼🏊

14 RICHBOROUGH FORT & AMPHITHEATRE
Looms unexpectedly above the Kent fields and marshes. Hugely important throughout the Roman occupation, the site is now maintained by English Heritage. Small entry cost to fort but the nearby amphitheatre remains are free to explore.

→ Well signed off A256, just N of Sandwich (CT13 9JW). 300m before the fort entrance track, on the L, find the footpath that leads 200m to the amphitheatre earthworks on R (51.2905, 1.3263).
1 min, 51.2936, 1.3313 🖼🖼

15 ST JOHN'S COMMANDERY, SWINGFIELD
Medieval chapel house and hall, later converted into a farmhouse and surrounded by sheep fields. English Heritage, free.

→ Signed Swingfield Street/Lydden from A260, 2 miles N of Densole, then on R after a

mile. Or 2 miles SW of Lydden. Internal viewing by appointment only (01304 211067).
1 min, 51.1514, 1.1924 🖼

WOODLAND & WILDLIFE

16 FREDVILLE PARK CHESTNUTS & OAKS
Many ancient gnarled chestnuts and oaks are found on this parkland. The colossal Majesty Oak (not on the footpath) is often said to be the most beautiful tree in England, and is the UK's largest surviving maiden oak.

→ Turn R out of the Royal Oak in Nonington (CT15 4HT, 01304 841012) find the lodge cottage and entrace to park on L after 100m. After ½ mile, at junction to the house, bridleways bear to L. Majesty is off to R after 100m.
10 mins, 51.2152, 1.2304 🖼❓

17 WILDWOOD, HERNE COMMON
Wildlife park and conservation charity set in 40 acres of ancient woodland. Meet Britain's past and present wildlife, including wolves, deer, wild boar, badgers and lynx.

→ Herne Common, CT6 7LQ, 01227 712111. Signposted from the A291. 10am-3pm daily. £11.45 ticket price.
1 min, 51.3311, 1.1190 🐾🅱🖼

16

18 BLEAN WOODS, CRAB AND WINKLE WAY

Varied and mainly traffic-free seven-mile cycle and walking route through southern Britain's largest ancient broadleaved woodland, famous for spectacular displays of wood anenomes. Route follows the disused Crab and Winkle railway line between Canterbury and Whitstable, which itself followed an ancient salt route. The railway originally opened in 1830 and was the UK's first ever regular passenger service. From the highest point expect fantastic views across Whitstable and out to sea.

→ Follow the well-signposted route from Oaks Nursery, Parkwood Road, Canterbury, CT2 7FL
1 min, 51.2982, 1.0539 🚲♿🚶📷🔵📷

19 STODMARSH NATURE RESERVE

Quiet nature reserve, with the chance of seeing water voles, weasels and otters.

→ Bumpy track to car park. Turn L after the Red Lion in Stodmarsh village (CT3 4BP, 01227 721339).
2 mins, 51.3016, 1.1828 🚶📷

SLOW FOOD

20 BLUE BIRD TEA ROOMS

Tuck into a pot of tea and a slice of home-made cake in this little café perched high on a cliff overlooking the English Channel. On a clear day you can see France.

→ 79 Granville Road, CT15 6DT, 01304 852843.
51.1569, 1.3935 🍴🔵

21 THE CLIFFTOP CAFÉ, CAPEL-LE-FERNE

Secret café hidden beneath the cliff edge. Fantastic views along the coast. Great for a quick cup of tea to revive you on a windy clifftop walk. Leads down to Abbot's Cliff beach.

→ Old Dover Road, CT18 7HT, 01303 255588.
51.1011, 1.2184 🅱

22 THE DUCK INN, PETT BOTTOM

Tucked away in a little village in the heart of the Kent countryside, the Duck Inn is the fictional childhood home of James Bond, where he stayed with his aunt. Author Ian Fleming is said to have written *You Only Live Twice* when he stayed here.

→ Pett Bottom Road, Bridge, CT4 5PB, 01227 830354.
51.2268, 1.0936 📷

23 THE GOODS SHED, CANTERBURY

Food hall, restaurant and daily farmers' market in old railway goods shed. Vegetables sourced within 12 miles, artisanal foods and a restaurant with an incredible seasonal menu.

→ Station Road West, CT2 8AN, 01227 459153.
51.2845, 1.0762 🍴

24 FERGUS THE FORAGER

Learn to forage with this expert on a 12–13 hour long day course. Expect two foraged three-course meals, tasters throughout the day, and a drink and pickle to take home. Not cheap, but past participants say it's worth every penny. Advance booking essential.

→ Meeting place varies between Herne Bay and Canterbury, depending on the course. Fergustheforager.co.uk
51.3728, 1.1233 📷

25 THE OLD LANTERN INN, MARTIN

Atmospheric 'olde worlde' pub in converted farm buildings. Deservedly popular, the food is excellent, as is the range of real ales.

→ The Street, CT15 5JL, 01304 852276.
51.1744, 1.3435 📷

26 THE TIGER INN, STOWTING

Traditional, rustic pub in a small village.

Great choice of real ales and whiskies. Kitchen focuses on local, organic food.

→ Whiteways, Stowting, TN25 6BA, 01303 862130.
51.1326, 1.0291

27 YE OLDE YEW TREE, WESTBERE
Heavily beamed 14th-century pub in pretty village, with simply furnished bare-boards bar, an inglenook log fire and local food.
→ Westbere, CT2 0HH, 01227 710501.
51.3062, 1.1466

CAMP & STAY

28 SOUTH FORELAND LIGHTHOUSE
East Cottage is the former lighthouse keeper's house high on the White Cliffs of Dover. Spectacular views across the Channel. Free lighthouse tours for guests. Mrs Knott's Tea-room is right on your doorstep if you fancy a proper cup of tea and a slice of cake (opening hours are limited).
→ St Margaret's Bay, CT15 6HP, 01304 852463. Nationaltrust.org.uk
51.1404, 1.3711

29 GREAT BROXHALL FARM B&B
Cosy B&B on a traditional working cattle farm. Delicious homemade breakfast – much of the food comes from the farm itself.
→ Great Broxhall Farm, Pett Bottom, CT4 5PE, 01227 700205.
51.2206, 1.0890

30 NETHERGONG NURSERIES, UPSTREET
Deservedly popular campsite with lots of space for kids to play.
→ Nethergong Hill, CT3 4DN, 07901368417.
51.3271, 1.1936

31 PARAMOUR GRANGE, ASH
Tudor beams, fireplaces and frescoes make this a rather special B&B to stay at, set in deeply rural Kent.
→ Paramour Street, CT3 2NE, 01304 813927.
51.3025, 1.2825

32 THE WARREN, FOLKESTONE
Rambling camping and caravan site with easy access to the beach and stunning views across the Channel. It can get crowded in good weather but the location is fantastic.
→ Folkestone Camping and Caravanning Club Site, CT19 6NQ, 01303 255093.
51.0943, 1.2072

33 WALLETT'S COURT, WESTCLIFFE
Spacious tipis with luxurious queen-sized beds and Siberian goose down duvets. Or for something a little different, there is a Victorian bathing hut converted into a luxury sleeping space.
→ St. Margaret's-at-Cliffe, Dover, CT15 6EW, 01304 852424.
51.1537, 1.3575

34 WITHERDENS HALL ORGANIC B&B
Luxury B&B with a focus on organic, from the Egyptian cotton bed linen to the chickens that can be seen pecking about outside.
→ Popsal Lane, Wingham CT3 1AT, 01227 720543.
→ 51.2656, 1.2222 g

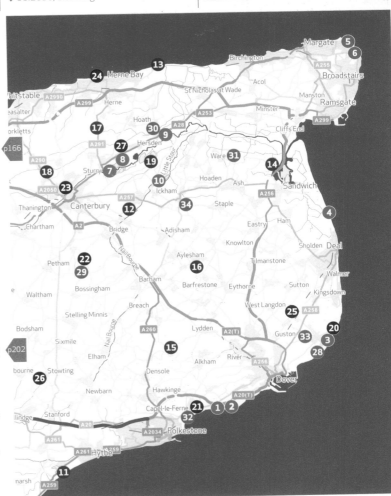

NEW FOREST

Our perfect weekend

→ **Climb** ancient pollarded oaks at the remote Sloden Inclosure, site of a royal hunting lodge.

→ **Paddle** and swim from the grassy banks at Bolderford Bridge or Balmer Lawns.

→ **Leap** from the rope swing into the beautiful river Avon from Castle Hill woods.

→ **Cycle** miles of traffic-free trails, and stop off for tea at the Old Station Tea Room.

→ **Toast** marshmallows over the campfire before snuggling down in your tent at Embers Camping.

→ **Puzzle** over the labyrinth of Breamore mizmaze, enclosed by a grove of yew trees.

→ **Dip** in the Beaulieu River at high tide after admiring the ship-building village of Buckler's Hard.

→ **Sample** cider straight from the barrel at New Forest Cider.

→ **Gaze** out across the Solent as you walk out on Hurst Spit towards the castle.

→ **Tuck** into locally-sourced food at The Pig, or gather your own with their master forager.

→ **Fall** asleep surrounded by ancient oak trees at Roundhill Campsite.

The New Forest covers 150 square miles of southwest Hampshire, from the Hampshire River Avon in the west to Southampton in the east, and from the borders of Wiltshire all the way south to the shores of The Solent.

The New Forest was 'new' almost a thousand years ago, declared a royal hunting reserve by William the Conqueror. 'Forest' at that time meant an area reserved for hunting, rather than a woodland, and there is more heathland and marshy field than trees across the whole area. There are numerous sites of medieval hunting lodges that provided temporary accommodation for visiting royalty or nobility throughout the forest, such as the 'churchyard' near the Sloden Inclosure.

The most famous forest-dwellers are the ponies. They are privately owned but free to roam, and along with roe and fallow deer often cause traffic to slow to a halt while they cross the road. Life is generally a bit slower and more relaxed here, and animals rule. In fact, the penalty for disturbing the deer used to be blinding. Stories of New Forest ponies live on in some of the names in the area.

There are so many places here that go out of their way to serve seasonal and local food, but The Pig in Brockenhurst stands out, despite being somewhat pricey. Much is grown in their own garden or foraged locally, and everything else comes from within a 25-mile radius. Also worth visiting is New Forest Cider, where you can sample local cider. There are five campsites that are beautiful, wild and spacious – Aldridge Hill, Denny Wood, Matley Wood, Longbeech and Setthorns – but all require you to bring a chemical toilet with you. All five sites are run by Camping in the Forest, and it's a shame that they don't offer compost toilets or another more eco-friendly option, as they really are gorgeous.

Bordering the New Forest to the west, the River Avon offers wild swimming ranging from wide meanders in empty meadows to fun rope swings and deep swimming. To the south, the high shingle bank of Hurst Spit runs from the mainland out to Hurst Castle, part of a chain of defences built by Henry VIII along the Solent. There is some salt marsh and a shallow harbour behind the spit, which has been built up by the tidal race from the Solent.

10

WILD BEACHES

1 HURST SPIT & CASTLE, KEYHAVEN

Long, bleak shingle headland with views across the Solent to the Isle of Wight. Worth visiting at the end of the spit is Hurst Castle, which was used as a prison for eminent captives in the 17th century (English Heritage, entry fee).

→ 1½ mile walk along the shingle spit. Parking at Milford seafront (The Marine Restaurant, SO41 0PY, 01590 644369) or, slightly closer, Keyhaven (on Saltgrass Lane, SO41 0TQ, then cross footbridge). Powerful tidal current at the beach.

30 mins, 50.7064, -1.5515

2 HENGISTBURY HEAD POND & BEACH

Dotted with prehistoric barrows and pitted by Victorian mining remains, this is a wonderfully wild spit of undulating heath and dunes tumbling into the sea from Warren Hill. It is a popular holiday spot with a good sand-and-shingle shorefront, the E beach lined with many beach huts. The quarry lake is an ethereal blue and makes a beautiful dip.

→ Park by the Hengistbury Head Visitor centre (BH6 4EN) and walk E along the spit.

5 mins, 50.7169, -1.7547

RIVERS & LAKES

3 BALMERLAWN, BROCKENHURST

Very popular for picnics and paddling, right by the road. Grassy banks with deeper pool near the bridge.

→ ½ mile N of Brockenhurst on the A337, turn R onto the B3055 to find car park immediately on R before SO42 7TS.

2 mins, 50.8266, -1.5707

4 BOLDERFORD BRIDGE & QUEEN BOWER

Footbridge and paddling from a shingle beach. Upstream are ancient oaks in a grassy clearing, close to the site of a royal hunting lodge.

→ Just as you leave Brockenhurst to NW on Rhinefield Rd (past SO42 7QF) the heath opens up ahead and there is a road bearing to R with a car park (cycleway 28 sign). Continue to end approx 1 mile to park at Ober Corner then walk ½ mile on gravel track to the bridge. The bower clearing is 200 m upstream on near bank.

15 mins, 50.8360, -1.5881

5 KING'S HAT, R BEAULIEU

Pools and paddling in the little stream, deep in the enchanted woods. Children love it.

→ A mile N of Beaulieu on B3056, before SO42 7YP, turn R (signed Ipley Cross). Large Kings Hat car park after a mile on the L in the woods. From here follow the path to the river and footbridge.

2 mins, 50.8462, -1.4543

6 BUCKLERS HARD, R BEAULIEU

A short walk upstream from this famous 18th-century boat-builders' village are quiet wooded bends in the river, perfect for a secluded dip at high tide. A bit muddy.

→ Well signed from B3056 just S of Beaulieu. From the shore (Master Builder's Hotel dining, SO42 7XB, 01590 616253) follow the Solent Way footpath upstream, past all the boats and boatyard. 500m beyond the last find a little path on the R, to a bird hide which leads to the shoreline beyond. High tide only.

10 mins, 50.8053, -1.4249

7 EYEWORTH POOL, FRITHAM

A little lane leads down to this shallow warm lake by the car park.

→ Leaving Fritham past the pleasant Royal Oak pub (SO43 7HJ, 023 8081 2606, large garden) continue just under ½ mile down the hill to the pond car park.

1 min, 50.9308, -1.6761

8 CASTLE HILL, R AVON

A very steep, remote and wooded descent leads to rope swings and deep swimming.

→ Heading S out of Woodgreen, turn R signed Castle Hill. Continue ½ mile, past main car park, to find layby on R (before SP6 2LU). Descend to river. Or dip at the bridge N of Woodgreen (50.9672, -1.7491) or at Sandy Balls camping (SP6 2JZ, 0844 693 1050).

5 mins, 50.9468, -1.7624 🍴⛺🛶🏕❓

9 IBSLEY BRIDGE, R AVON

The weir pool is fenced, but continue downstream to find deep river meaders in this pretty meadow.

→ 3 miles N of Ringwood on A338, turn L signed Harbridge (BH24 3PP). Find path on L by bridge.

5 mins, 50.8866, -1.7881 ❓🚶

10 RINGWOOD, R AVON

Wonderful wide meaders in wide open water meadows.

→ From A31 follow B3347 a mile S. Turn R (dead end) just after L turn Moortown Lane, poorly signed Burley. Continue a mile down Hampshire Hatches Lane until parking at bend and follow path N over footbrige 300m.

5 mins, 50.8352, -1.7913 🛶⛺❓

11 WATTON'S FORD, R AVON

An old ford and byway lead to the beautiful shore of the Avon.

→ Heading S on the B3347 from Ringwood, before Bisterne, and after the converted chapel (BH24 3BJ) find unsigned lane on R. Byway continues from far end to the river. Or the W shore via Watton Ln (near BH24 2BP) from A338.

3 mins, 50.8156, -1.8064 ⛺🛶

12 EAGLE OAK, KNIGHTWOOD

Hidden in the Knightwood Inclosure (near the better-known but popular Knightwood Oak) is one of the largest trees in the New Forest. So named because England's last sea eagle was shot from its braches in 1810.

→ Turn onto Bolderwood Arboretum Ornamental Drive over cattle grid from the A35 approx 2¼ miles SW of Lyndhurst. After 300m, park in the Knightwood Oak car park on L. Take the footpath heading SW (away from road) and after 200m turn R at junction. Turn L at crossroads after 100m and R again after 200m. Follow path as it bends round to the L and look for the Eagle Oak L after 250m.

10 mins, 50.8543, -1.6391 🌳

13 POLLARDED OAKS, SLODEN INCLOSURE

Brilliant tree climbing at the end of a lovely walk past the ancient site of a royal hunting lodge and churchyard. Look for the bumpy remains then climb into huge trees for wonderful views out over wild heathland.

➔ From the far end of the Fritham car park (90m from Royal Oak, SO43 7HJ) follow track SW across moorland for one mile. As you enter the woods take the second, smaller track bearing R after 200m. Continue for 500m, staying on the ridge top.

40 mins, 50.9117, -1.7018

14 RIDLEY WOOD HOLLOWAY

Glorious pocket of ancient woodland with bilberries in early summer. Secluded holloway known as the 'market place'. Find tree swing from the tangled roots of a tree hanging over the sunken way.

➔ ¾ mile N of Burley Street (BH24 4DD) dir Picket Post and A31, find Vereley car park on R by transmitter (immediately after Vereley Hill car park on L). Take footpath N to skirt around trees. At end of trees continue NE over ridge through crossroads approx. 500m to T-junction at stream. Take R path over stream and continue into the wood.

15 mins, 50.8520, -1.7135

15 NETLEY ABBEY, SOUTHAMPTON

Captivating ruins of a 13th-century Cistercian monastery. A source of inspiration for Romantic writers and artists; John Constable painted here, and Jane Austen was said to have found inspiration for her novel *Northanger Abbey*.

➔ Abbey Hill, Netley Abbey, Southampton, Hampshire SO31 5GA, English Heritage, free. 0370 333 1181

1 min, 50.8781, -1.3576

16 BREAMORE MIZMAZE AND YEWS

On the lonely summit of Breamore Down is a labyrinth where all paths lead to the centre. Originally used on holy days or for penances, with prayers said at fixed points along the path. The mizmaze is enclosed by a grove of yew trees and is fenced for preservation. A Bronze Age barrow lies just SW.

➔ Take the well-trodden, mile-long footpath NW from Breamore House and museum (Breamore, SP6 2DF, 01725 512858). Pass through woodland and then out onto the down to find the mizmaze within a copse.

20 mins, 50.9816, -1.8001

17 COLD PIXIES CAVE

A Bronze Age barrow rather than a cave, where an amber necklace was excavated with no sign of a body. The name might originally have been Colt Pixies Cave, after ghostly pixies that take the form of a horse and lead New Forest wild ponies into danger and trouble.

➔ Take the B3055 towards Beaulieu from Brockenhurst for 3½ miles. Immediately after a red brick house R as you come out of the trees is Stockley car park. The barrow is at the next R at the staggered crossroads onto a small road with a gate across it, 1¼ miles W of the turning to SO42 7WB. Facing down the small road (with the B0355 behind you) look for the barrow immediately R.

1 min, 50.8132, -1.5046

18 THE OLD RAILWAY CYCLE ROUTE

Make the most of over 100 miles of traffic-free cycle trails throughout the New Forest. One of the best is the flat, disused railway line. Setting out at dusk or dawn can also be a good way to experience the autumn deer rut, when stags lock horns and bellow through the woods from Sept to Oct.

→ Head out of Burley SW on Pound Lane, directly opp Forest Leisure Cycling (BH24 4AB, 01425 403584). After a mile turn L into Burbush car park and continue onto cycle path. Passes the popular Old Station Tea Rooms (BH24 4HY, 01425 402468).
1 min, 50.8153, -1.7153

19 COCKLEY PLAIN

One of the least frequented parts of the New Forest, this is an especially good place to see the famous New Forest ponies.
→ Head NE along the B3078 from the Fighting Cocks Pub in Godshill (SP6 2LL). After ¾ mile look for Ashley Walk car park R. Follow footpath E away from road for ½ mile to reach the wilder part of the Plain.
10 mins, 50.9363, -1.7211

SLOW FOOD

20 NEW FOREST CIDER, BURLEY

Sample cider straight from the barrel in the little shop, or visit the Cider Pantry for tea and cake (and, of course, cider). Accommodation available in the cottage.
→ Pound Lane, BH24 4ED, 01425 403589.
50.8235, -1.7043

21 OTTERBOURNE PARK WOOD

The steep public footpath through the NE corner offers a wealth of foraging opportunities: elderflowers in the spring, wild cherries in July, and shiny elderberries in the late summer, just waiting to be made into jams.
→ Exit R from The Otter pub (Boyatt Lane, SO21 2HW), follow road for 70m and take second L (Chapel Ln). Stay R at fork and find footpath L through wooden gate beneath trees. Follow into wood.
50.9984, -1.3490

22 THE COMPASSES INN, DAMERHAM

Good choice of well-thought-out meals, including local fresh fish and meat. Slightly pricey option but an excellent treat.
→ East End, SP6 3HQ, 01725 518231.
50.9450, -1.8508

23 THE ROYAL OAK, FRITHAM

One of the New Forest's best-known pubs, this traditional establishment has a thatched roof and good selection of cask ales. Simple meals served at lunchtime only. Pleasant garden.
→ Lyndhurst, SO43 7HJ, 023 8081 2606.
50.9262, -1.6709

24 THE FILLY INN, BROCKENHURST

Scenic gastropub serving free-range local food.
→ Lymington Road, Setley, SO42 7UF, 01590 623449.
50.8010, -1.5721

25 THE FORESTERS ARMS, FROGHAM

Rustic pub with woodburner. Dogs welcome.
→ Abbotswell Road, Fordingbridge, SP6 2JA, 01425 652294.
50.9151, -1.7555

26 THE OAK INN, LYNDHURST

Old fashioned, cosy pub serving traditional food with a modern twist, and a good range of real ales. Dog- and horse-friendly.
→ Pinkney Lane, Bank, SO43 7FD.
023 8028 2350.
50.8634, -1.5951

27 THE PIG, BROCKENHURST

If you're a fan of New Forest produce, this is the place for you, with ingredients either plucked from the pub garden, foraged or sourced from within a 25-mile radius. Ask to go out and forage with The Pig's forager, who can teach you how to identify wild food.
→ Beaulieu Road, SO42 7QL, 01590 622354.
50.8256, -1.5523

CAMP & STAY

28 ACRES DOWN FARM CAMPSITE

Basic campsite on a Commoner's working farm. Farm shop sells home-made sausages and burgers, and charming tea room offers home-baked cakes. Showers charged at £1.
→ Minstead, SO43 7GE, 023 8081 3693.
50.8871, -1.6184

29 ALDRIDGE HILL, BROCKENHURST

Stunning campsite set in a heathland clearing, bordered by two rivers. Very basic facilities with no showers or toilets - just a tap and bins.
→ Just as you leave Brockenhurst to NW on Rhinefield Rd (past SO42 7QF) and the heath opens up ahead, take road bearing to R with (cycle way 28 sign) and find Beachern Wood car park immediately on L. Follow signs to campsite (SO42 7QD), 01590 623152.
50.8258, -1.5995

30 EMBERS CAMPING, BEAULIEU

Campfires are at the heart of this site, and every pitch has a purpose-built fire pit. Children can choose their eggs for breakfast from the farm chickens, and feed the other animals. Kayaking, horse riding and cycle tracks on site.

➜ Palace Lane, Beaulieu, SO42 7YG, 0845 257 2267.
50.8209, -1.4417

31 HOLLANDS WOOD CAMPSITE
Set in 54 acres of oak woodland, bordered by heathland. A popular, family-friendly site, so book ahead during peak summer season.

➜ Lyndhurst Road, SO42 7QH, 01590 622967.
50.8298, -1.5717

32 LUTTRELL'S TOWER, EAGLEHURST
Georgian folly on the shore of the Solent. Treat yourself to a stay here with friends and enjoy private beach access down a tunnel said to have been used by smugglers.

➜ Calshot. Exact address given on booking, 01628 825925. Landmarktrust.org.uk
50.8062, -1.3249

33 ROUNDHILL, BROCKENHURST
Spacious campsite with pine trees and sweeping grassy areas. Choose any spot to pitch your tent but watch out for stony ground and tree roots in places.

➜ Leave Brockenhurst on the B3055 following signd for Beaulieu. After approx 1.5 miles turn R at bend into campsite (SO42 7QL). 01590 624344.
50.8184, -1.5464

34 THE BEECH HUT, NR SOPLEY
Cheerful blue cabin by a lake, hidden between mature trees on a fruit farm. PYO on the farm or enjoy the birds, butterflies and wild flowers. Camping also available.

➜ Exact location revealed on booking, 01348 830922.
50.7746, -1.7633

35 TOM'S FIELD, FORDINGBRIDGE
Quiet, family-friendly campsite. The area known as 'The Copse' is reserved for adults and is popular with couples.

➜ Godshill Pottery, The Ridge, SP6 2LN, 07759 474158.
50.9369, -1.7402

36 ASHURST CAMPSITE
Free-roaming ponies, woodland glade and surrounded by ancient oak trees. Five minutes walk from Ashurst, so good if arriving by train. Potential for noise from

road and railway.

➜ Lyndhurst Rd, SO40 7AR, 023 8029 2097.
50.8893, -1.5303

37 HOLMSLEY CAMPSITE
Intriguing and beautiful campsite on part of an old WWII airfield. Can get busy.

➜ Forest Road, BH23 8EB, 01425 674502.
50.7923, -1.6964 B

38 OCKNELL CAMPSITE, FRITHAM
Quiet campsite on a breathtaking expanse of heathland, with easy access to the forest by foot or bike.

➜ Fritham, SO43 7HH, 023 8081 2740.
50.9061, -1.6464

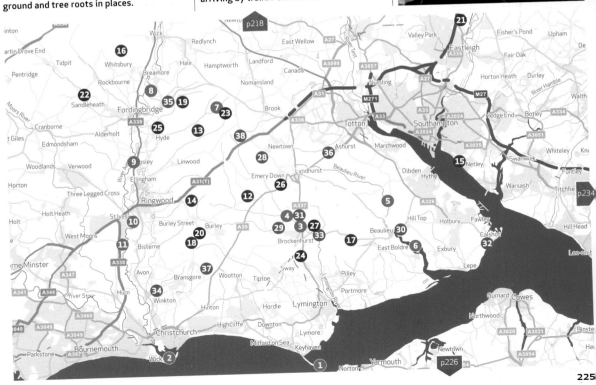

225

ISLE OF WIGHT

Our perfect weekend

- → **Descend** deep down into a chine in search of the island's wildest beaches.
- → **Coasteer** or kayak around to the secret coves, caves and smugglers' passages from Freshwater Bay.
- → **Watch** the sunset over the Needles from the abandoned rocket base on Tennyson Downs.
- → **Bivvy** and stargaze high on the remote downs at Gallibury Hump for sensational views.
- → **Wonder** at the ancient Long Stone of Mottistone.
- → **Scramble** down to the beach from your cliff-top tent at Bank End Farm.
- → **Swim** at Newport ancient harbour, now a nature reserve but once the island's first port town.
- → **Look** out for the elusive red squirrels in Borthwood Copse.
- → **Tuck** into delicious seafood at the shoreside Beach Hut, some of the best food on the island.
- → **Fall** asleep in the quirky luxury of The Shack after a final evening dip in the sea.
- → **Search** for enormous dinosaur fossils around Culver Cliff.

Officially the sunniest place in Britain, with large stretches of undeveloped coast to ensure its popularity, as well as white cliffs and landslip jungles, remote ravines or 'chines' and sleepy coves.

Along the south-west coast, high cliffs protect around 12 miles of shingle and sand with access only possible by descending the sheer ravines or chines that streams and waterfalls have cut through the soft clay and chalk cliffs. Shepherd's Chine and Whale Chine are the most dramatic – perfect places to watch the sunset over the western Needles and swim.

Steephill Cove, just outside Ventnor, welcomed many royal visitors in its heyday but has reverted to a backwater with a handful of deckchairs, beach huts and crab shacks serving freshly caught and dressed crab in sandwiches. It's just one home to the many lesser-known beach-shack style café locations that pop up in the summer.

The Needles are probably the most famous coastal landmark around the Isle, and the Cold War rocket-testing station behind them is its most unusual site (the Old Battery). The best approach is the three-mile blustery walk along Tennyson Down from Freshwater Bay. Bembridge and Culver Downs are also fascinating to explore, with dramatic views and numerous First World War fortifications. For something more ancient, head to Five Barrows to see the ancient Bronze Age barrows laid out in a line from east to west.

The Isle of Wight is unusual in England in that its squirrel population is entirely comprised of red squirrels. To ensure the red squirrels' protection, it is an offence to introduce grey squirrels to the island, and there are stories of ferries being turned back when a grey squirrel was found among their passengers.

The sleepy hamlet of Newtown, on a remote tidal estuary in the north-west of the Isle, is a good place to end your explorations. In the 13th century, Newtown was the Isle's biggest town and harbour. Today only its crooked town hall remains, perched alone on the village green, a relic of a once-thriving port that slowly silted up. The old port, a mile's walk across the wetlands, has long since been submerged under marsh grass and mud, but it still has a quay and now provides a peaceful and magical place to swim.

8

HIDDEN BEACHES

1 PRIORY BAY, ST HELENS
Quiet, golden sands with shallow lagoons set beneath woods.

→ Pass through St Helens on the B3330, staying R to take Duver Road (dead end) to the shore, car park and the ruined church (PO33 1XZ). Walk N ½ mile through woods to bay. Or access direct from Priory Bay Hotel/restaurant (PO34 5BU, 01983 613146, patrons only).

15 mins, 50.7067, -1.1006 🅿️

2 LUCCOMBE CHINE, VENTNOR
Steep path and wooden steps lead down to this dramatic cove beneath the cliffs. There is some low tide sand. Sunny in morning only.

→ A mile E of Ventnor park at Smuggler's Haven car park (The Landslip) close to PO37 6RH and descend.

10 mins, 50.6105, -1.1768 🅿️

3 SIR RICHARD'S COVE, VENTNOR
Lovely shingle beach hidden beneath the Botanic Gardens, also called Mount Bay or Battery Bay after Sir Richard Worseley mounted a battery of guns here in the Napoleonic Wars.

→ Pass E through St Lawrence/A3055 and park in Inglewood Park on L. Cross road and follow path to coast and then bear R 300m. Or ½ mile from Steephill or from Botanic Gardens (PO38 1UL, 01983 855397).

5 mins, 50.5862, -1.2349 🅿️🔔🐚

4 ROCKEN END, ST CATHERINE'S
The Isle's most remote beach, at the bitter end of Chale Bay, Blackgang cliffs.

→ Heading downhill E out of Niton A3055, turn R signed for lighthouse and Inn (PO38 2NE, 01983 730243) down St Catherine's Rd,, pass pub, follow R-signed 'All traffic' then L to parking at end of Old Blackgang Rd. Bear down to sea R, crossing stream at bottom. Scramble across mud and rock slide to find beach.

10 mins, 50.5801, -1.3086 🅿️🏕️🔔🐚🌊

5 SHEPHERD'S CHINE, CHALE
Small stream leads to shingle beach below cliffs on wild Brighstone Bay.

→ On A3055, 6 miles NW from St Catherine's Point, find footpath to coast from road, 500m beyond Chine Farm (PO38 2JH, 07929 765747). There is camping at Grange Farm (PO30 4DA, 01983 740296) also on A3055.

5 mins, 50.6164, -1.3702 🅿️🔔🏕️🌊

6 WHALE CHINE, CHALE
Wooden steps used to lead down to very remote beach but people still descend.

→ On A3055, 600m N of turning for Atherfield Green, 2 miles SE of Chine Farm (PO38 2JH) find lay-by on R. Staircase has collapsed at but an informal path exists along the stream.

10 mins, 50.6021, -1.3395 🅿️🔔❓

7 NEWTOWN QUAY, SHALFLEET
High tide swimming at medieval quay which used to be the island's main port. Salt marsh, mudflats and nature reserve.

→ From Old Town Hall, Newtown (PO30 4PA) bear L, past church to road end and across meadow ½ mile to quay. New Inn (Shalfleet, ½ mile E of PO30, 01983 531314).

20 mins, 50.7183, -1.4083 🍽️🔔🏕️🐾

KAYAKING & COASTEERING

8 WATCOMBE BAY, FRESHWATER
The adventurous can swim around Fort Redoubt to Watcombe Bay with sands, stacks and many sea caves to explore. A secret tunnel connects to the cliff above.

→ Freshwater Bay is a fun family beach with a waterside café and car park (PO40 9QU).

10

1

Scramble along rocks to far W end of the bay, past the timber staircase, then swim, wade or scramble to headland, followed by 150m swim into Watcombe Bay. Raised cave leads up into a smugglers' tunnel emerging on cliff top. Many more interconnected caves and lagoons at far end. Hire paddleboards from Isle of Wight Sea Kayaking by beach (01983 755838).

30 mins, 50.6682, -1.5162 🌊🪨⛺⛰🏖

9 THE NOSTRILS, CULVER CLIFF

Partially submerged at high tide are two caves known as The Nostrils. Definitely worth the scramble over rocks to get to, but

keep watch for falling rocks from above, and the rising tide below.

→ From Whitecliff Bay (500m S of Hillway, footpath through holiday park at PO35 5PL), head S along beach and walk/scramble around the base of the cliffs until you see the caves. Or scramble down SE from Culver Battery car park near PO36 8QT (Bembridge Fort). Only begin as the tide is falling, and keep an eye on the water to avoid getting cut off.

15 mins, 50.6652, -1.0982 🅅📷♿

10 SEA KAYAKING EXPEDITION

Wild camp on beaches, cook over an open fire and explore the shoreline for two, three or four days – if the conditions are right, maybe even circumnavigate the island!

→ Book in advance with Isle of Wight Adventure Activities, Freshwater, 01983 755838.

1 min, 50.6770, -1.5068 🏖⛺🪨

SACRED & ANCIENT

11 ST CATHERINE'S ORATORY, CHALE

This medieval tower, said to have been a lighthouse, stands tall and lonely on one of highest points of the Isle of Wight. Maintained by English Heritage and known

locally as The Pepperpot, this is a well-known landmark.

→ Take the A3055 SE from Chale, cross roundabout, and park in car park R (PO38 2JB). Cross road and follow signed footpath to the oratory.

10 mins, 50.5919, -1.3048 🏞📷🚶

12 THE LONG STONE, MOTTISTONE

Standing stones, an ancient burial mound and a place of worship where solstices and equinoxes are still celebrated. Legend says that St Catherine and the Devil were fighting for control the island; St Catherine threw the tall sandstone, while the Devil's smaller stone fell short.

→ From Mottistone Manor (PO30 4ED), or turn N on Strawberry Ln from the B3399, E of Mottistone. After 100m park in small, free NT car park L. Continue up track 600m, sticking to the main path. At fork, continue R up hill for 300m (near PO30 4EB).

15 mins, 50.6562, -1.4254 🏞💠🚶

13 FIVE BARROWS

Actually eight Bronze Age barrows, laid out in an east-west direction, with visible remains of a rampart and ditch. Fantastic views in all directions.

18

→ Take the B3399 from Brook towards Shalcombe. As the road bends to the L then R look out for a track L, signposted Tennyson Trail. Follow track for 30m to small parking area and take marked pathway L through wooden gate. After 40m take R track uphill when path divides. After 200m, the barrows are on the highest point of the down.
10 mins, 50.6650, -1.4497 📷✦

14 ST HELEN'S OLD CHURCH
Church tower destroyed by huge waves in the 18th century, now painted white as a sea mark. Admiral Nelson's final view of England.
→ As for Priory Bay, St Helen's (see entry).
1 min, 50.7013, -1.0993 ✝B

11

SUNSET HILLTOPS

15 BEMBRIDGE & CULVER DOWNS
Dramatic promontory with views across the Solent. Numerous remains of 19th-century and First World War fortifications on Bembridge Down. Fossils.
→ From Brading take the B3395 E towards Bembridge. 500m after mini-roundabout for Yaverland turn R up small road signed Culver Down. Find Bembridge Down L after ¾ mile and Culver Down at end of road after 1½ miles

(near PO36 8QT). Yaverland beach is well known for fossils (50.66563, -1.11072).
1 min, 50.6680, -1.1083 🏖🚶

16 TENNYSON DOWN AND THE NEEDLES
The 'pleasure park' approach from Alum Bay is easily avoided by arriving on foot along the Tennyson Trail coastal path for views from The Old Battery Victorian fort, once used as a Cold War test station.
→ From the Highdown Inn (Totland, PO39 0HY, 01983 752450), head S down Highdown Lane. Follow road to end (500m). A few metres before the car park is a footpath R, past wooden barrier. Follow for 500m to crossroads. Continue straight for 1½ miles.
40 mins, 50.6631, -1.5865 📷B🚶

17 GALLIBURY HUMP, BRIGHSTONE DOWN
Fantastic viewpoint for looking over the north of the island, the Solent and out to the mainland of England. One of the largest and most obvious tumuli on Brighstone Down.
→ Just off the Tennyson Trail. From the free NT car park on Lynch Lane between Brighstone and Calbourne (50.6592, -1.4067, near Strawberry Lane junction, ¾ mile S of PO30 4JH). Bring a map.
45 mins, 50.6669, -1.3776 🏔📷🏖✦

12

WOODLAND & WILDLIFE

18 BORTHWOOD COPSE, WINFORD

Ancient oak and beech woodland with sunny glades. Stay very quiet while looking out for red squirrels in their natural habitat.

→ In Winford take Alverstone Rd NE and shortly after junction with Forest Rd look for car park R by bus stop and sign for Queen's Bower (near PO36 0LD). Follow footpath into woods from car park.

2 mins, 50.6561, -1.1987 🚶🐾🅱

19 GOODLEAF TREE CLIMBING, RYDE

Adventurous, family-friendly day of climbing trees with ropes. Tree hammocks with sea views. Drinks and climbers' flapjack. Near Appley Sands for a post-climb swim.

→ Main tree-climbing location is in Appley Park, Appley Lane, Ryde, PO33 1ND. Booking required 0333 800 1188.

1 min, 50.7256, -1.1401 🅱🔄🐾

SLOW FOOD

20 CAFÉS AND CRAB SHEDS, STEEPHILL

There are many lovely cafés in the tiny and old-fashioned Steephill Cove, most only open in summer. There is a lovely little beach too, perfect for children, and no cars. The Crab Shed sells crab, lobster and mackerel caught on the café's own fishing boat. The Beach Shack also serves crab, along with sandwiches and salads, and The Boathouse (01983 852747) serves fresh fish and shellfish.

→ Heading into Ventnor from W (A3055) look for tiny Love Lane (no cars) on R by cricket club (PO38 1AF). The cove has no direct road access, so you could park nearby and walk, or walk from Ventnor along the coastal path W for ½ a mile.

50.5888, -1.2240 🍴🔄🐚

21 BEACH HUT, FORELANDS BEACH

Quirky, al fresco beach café open on sunny days 12–3pm Easter to Xmas. Seasonal, local, healthy, non-fried food. Bring your own wine. Afternoon tea of scones. Passionate staff, tiny kitchen. A gem of a place which gets booked up quickly. Opens onto Black Rock Ledge sands S of Bembridge.

→ Forelands Field Road, Bembridge, PO35 5TR, 07832 127737 (or No 8 bus from Ryde). 50.6813, -1.0745 🐚

22 THE BUDDLE SMUGGLER'S INN, NITON

Historic pub with roaring fires and lovely sea views from the garden. Serves tasty local food.

→ St Catherine's Road, PO38 2NE, 01983 730243.

50.5792, -1.2913 🍴🐚

23 THE GARLIC FARM, NEWCHURCH

THE place for garlic lovers. The small restaurant uses locally sourced ingredients, including their own Highland beef. The farm shop and the Taste Experience are also worth it to discover their full range of garlic-related produce.

→ Mersley Lane, PO36 0NR, 01983 865378. 50.6793, -1.2154 🍴

24 THE HUT, FRESHWATER

Seasonal 'beach hut'-style restaurant right on the beach. Menu specialises in fresh fish and seafood. If you arrive by boat they will collect you in a dinghy.

→ Colwell Chine Road, Colwell Bay, PO40 9NP, 01983 898637.

50.6895, -1.5380 🍴

25 THE NEW INN, SHALFLEET

Historic inn with inglenook fireplaces and flagstone floors. The food is local, and the fish particularly good. Booking often necessary during high season.

→ Main Road, PO30 4NS, 01983 531314. 50.7016, -1.4149 🐚

26 THE SUN INN, HULVERSTONE

600-year-old thatched, local-food country pub, which allegedly once served as a smugglers' base for trading illicit goods.

→ PO30 4EH, 01983 741124. 50.6545, -1.4390 🐚🍴

27 THE TAVERNERS, GODSHILL

Serves (mainly) locally sourced, caught or foraged food. Fine selection of real ales includes the Taverners own brew. Veg patch and chickens outside.

→ High Street, Godshill, PO38 3HZ, 01983 840707. 50.6329, -1.2540 🍴

28 WARREN FARM CREAM TEAS, ALUM BAY

Delicious home-made cream teas using local produce and cooked on the farmhouse Aga. On the 15-mile Tennyson Trail footpath in a beautiful rural location.

→ Signposted off the B3322, where Alum Bay New Road and Alum Bay Old road meet, PO39 0JB, 01983 753200. 50.6672, -1.5593 🍴

29 STOATS FARM, TOTLAND
Small and friendly campsite set in open farmland at the foot of the Tennyson Downs. The facilities are basic and the views are stunning.
→ Weston Lane, PO39 0HE, 01983 755258.
50.6721, -1.5425

30 BANK END FARM CAMPING
Simple and secluded camping and caravanning with sea views and easy beach access. Only open to Camping and Caravanning Club members, but easy to join when you arrive.
→ Undercliff Drive, St Lawrence, Ventnor, PO38 1UW, 01983 852649.
50.5888, -1.2321

31 GRANGE FARM, BRIGHSTONE BAY
100 yards from the sea on a small, family-run farm, this friendly site has space for tents, caravans and touring vans. Eco-pods also available.
→ Military Road, Brighstone, PO30 4DA, 01983 740296.
50.6363, -1.4071

32 COMPTON FARM, NEWPORT
In a fold of the Downs, 5 mins walk from the beach, this is a peaceful, uncommercial site, with caravans and tents in separate fields. Children can feed the ducks, collect eggs and play on old tractors.
→ Compton Farm Brook, PO30 4HF, 01983 740215.
50.6645, -1.4731

33 HARBOUR HOUSEBOAT, BEMBRIDGE
Stay on your own spacious houseboat with a telescope for keeping watch on harbour life.
→ Houseboat 'Sturdy', Embankment Road, PO35 5NS, 0117 204 7830.
Canopyandstars.co.uk
50.6909, -1.0998

34 THE REALLY GREEN HOLIDAY
Eco glamping at its best. Grab a meal at The Hut (see entry) before coming 'home' to your comfortable furnished yurt.
→ Yurts are at Copse Lane, opposite PO40 9TL, 07802 678591.
50.6893, -1.5104

35 THE SHACK, COWES
Hidden away near the sea, this wooden summerhouse is in its own little dell. There is a wood burner, composting toilet and solar-powered lighting.
→ Cowes. Exact location is secret until you book. 07802 758113.
50.7623, -1.2965

36 TOLLGATE COTTAGES, FRESHWATER
Idyllic, rural B&B with easy access to the Tennyson Trail and sweeping countryside views from the bedroom windows.
→ Wilmingham Lane, Freshwater, PO40 9UX, 01983 756535.
50.6779, -1.4959

37 TOM'S ECO LODGE, YARMOUTH
Safari-tents on a lovely old dairy farm.
→ Tapnell Farm, Newport Road, PO41 0YJ, 01983 897089.
50.6805, -1.4724

38 WIGHT BELLS, SANDOWN
Luxury vintage glamping in bell tents, run by three sisters.
→ Old Barn Touring, Cheverton Farm, Newport Road, Apse Heath, PO36 9PJ, 07811 706921.
50.6470, -1.1923

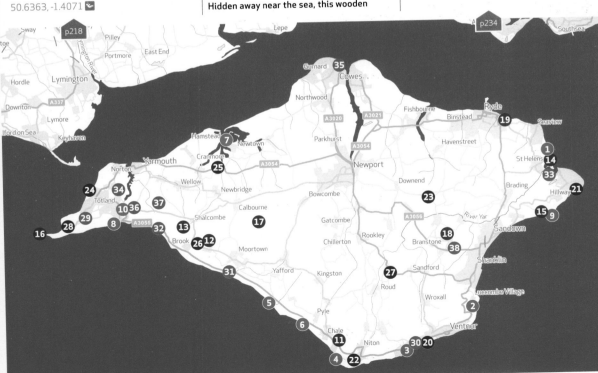

WEST SUSSEX DOWNS

Our perfect weekend

→ **Cycle** the Salterns Way from Chichester train station to the dunes of East Head, slide down the mud chutes or head out onto Winner sand bar.

→ **Swim** in the secret waters of the Rother at Stedeham, or find the Thai monk's hidden swimming pond at Chithurst.

→ **Forage** on remote Pagham Beach, with its colonies of sea kale and sea lavender.

→ **Camp** deep in the folds of the South Downs at New House Farm, and enjoy two excellent pubs.

→ **Align** the setting sun on the Devil's Jumps on midsummer's day then enjoy some Exmoor Beast beer at the woodland Royal Oak.

→ **Commune** with some of the most ancient things living in Britain at the yew grove in Kingley Vale.

→ **Approach** old Halnaker Windmill through the magical tunnel of trees on ancient Stane Street.

→ **Choose** from the tasty seasonal menu at the arty, quirky Horse Guards Inn.

→ **Stargaze** from your tent door in the gorgeously remote Gumber Farm campsite at Slindon.

Rolling green downs meet flat, glistening saltmarshes, islands and gorgeous sandy beaches at this most westerly portion of the South Downs. This area is rich in history and wildlife.

The Bronze Age left its mark on West Sussex in a series of spectacular hillforts. Beacon Hill is a steep climb to the top, but affords glorious views on a summer's evening. The nearby Devil's Jumps has five barrows, which align with the position of the setting sun on midsummer's day and are easily visited as part of a hike along the South Downs Way. The Devil's Jumps are not to be confused with the nearby Devil's Humps, on Bow Hill at the Kingley Vale Nature Reserve, also Bronze Age burial mounds. Kingley Vale has one of the finest yew woods in Europe, including one particular grove of ancient trees that are said to be some of the oldest living things in Britain. Although not quite as ancient, the Queen Elizabeth Oak in Cowdray Park nonetheless has its own particular history, being named for a royal visit on a hunt in 1591.

Besides the spectacular hillforts, there are other intriguing landmarks dotted about. The Halnaker Windmill stands high on a ridge surrounded by wild flowers, and can be reached through a glorious tunnel of trees. This is also a section of the ancient Roman road, Stane Street, and is an experience not to be missed. The tiny medieval Shepherd's Church at Didling is less visible, but is also a reminder of how little some things have changed here over the centuries. There is still no electric lighting there – the church is lit entirely by candles.

Chichester Harbour's wide expanses and intricate creeks are major wildlife havens, and here is the legendary scene of King Canute's stand against the incoming tide. One of the least developed sites on the south coast, this is a paradise of muddy tidal creeks and perfect white sandbars. Pilsey Island is perhaps the most remote of the harbour's beaches, and beachcombers will find little treasures such as pearl-lined limpet shells, razor clams and whelks. The bird life is also outstanding.

Probably the most spectacular of any beaches within two hours of London are the famous West Wittering beaches. Make for East Head, a long spit of white sands, dunes and marram grass. By far the best way to reach the Witterings is to take the train and then use the brilliant 11-mile Salterns rural cycle route from Chichester train station.

HIDDEN BEACHES

1 EAST HEAD, WEST WITTERING
A sand-dune peninsula to the N of popular Witterings. Warm lagoons, crabbing and mud slides on the inner shore, deep shelving for the best swimming at the spit head, Winner sand flats uncovered at LT on the outer shore. The Salterns Way cycle route links to Chichester centre.

→ From Chichester take A286 S following signs to Birdham, then B2179 to West Wittering beach (PO20 8AU). Often very busy here. Park at far end of beach car park (½ mile) and walk R onto dunes N ½ mile, past crabbing pools and away from main beach, onto East Head.
20 mins, 50.7892, -0.9134 🌊🏖🏊

2 CHURCH NORTON, SELSEY
Wild shingle beach beyond tiny church next to Pagham Harbour Nature Reserve.

→ Turn off B2145 for Church Norton on bend shortly before entering Selsey. Park by church (PO20 9DT) and follow path to R alongside natural harbour/mud flats to shingle sea beach.
15 mins, 50.7483, -0.7621 🏔🚶🌿

3 PRINSTEAD COVE, SOUTHBOURNE
High-tide only cove by car park. Water warms nicely as the tide rises.

→ On A259 miles E of A27 junction, look for Prinstead Lane on R (opp PO10 8ET). Follow down to marina and car park.
1 min 50.8401, -0.9134 🛶

4 BOSHAM QUAY
Ancient harbour village of King Canute. Kids enjoy jumping from quay at high tide.

→ Halfway between Emsworth and Chichester on A259, signed to Bosham at roundabout. Head down to Shore Road, past the lovely Anchor Bleu inn (PO18 8LS, 01243 573956) to far end of quay, by black building. Do not impede boats. Also try Ferry Barn shingle beach at West Itchenor (PO20 7AW), 1½ miles S to ferry boat crossing in summer.
2 mins, 50.8280, -0.8609 🍴🏖🚣🌊

5 EMSWORTH HARBOUR
Steps lead down to estuary for high tide swim. Just off the causeway.

→ Follow Thorney Island/Thorney Rd for Emsworth Yacht Harbour (PO10 8BP) then follow harbour wall S 500m to steps.
10 mins, 50.8381, -0.9333 🏊

6 PILSEY ISLAND, THORNEY ISLAND
Very remote beach and nature reserve.

→ Continue on Thorney Rd past Emsworth yacht club (above) then next L (300m) to Thornam Marina (PO10 8DD). Follow coast path 2½ miles S, crossing at SE tip onto remote Pilsey Island.
60 mins, 50.8003, -0.9066 🏔🏖🏞🌿

7 RIVER HAMBLE, HEDGE END
Tree-lined shingle beaches on this hidden river estuary.

→ J8 off the M27, signed Manor Farm Country Park (SO31 1BH, 01489 787055). Go ½ mile beyond gates to park at Barnfield car park, then to river upstream of pontoon. High tide swimming only.
10 mins, 50.8935, -1.2892 🏔🏖

RIVERS & LAKES

8 STEDHAM, R ROTHER
A beautiful section of river in deep countyside. Deep bays and pools. Quiet.

→ Signed off A272 1½ miles W of Midhurst centre. Continue through village (GU29 0NW) and over bridge to find a fishermen's parking area in field on R. Explore for up to 15 mins

downstream where there are stepping stones and a weir below Stedham Mill.
5 mins, 50.9977, -0.7718 ▲🏊

9 MIDHURST, R ROTHER
Sandy Bay is the traditional place for a paddle and dip, in front of the wonderful Cowdray ruins. Or for much deeper swimming explore upstream.
→ From main car park in Midhurst (GU29 9DJ) walk to ruins. Swim spot is 100m upstream from the bridge. To explore the deep and secret wooded river upstream head NE out of Midhurst, L at roundabout signed Fernhurst and Haslemere and take the footpath by the medical centre after 50m (GU29 9AW)
10 mins, 50.9890, -0.7329 🏊📷

10 HORN MILL HAMMER POND, CHITHURST
Lost in the woods, a wild old pond, part of Chithurst Buddhist Monastery, who follow the Thai forest tradition of living secluded in the forest. Be peaceful and quiet.
→ Signed Chithurst off A272, 3 miles W of Midhurst. Pass the monastery (GU31 5EU), follow orad to R and after 300m find footpath up to lake (200m). Or continue R instead for easier entry to L behind cabin after 400m.
5 mins, 51.0062, -0.7943 ▲🍴🏊📷

11 UPPER POND, PETWORTH PARK
Beautiful, graceful lake with views of National Trust parkland. Be discreet.
→ Main car park is at GU28 9NL at N end of the village (A283). Head SW across the park for 300m. Also via S gatehouse, off A272 to Midhurst.
10 mins, 50.9902, -0.6182 🍴❓

ANCIENT & SACRED

12 THE SHEPHERD'S CHURCH, DIDLING
Tiny medieval church that has changed little over the centuries. Lit entirely by candles, as there is no electricity. An ancient yew tree stands in the churchyard.
→ On the northern slope of Didling Hill. Signposted at triangle (GU29 0LG) S of Didling, go 200m S then along a short track L at bend. Very limited parking.
1 min, 50.9564, -0.8123 🍴▲✝

13 RACTON FOLLY
Abandoned ruins of a late 18th-century folly, said to be haunted, with sweeping views down to Chichester Harbour. It is privately owned, but is clearly visible from the bridleway.

→ Take the B2146 S from Walderton (PO18 9EA). After nearly a mile, just after turnoff L to Chichester, find bridleway on R, by postbox and flint buildings. Follow bridleway for 600m and look for ruin L, partly hidden by trees. Also N from Emsworth/A27 on B2147

10 mins, 50.8794, -0.8975 🚉❓

SUNSET HILLFORTS

14 BEACON HILL, EAST HARTING

Bronze Age hillfort with glorious views, perfect for watching the sunset. The trek to the top is particularly steep.

→ On the B2141 from North Marden to South Harting, look for Harting Down car park R, some 3½ miles NW of Chilgrove (before turn to GU31 5PN). Pick up the South Downs Way heading NE. This is a tough walk with a number of steep climbs.

35 mins, 50.9590, -0.8520 🏞🚶🏞✤

15 THE DEVIL'S JUMPS, TREYFORD

Five Bronze Age barrows, aligned with the position of the setting sun on midsummer's day. Drink Exmoor Beast at the woodland pub.

→ From the Royal Oak, Hooksway (PO18 9JZ) follow footpath NE up into downs for a mile to find the barrows on L, in open field after the

woods. Also via rough byway (partly driveable) from dead end road in Treyford (S of GU29 0LD).

20 mins, 50.9489, -0.8268 🚶🍴🏞🏞🏕✝

16 OLD WINCHESTER HILL

Chalk hill with an Iron Age hillfort and a Bronze Age cemetery at summit. Breathtaking views of the Isle of Wight on clear days. Two long-distance footpaths, South Downs Way and Monarch's Way, cross the summit.

→ Signposted SE from A32 in Warnford (SO32 3LD) on Hayden Lane. Park in the small car park R about ¼ mile after Old Winchester Hill Lane joins on L. Follow South Downs Way ¾ mile to summit.

15 mins, 50.9806, -1.0875 🚶🏞

ANCIENT TREES

17 QUEEN ELIZABETH OAK, COWDRAY

Wide, squat, fenced hollow oak, one of the greatest girthed in the UK. Queen Elizabeth I stood beneath it in 1591 with an arrow in her bow, waiting (fruitlessly) for a stag to be driven within range. The park also contains many other ancient trees.

→ Heading from Easebourne (GU29 0AG) towards Petworth on the A272, turn L into

Benbow Pond after 1¼ miles, and park in small car park. Head N and through the gap next to a wooden gate onto a grassy path by golf course. Bear L as path opens out, past Steward's Pond.

10 mins, 50.9961, -0.7007 🌳🅱

18 KINGLEY VALE NATURE RESERVE

One of the finest yew woods in Europe, includes a grove of ancient trees which are among the oldest living things in Britain. Also find the Devil's Humps Bronze Age burial mounds on Bow Hill within the reserve.

→ A286 N from Chichester to Lavant, then L for East Ashling and Funtington. Follow to West Stoke (PO18 9BE) and park in car park immediately W of St Andrew's Church. Reserve is signposted from car park.

15 mins, 50.895, -0.8290 🌳

19 HALNAKER WINDMILL AND 'TUNNEL'

This well-known landmark stands high on a ridge of wildflower-rich chalk grassland with fantastic views to the Isle of Wight. Look out for buzzards and listen for skylark song. Reached through a magical tree tunnel along a section of the ancient Roman Stane Street.

→ From the Anglesey Arms in Halnaker (PO18 0NQ) head NE on the A285. Look for layby and

19

26

20

33

lane going straight on L at Warehead Farm as road bears R after ½ mile. Follow lane/footpath for 500m through tunnel of trees, and then path N for 500m to windmill.
15 mins, 50.8788, -0.6935 🥾🖼

WILDLIFE & MEADOWS

20 TERWICK CHURCH & LUPINS
Remote church with meadows of lupins in June.
→ Signed St Peter Church, off A272, a mile E of Rogate (near GU31 5EQ).
2 mins, 51.0049, -0.8357 🏞✝

21 PAGHAM HARBOUR BRENT GEESE
Peaceful nature reserve on the Sussex coast. Watch and listen for flocks of Brent geese returning from the arctic each autumn to feed on the saltmarsh throughout winter.
→ Head S from Sidlesham for ½ mile – signposted Visitor Centre car park on L (PO20 7NE).
1 min, 50.7626, -0.7865 🐾

SLOW FOOD

22 WEALD & DOWNLAND MUSEUM
40 acres of traditional rural buildings with woodland walks and lakeside café. Entry fee.
→ Town Lane, Singleton, West Sussex, PO18 0EU, 01243 811363
50.9073,-0.7564

23 ANCHOR BLEU, BOSHAM
Right on the water's edge, this historic pub has a harbourside patio. The traditional menu focuses on seasonal and local produce.
→ High Street, Bosham, PO18 8LS, 01243 573956. If parking on the shore, keep an eye on the tides.
50.8285, -0.8582 🍴

24 DURLEIGHMARSH FARM PYO
Range of fruit, veg and flowers to pick in idyllic countryside. There is also a tea barn and a farm shop, with food from within a 20-mile radius. Seasonal opening hours.
→ Durleighmarsh, GU31 5AX, 01730 821626.
51.0069, -0.8829 🍴

25 NORTHNEY FARM TEA ROOMS
Village tea rooms with views to Chichester Harbour. Serves light lunches and ice-creams made from the dairy farm's own milk.
→ St Peters Road, Hayling Island, PO11 0RX, 023 9246 7607.
50.8280, -0.9628

26 THE HORSE GUARDS INN, TILLINGTON
Quirky, arty and wonderful inn. Small menu that reflects the seasons and whatever can be foraged, grown or caught locally. Log fires, chestnut-roasting and board games in winter, deckchairs and straw-bale seats outside in summer.
→ Upperton Road, Tillington, Nr Petworth GU28 9AF, 01798 342332
50.9897, -0.6296 🍴🛏

27 THE ROYAL OAK, EAST LAVANT
Nestled at the foot of the South Downs, this is an ideal base for walkers. Enjoy local food, including venison and pheasant supplied by the local herdsman. Accommodation also available.
→ Pook Lane, East Lavant, Chichester, PO18 0AX, 01243 527434.
50.8696, -0.7741 🍴

28 ROYAL OAK, HOOKSWAY
Remote, haunted traditional pub right in the woods at the heart of the Downs.
→ Off B2141, between Chilgrove and South Harting, PO18 9JZ, 01243 535257.
50.9398, -0.8405 🏔

29 THE SHIP INN, LANGSTONE
Lovely waterside location means you can arrive by boat. Patio gives views of Hayling Island. Menu focuses on locally caught fish.
→ Langstone Road, Langstone, PO9 1RD, 023 9247 1719.
50.8376, -0.9805

30 THE SHOE INN, EXTON
Relaxing pub in the heart of the Meon Valley. The kitchen garden, ducks and hens provide much of the menu, along with locally caught game.
→ Shoe Lane, Exton, SO32 3NT, 01489 877526, Signposted off the A32.
50.9840, -1.1288 🍴

31 THE THOMAS LORD, WEST MEON
Lovely pub with candles and cricketing memorbilia, set in a small village near the Meon Valley. Much of the food sourced from the pub's own veg garden and chickens.
→ The High Street, West Meon, GU32 1LN, 01730 829244.
51.0122, -1.0853 🍴🛏

32 THE WHITE HORSE, CHILGROVE
Boutique inn with village-pub roots on the edge of the South Downs. Menu takes a

'forest to fork' approach, and includes game shot on the Chilgrove Estate. Rustic but luxurious accommodation.

➔ 1 High Street, Chilgrove, PO18 9HX, 01243 519444. Immediately off the B2141 to Chichester.
50.9235, -0.8235

CAMP & STAY

33 CEDAR VALLEY, EAST MEON

Camping and glamping in the 2,500-acre Bereleigh Estate. Camp around a field edge, or stay in a safari tent, yurt or converted Bedford truck. Hire mountain bikes to explore the estate.

➔ Bereleigh Estate, Nr Petersfield, GU32 1PH, 07557 798857.
51.0080, -1.0354

34 GUMBER FARM, SLINDON

Remote NT campsite on the 3,500-acre Slindon Estate with a Roman road and Bronze Age burial sites. Pitch in a field near an old flint bothy with kitchen and lounge (great in wet weather). Sheep, deer and woodland surround you, and the unpolluted night sky is perfect for stargazing.

➔ Slindon, BN18 0RG, 01243 814484. A 2-mile walk from the nearest car park at Bignor Hill (50.9075, -0.6170), the closest you can get by car. For walkers, it is signposted off the South Downs Way.
50.8979, -0.6333

35 MEON SPRINGS, EAST MEON

Six authentic Mongolian yurts on a working dairy farm. Set beside a lake, with bike hire, fishing and a bar on the farm. Lots of walking and cycling nearby.

➔ Whitewool Farm, Hampshire, GU32 1HW (be careful satnav misleading), 07500 947810.
50.9878, -1.0636

36 NEW HOUSE FARM, EAST DEAN

Basic camping in several acres of fields, hidden deep in the Downs and surrounded by woods. Up a long farm track from a beautiful pub and village.

➔ East Dean, Chichester, PO18 0NJ, 01243 811685. Nearby, The Fox Goes Free (01243 811461) and the Star and Garter (01243 811318) are both excellent pubs.
50.9116, -0.7120

37 STUBCROFT FARM CAMPSITE

Close to sandy beaches on a sustainable sheep farm, this little camping field is encircled by trees, hedgerows and wildlife. B&B option for non-campers.

➔ Stubcroft Farmhouse, Stubcroft Lane, East Wittering, PO20 8PJ, 01243 671469.
50.7741, -0.8586

38 SUSTAINABILITY CENTRE, EAST MEON

Sustainable sleeping options on the South Downs Way – camping, self-catering, tipis and yurts. Small, family-friendly site with compost toilets, solar showers, fire pits and a clay pizza oven.

➔ Droxford Road, East Meon, GU32 1HR, 01730 823166.
50.9673, -1.0376

39 UPPER PARSONAGE FARM, EAST MEON

Tiny campsite with swings. Animals in neighbouring fields. Glamping and B&B also available.

➔ Harvesting Lane, East Meon, GU32 1QR, 01730 823490.
50.9777, -1.0015

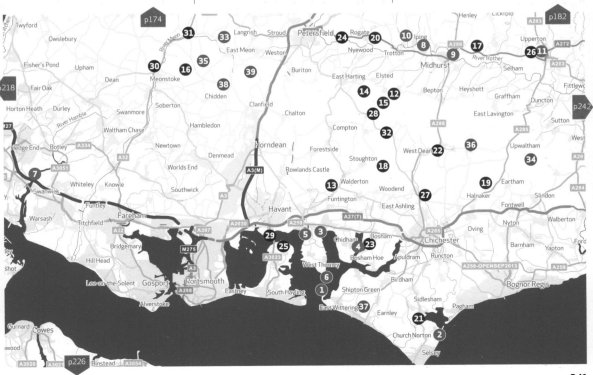

MID SUSSEX DOWNS

Our perfect weekend

→ **Canoe** or swim with the tide from Arundel to Greatham Bridge.

→ **Climb** to the top of Cissbury Ring hillfort and gaze out towards the Isle of Wight.

→ **Marvel** at the spectacle of the murmurations over Brighton Pier.

→ **Pitch** your tent in The Secret Campsite meadows and forage for your supper.

→ **Taste** seasonal food at the Half Moon in Plumpton.

→ **Refuel** at the Hiker's Rest on the South Downs Way with organic cakes and tea.

→ **Explore** Mount Caburn's orchid-rich grassland.

→ **Row** your boat upstream from the Anchor Inn to Isfield, swimming and picnicking along the way.

→ **Play** in the dunes at Littlehampton, just ten minutes from the train station.

→ **Sleep** wild at Castle Rings, the wilder alternative to the popular Devil's Dyke.

Despite the proximity of Brighton and other coastal towns, the great, green, rolling downs of Mid Sussex, alive with salty sea air, exude a sense of ancient mystery.

A profusion of ancient sites and hillforts crown the countryside, overhung with legend and providing sublime spots to escape from the everyday world. Chactonbury Ring is a great choice (as long as you avoid summoning the devil by running backwards round the site in circles), as well as the lesser-known Wolstonbury Hill. Head up the hills as the day draws to a close to bivvy out under the stars. From ancient forts to ancient trees – head into The Mens woodland in search of the centuries-old Idehurst Oak, whose huge fallen branch provides a habitat for insects and newly-grown plants.

Three cool rivers run north to south, like prongs of a fork, offering swimming and kayaking galore. You can canoe on the Adur, but to the west the Arun provides the better swimming, both near Arundel Castle and on the meadows of Waltham Brooks at Greatham. To the east, the Ouse was made famous by the Bloomsbury Group, near Virginia Woolf's house at Rodmell. Upstream on the Ouse, the open fields of Barcombe Mills are a perfect place for cricket, leapfrog and other riverside games. The Ouse here is deep, with pretty grassy banks, ideal for cooling down after cartwheels or diving in for a long swim among the rushes. The well-known Anchor Inn is nearby, just a mile upstream, at the bottom of a dead-end lane. You can hire one of its fleet of blue rowing boats or swim for over two miles through remote countryside, the spire of Isfield church the only building in sight for the entire journey.

Much of the coastline is dominated by towns and cities, but head west towards Littlehampton for more rural beaches. Climping is at the end of a lane with only a pub and a mobile café in the tiny car park for sustenance. Here, a dedicated group of sea-swimmers gather every morning to dive from the groynes, swim the length of the beach and then huddle together in front of steaming mugs of tea. The fields and woodlands around here are alive with birdsong, while the dunes stretching toward Littlehampton offer a small oasis to those seeking solitude.

MID SUSSEX DOWNS

Our perfect weekend

→ **Canoe** or swim with the tide from Arundel to Greatham Bridge.

→ **Climb** to the top of Cissbury Ring hillfort and gaze out towards the Isle of Wight.

→ **Marvel** at the spectacle of the murmurations over Brighton Pier.

→ **Pitch** your tent in The Secret Campsite meadows and forage for your supper.

→ **Taste** seasonal food at the Half Moon in Plumpton.

→ **Refuel** at the Hiker's Rest on the South Downs Way with organic cakes and tea.

→ **Explore** Mount Caburn's orchid-rich grassland.

→ **Row** your boat upstream from the Anchor Inn to Isfield, swimming and picnicking along the way.

→ **Play** in the dunes at Littlehampton, just ten minutes from the train station.

→ **Sleep** wild at Castle Rings, the wilder alternative to the popular Devil's Dyke.

Despite the proximity of Brighton and other coastal towns, the great, green, rolling downs of Mid Sussex, alive with salty sea air, exude a sense of ancient mystery.

A profusion of ancient sites and hillforts crown the countryside, overhung with legend and providing sublime spots to escape from the everyday world. Chactonbury Ring is a great choice (as long as you avoid summoning the devil by running backwards round the site in circles), as well as the lesser-known Wolstonbury Hill. Head up the hills as the day draws to a close to bivvy out under the stars. From ancient forts to ancient trees – head into The Mens woodland in search of the centuries-old Idehurst Oak, whose huge fallen branch provides a habitat for insects and newly-grown plants.

Three cool rivers run north to south, like prongs of a fork, offering swimming and kayaking galore. You can canoe on the Adur, but to the west the Arun provides the better swimming, both near Arundel Castle and on the meadows of Waltham Brooks at Greatham. To the east, the Ouse was made famous by the Bloomsbury Group, near Virginia Woolf's house at Rodmell. Upstream on the Ouse, the open fields of Barcombe Mills are a perfect place for cricket, leapfrog and other riverside games. The Ouse here is deep, with pretty grassy banks, ideal for cooling down after cartwheels or diving in for a long swim among the rushes. The well-known Anchor Inn is nearby, just a mile upstream, at the bottom of a dead-end lane. You can hire one of its fleet of blue rowing boats or swim for over two miles through remote countryside, the spire of Isfield church the only building in sight for the entire journey.

Much of the coastline is dominated by towns and cities, but head west towards Littlehampton for more rural beaches. Climping is at the end of a lane with only a pub and a mobile café in the tiny car park for sustenance. Here, a dedicated group of sea-swimmers gather every morning to dive from the groynes, swim the length of the beach and then huddle together in front of steaming mugs of tea. The fields and woodlands around here are alive with birdsong, while the dunes stretching toward Littlehampton offer a small oasis to those seeking solitude.

5

WILD BEACHES

1 LITTLEHAMPTON WEST BEACH
Wonderful dunes, just a stone's throw from the station – nature reserve and naturists here. Gently shelving beach for children.

→ Turn R out of the station then take the first L over the footbridge, by the Arun View Inn (BN17 5DD, 01903 722335). Then bear L down to beach.

15 mins, 50.7992, -0.5451

2 ATHERINGTON BEACH, CLIMPING
A quiet rural shingle and sand beach. There's a van selling teas, and a sea swimming club meets here regularly.

→ Between Bognor and Littlehampton (A259), turn L by farm shop into dead-end Climping Street, signed Climping Beach. Pass palm-decked Black Horse Inn (BN17 5RL, 01903 715175) to car park at beach. Walk E up to a mile for rural dunes and sand (West Beach).

1 min, 50.7978, -0.5721

RIVER SWIMS & KAYAKING

3 BARCOMBE MILLS, R OUSE
Popular stretch of grassy river bank and meadows. Steep banks and deep water.

→ 2 miles N of Lewes, turn L signposted Barcombe off A26. Find car park on R after a mile, after road to BN8 5BY, and head upstream past sluices to meadow.

5 mins, 50.9151, 0.0411

4 ANCHOR INN, R OUSE
Remote riverside pub. Bucolic swimming and boating for two miles upstream to Isfield. Hire boats from the Anchor and paddle by grassy meadows for the afternoon.

→ Leave Barcombe Cross dir Spithurst, after ½ mile turn R down single-track dead-end Anchor Lane to find pub at end past BN8 5EA (01273 400414). Or walk upstream 1 mile from Barcombe Mills (above).

5 mins, 50.9264, 0.0513

5 ISFIELD, OUSE
Park in Isfield and enjoy a short walk to the river, then follow the footpath downstream until you find a suitable place to get in.

→ Go down Station Rd at the Lavender Line, past the Laughing Fish pub, to find the bridleway track on the L after 500m. Follow it to the river ½ mile (TN22 5XJ) and head up or downstream. Anchor Inn (see entry) is about 1 mile downstream.

10 mins, 50.9366, 0.0550

6 KNEPPMILL POND, DIAL POST
Hilltop ruin and one of the largest stretches of water in Sussex, believed to have been created in the 16th century to power a furnace mill.

→ Leave Dial Post village N on Swallows Lane. After ¾ mile go on foot through signed wooden gate and follow bridleway across field, over River Adur, and slightly right to meet up with Castle Lane bridleway. Ruins of Knepp Castle are on hill to R (RH13 8LH). Follow Castle Lane L ¼ mile to S edge of lake. Be discreet.

5 mins, 50.9783, -0.3542

7 BURY, R ARUN
A tiny dead end hamlet with lovely grassy riverbanks downstream. Some people like to swim with the current up or downstream depending on the tide.

→ 4 miles N of Arundel on A29, turn R at Squire & Horse (RH20 1NS) down into Bury and then Houghton dead-end hamlet (limited parking). Take footpath downstream 300m. Or explore upstream from Amberley riverside park (BN18 9GY).

5 mins, 50.9055, -0.5562

7

11

8 GREATHAM BRIDGE, R ARUN
Good access to Arun and views of the medieval stone bridge. Steep banks. Leading to Waltham Brooks Nature Reserve.
→ A mile E of Coldwaltham (A29). Parking by bridge (before RH20 2ES).
5 mins, 50.9363, -0.5336 🐾🏊🏕

9 SOUTHSTOKE BRIDGE, R ARUN
Quiet hidden stretch of the Arun, up narrow lanes N of the castle, or a pleasant walk upstream from the castle. White metal footbridge. High tide only.

→ From Arundel, follow Mill Rd past castle and lake, for a mile until T junction. Turn L signed 'S Stoke' and continue a mile to church (BN18 9PF). Limited parking.
5 mins, 50.8817, -0.5417 🏊👫🏕

10 KAYAK THE RIVER ADUR
Put your kayak in at Shoreham, an hour before high tide, and paddle upstream to Upper Beeding, or further to Ashurst. Look for herons, buzzards and damselflies.
→ Enter the river just E of Old Shoreham footbridge (near BN43 5DR).
2 mins, 50.8315, -0.2739 🏊

RUINS & ANCIENT PLACES

11 BRAMBER CASTLE, BRAMBER
Remains of a Norman castle on the edge of Bramber village. Gatehouse still very visible, with wonderful views of the surrounding South Downs.
→ Castle Lane from roundabout on A283 for Steyning and Bramber villages, off A283 (near BN44 3WE). Signposted. Park in car park and continue up the path on foot.
3 mins, 50.8832, -0.3155 🏯 B

12 BIGNOR ROMAN VILLA
Remains of a Roman home with striking mosaic floors in a rural setting. Pop into the Museum tea rooms afterwards for tea and cake. Open March–October, entrance fee. Lovely walks nearby, including Stane Street, a 56-mile long Roman road that once linked London and Chichester.
→ Bignor, Pulborough, RH20 1PH, 01798 869259
1 min, 50.9231, -0.5955 🚩🏠🚶

SUNSET HILLTOPS

13 CASTLE RING, EDBURTON HILL
The Devil's Dyke is one of the best hillforts on the Downs, and well worth visiting mid-week for sunset, but it gets very busy at weekends. Castle Ring, to the W, is wilder and also impressive. Enjoy the striking views as the sun dips below the horizon on summer evenings or stay out all night under the stars.
→ A beautiful 2-mile ridge walk W from Devil's Dyke (with café/pub, 01273 857256, well signed from the A27 Brighton), via Fulking Hill and several ancient earthworks. Or you can climb straight up the N escarpment on the bridleway near church in Edburton (BN5 9LN).
40 mins, 50.8850, -0.2414 📷🚶🏕

17

13

14 CHANCTONBURY RING, SOUTH DOWNS

Iron Age hillfort, distinctive for its circle of beech trees, with stunning views across to the sea. Legend has it that on a midsummer's night you can summon the devil from the underworld by running backwards around the ring six times.

→ Follow the footpath and signs from Chanctonbury car park and picnic site (Chanctonbury Ring Road, BN44 3DR, signed off the A283 near BN44 3DE). Also a longer but lesser-used approach from Washington car park, off the A24 a mile S of Washington (RH20 4AX).

30 mins, 50.8966, -0.3816 🚶📷

15 CISSBURY RING, FINDON

The largest hillfort in Sussex gives views as far as the Isle of Wight on a clear day. Many flint mines. Come here for dusk or dawn, or to fly your kite.

→ Heading S on A24, take L turn signed Nepcote, on very S edge of Findon. Continue ½ mile, around green, to turn R at 'dead end' (BN14 0SL) signed Cissbury Ring. Parking is on hilltop (50.8648, -0.3825).

20 mins, 50.8600, -0.3793 📷🐕🚶

16 MOUNT CABURN, GLYNDE

Thought to have been settled during the Bronze Age, with ramparts and a wooden palisade added by Iron Age dwellers to protect their settlement. The fort was occupied from 500BC to AD100 and used by Romans, Saxons and Normans as a lookout point. Sit by the remains and watch the paragliders, or see the orchid-rich grassland glowing at sunset.

→ Follow the public footpath starting almost opposite the village shop on Ranscombe Lane in Glynde village (BN8 6ST) for 600m and then bear L towards the summit.

20 mins, 50.8619, 0.0509 📷🌾🐕🚶

17 WOLSTONBURY HILL

Distinctive landmark with fantastic views. The walk up passes through beech woodland and spring wildflowers. Although the hill is sandwiched between two A-roads, they can't be heard or seen from the summit.

→ Heading S from Hassocks on the A273, turn R at the Jack and Jill Inn in Clayton (BN6 9PD, 01273 843595) into single-track New Way Lane. After 200m, take the bridleway on L, and follow 200m across field. Continue for 600m with copse on L and then bear W up to summit.

35 mins, 50.9086, -0.1769 📷🚶🏞

18 THE MENS & IDEHURST OAK

Atmospheric ancient woodland dominated by towering beech trees, interspersed with oak, hawthorn, ferns and flowers. The unusual name comes from the Anglo-Saxon word 'ge-mænnes', which means 'common land.' See if you can find the centuries-old Idehurst Oak, which lost a huge branch in 2011.

→ From Wisborough Green go SW on the A272 (dir Petworth). After approx 2 miles take the L turn for Crimbourne/Coldharbour at a small crossroads. After 150m, before RH14 0HR, find car park R, down a bumpy track. There are multiple footpaths into the woods from here.

5 mins, 51.0025, -0.5438 📷🚶

19 BRIGHTON OLD PIER, MURMURATIONS

Throughout autumn and winter evenings, watch the breathtaking spectacle of some 40,000 starlings wheeling and swooping in unison to create huge ribbons and pulsing swirls as they come in to roost above the burnt-out West Pier. Although in town, this is one of the best mumurations to be seen in the country.

→ Fantastic views on winter evenings, all along the beach near the West Pier (BN1 2FA).

The murmurations can start as early as 4pm. Hove end is somewhat quieter if the beach feels crowded.

1 min, 50.8209, -0.1500 🚃B

20 PARHAM GARDENS, PULBOROUGH

Impressive yet personal 16th-century stately home and gardens in 875 acres. Walled garden, parkland with deer and ancient trees, a maze and wildflower meadows. Look out for the Victorian 'Wendy' house in the walled garden.

➜ Main entrance is on the A283 between Storrington and Pulborough (RH20 4HR). Well signposted. 01903 742021.

1 min, 50.9186, -0.4931 ✿B⛲

SLOW FOOD

21 THE BUTTERCUP CAFE, LEWES

If you find yourself in Lewes for the day, this little café is the perfect place to while away the afternoon. Home-made local food and proper cream teas. Closed on Sundays. The Downs are just a short stroll out of Lewes to the W.

➜ At Pastorale Antiques, 15 Malling Street, BN7 2RA, 01273 477664.

50.8747, 0.0193 🍴

22 THE HALF MOON, PLUMPTON

Quirky country pub set beside the road in the South Downs. Open fires in winter and large, elevated garden out back for summer.

➜ On the B2116 (Ditchling Road), BN7 3AF, 01273 890253.

50.9025, -0.0623 🍴

23 THE HIKERS REST, BRIGHTON

Delightfully simple hut with picnic benches in a farmyard on the South Downs Way. Serves homemade organic cakes and teas from a hatch. Chimineas lit in colder weather to keep you warm.

➜ Saddlescombe Road, BN45 7DE, 01273 857712. One mile E of Fulking on the South Downs Way. Exit A27 near Brighton for Devils Dyke, but then stay on road where it bends R with Devil's Dyke Road signed left. Continue 2 miles to find Saddlescombe Farm entrance on R, parking on L. Closed Wednesdays.

50.8892, -0.1945 🏞

24 JOLLY SPORTSMAN, EAST CHILTINGTON

Updated country gastropub with fantastic seasonal food.

➜ Chapel Lane, BN7 3BA, 01273 890400.

50.9206, -0.0488

25 THE SHEPHERD AND DOG, FULKING

Tucked at the foot of the South Downs ridge in a higgeldy-piggeldy village, the real appeal of this quirky little pub is its secluded garden with pretty stream, which has striking views of the steep ridge behind it. South Downs walks surround.

➜ The Street, Fulking, BN5 9LU, 01273 857382. 50.8880, -0.2287 🏞🍴🚶

26 WOBBLEGATE JUICE AND CIDER

Family farm that grows and presses Sussex apples. You can taste the juices and ciders before buying.

➜ Old Mill Farm, Cowfold Road, Bolney, RH17 5SE, 01444 881356.

50.9953, -0.2196 🍴

27 HUNTER GATHERER COOK

Foraging and cooking school with focus on outdoor adventure and self-sufficiency. Expect to be thrown in at the deep end, get your hands dirty and have a go at everything from skinning wild meat to building the fire to cook lunch on.

➜ Barcombe, Lewes, 07921 863768. Exact location given upon booking.

50.9134, 0.0219 🏞

CAMP & GLAMP

28 BILLYCAN CAMPING, TORTINGTON

Rustic glamping set in 650 acres of farmland. A magical place with a fairy-lit bridge, communal campfire and delicious breakfast hampers delivered to your tent on Saturday mornings.

➜ Manor Farm, Arundel, BN18 0BG, 01903 882103.

50.8423, -0.5681 ⛺🏕

29 BLACKBERRY WOOD, STREAT

Quirky campsite full of surprises. Pitch your tent in a secluded woodland glade and light a campfire, or stay in a double decker bus, converted helicopter or gypsy caravan.

➜ Streat Lane, BN6 8RS, 01273 890035.

50.9168, -0.0792 ⛺🏕

30 BLACKLANDS FARM CAMPSITE

Large, family-run campsite in oak-fringed meadows by a lake. Both caravans and tents permitted. Great on-site shop with all the essentials.

➜ Wheatsheaf Road (B2116), Henfield, BN5 9AT, 01273 493528

50.9495, -0.2483

31 HOUSEDEAN FARM CAMPSITE, LEWES

Simple campsite on a traditional working farm with glorious views and open-air shower. Some traffic noise can be heard, but don't let this put you off this lovely site.

→ Housedean Farm, Brighton Road, BN7 3JW, 07919 668816.
50.8668, -0.0565

32 KITTS COTTAGE CAMPSITE, SCAYNES HILL

Camp in a huge meadow bordered by sheep fields and ancient woodland. New solar showers, numerous campfires, and breathtaking countryside views.

→ Freshfield Place Farm, Sloop Lane, RH17 7NN, 07733 103309.
50.997, -0.0210

33 KNEPP SAFARIS CAMPING, DIAL POST

In the heart of a 3,500-acre re-wilding project, on disused farmland, this wildflower meadow has space for ten tents, or hire one of their bell tents. Expect a wealth of wildlife and over 16 miles of permissive footpaths nearby. Children must be 12 or over.

→ 0117 204 7830 Canopyandstars.co.uk. New Barn Farm, Swallows Lane, RH13 8NN.,
50.9716, -0.3632

34 POP-UP BY THE RIVER, STEYNING

Up on the downs or down by the River Adur, life is peaceful for campers and glampers alike. Be lulled by the sounds of the river and the glow of the campfires.

→ New Wharf Farm, BN44 3AL, 0777 1535350. popupcampsites.com
50.9225, -0.3081

35 THE SHEPHERDS RETURN, SUTTON

Peaceful shepherd's hut on a private patch of green space. Organic breakfast hamper delivered each morning.

→ 1 The Hollow, Sutton End, Pulborough, RH20 1PY, 01798 869364.
50.9376, -0.6034

36 THE SECRET CAMPSITE, NR BARCOMBE

Pitch your tent in the overgrown meadow or stay in England's first tree tent, a suspended structure that resembles a harvest mouse nest. Fringed by ancient oak and hornbeam trees, it plans to become the first 'edible campsite', with everything from berries to edible flowers planted by the botanist owner.

→ Brickyard Farm, Town Littleworth, BN8 4TD, 01273 401100.
50.9398, 0.0089

37 WOWO CAMPSITE, UCKFIELD

A winning combination of luxurious glamping and a laid-back vibe. Rope swings, woodland adventures and free camping for musicians who perform around the campfire. Huge site with lots of surprises.

→ Wapsbourne Manor, Sheffield Park, TN22 3QT, 01825 723414.
50.9931, -0.0078

38 DITCHLING CAMP

Relaxed rural camping with South Downs views. Basic facilities add an extra sense of wildness. Pubs and cafés in nearby Ditchling.

→ One mile SW of Ditchling. Call for directions: 07733 103309.
50.9085, -0.1278

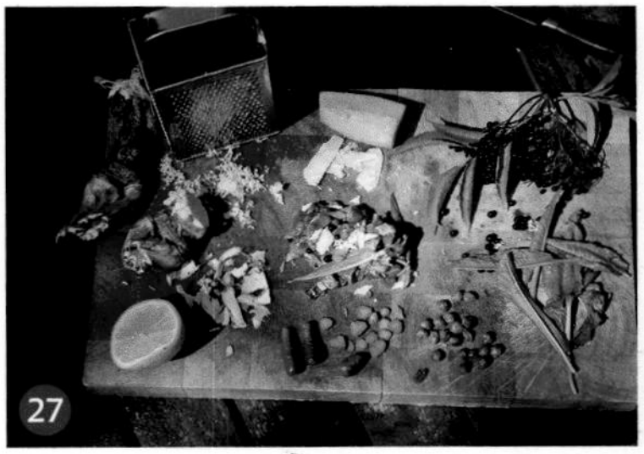
27

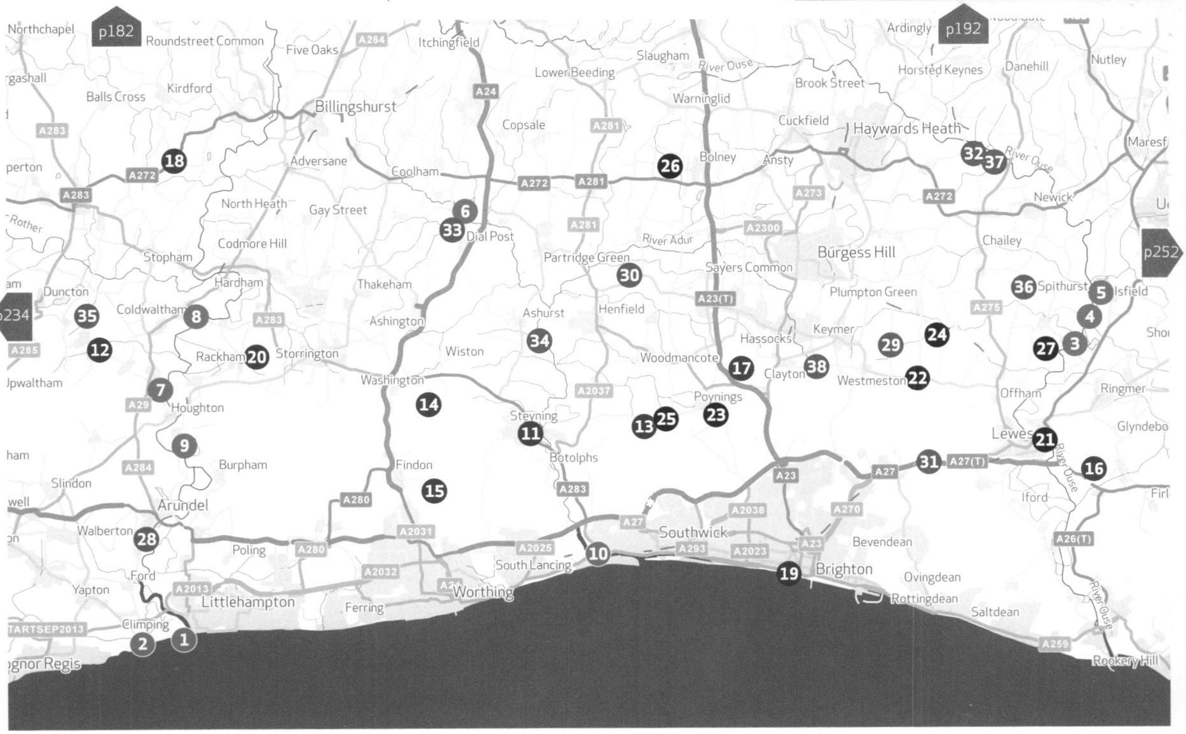

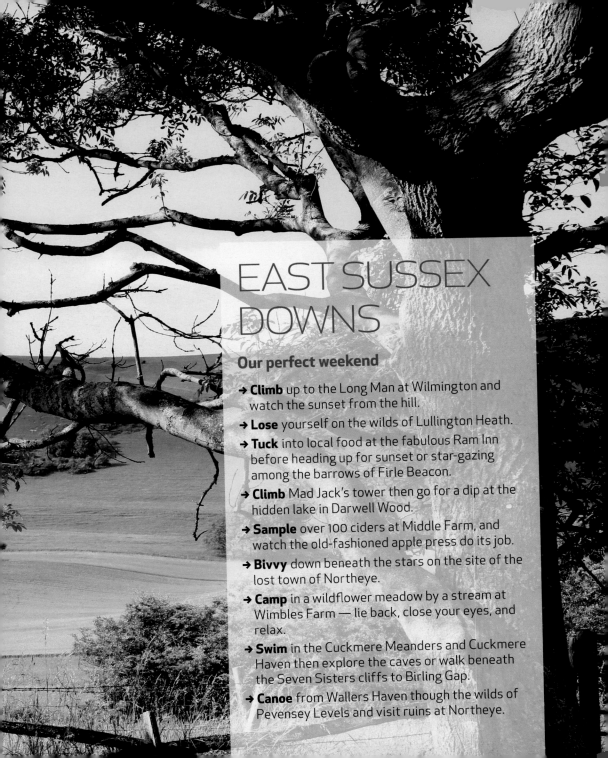

EAST SUSSEX DOWNS

Our perfect weekend

→ **Climb** up to the Long Man at Wilmington and watch the sunset from the hill.

→ **Lose** yourself on the wilds of Lullington Heath.

→ **Tuck** into local food at the fabulous Ram Inn before heading up for sunset or star-gazing among the barrows of Firle Beacon.

→ **Climb** Mad Jack's tower then go for a dip at the hidden lake in Darwell Wood.

→ **Sample** over 100 ciders at Middle Farm, and watch the old-fashioned apple press do its job.

→ **Bivvy** down beneath the stars on the site of the lost town of Northeye.

→ **Camp** in a wildflower meadow by a stream at Wimbles Farm — lie back, close your eyes, and relax.

→ **Swim** in the Cuckmere Meanders and Cuckmere Haven then explore the caves or walk beneath the Seven Sisters cliffs to Birling Gap.

→ **Canoe** from Wallers Haven though the wilds of Pevensey Levels and visit ruins at Northeye.

Where the Sussex chalk downs finally meet the sea there is a welcome sense of relief, as wild coast prevails after 30 miles of south-coast conurbations. The Seven Sisters chalk cliffs are the most famous site, marching along the coast, falling steeply away to rocky coves and remote beaches. There are wild downs and green inlands to discover and many fantastic campsites and places to stay.

Everyone should walk the Seven Sisters once in their lives, but the foot of these cliffs are perhaps the greater adventure – an inter-tidal no man's land of tiny coves and cliff tunnels. Here you'll find some of the most secluded beaches in southern England. Make sure you leave three hours before low tide to give yourself plenty of time for the slow three-mile return scramble to your starting point, or you'll risk being cut off. The Birling Gap is a good place to start exploring, and to swim. At this spot a narrow gut of sand opens up among the rock pools at low tide, and there is now a National Trust café perched high on the cliff. It's possible to walk east from the gap to Beachy Head, Britain's tallest chalk sea-cliff. The name comes from 'beau chef', or beautiful head(land), and this really is a glorious place to watch the sunrise. Or you can walk west to Cuckmere Haven, a majestic sweep of beach at the mouth of the Cuckmere River.

There are fantastic walks through the Seven Sisters Country Park from Cuckmere Haven past the Cuckmere meanders, with Firle Beacon and Wilmington Long Man making wonderful viewpoints. The Long Man was thought to originate in the Iron Age, or even the Neolithic period, as a symbol of an astral religion, though more recent archaeological work shows the figure may have been cut in the 16th or 17th century. These hills lead onto some of the wildest stretches of downs, such as Lullington Heath and Friston Forest, many miles from habitation.

Past Eastbourne the chalk turns to shingle and the land drops to the flatlands of the Pevensey Levels with its wide open swimming rivers. There are the remains of Northeye village, and those in search of peaceful shingle beaches might try Norman's Bay, site of the famous 1066 Norman landings.

Perhaps more than anywhere else in the South East, East Sussex has an impressive choice of places to stay, from tiny wild campsites like Wimbles Farm, to glorious glamping at Glottenham and the quirky Belle Tout Lighthouse high on Beachy Head. There is also delicious food at the Ram Inn and at Middle Farm to keep you going. Set up the tent, light the fire, and sit back to enjoy the peace and quiet of this corner of England.

WILD BEACHES

1 BIRLING GAP, EAST DEAN

Wild rocky beach at the foot of the Seven
Sisters chalk cliffs, accessed via steep
steps beneath a faded hotel. Great for a lazy
afternoon rock pooling and fossil hunting.

→ Signed from Friston (A259). Park at NT cafe
(BN20 0AB, 01323 423197).
3 mins, 50.7426, 0.2009 🐾🚗🏊🍴🎎

2 CUCKMERE HAVEN, SEAFORD

Rough shingle-and-sand beach at base of the
iconic Seven Sisters chalk cliffs.

→ Park at Exceat, 2 miles E of Seaford (A259).
Follow valley past meanders (on L Foxhole
camping) to E end of beach. Access W beach
via Golden Galleon pub (BN25 4AB) on other
side of bridge, or via Hope Gap ¾ mile W (from
Seaford follow signs for golf course, go to end
of Chyngton Lane BN25 4JE, then R to South
Hill Barn). Avoid river mouth in high swell.
30 mins, 50.7591, 0.1486 🏊🚗🎎🏕

3 NORMAN'S BAY CAMPING, BEXHILL

Shingle-and-sand beach, site of 1066
landing, remarkable for absence of buildings,
except for train station and hotel.

→ Just W of Bexhill, turn by Cooden Beach
Hotel (TN39 4TT, 01424 842281) to follow
coast road to Norman's Bay with large, windy
shoreside campsite (BN24 6PR, 01323
761190). Train is 1hr 40 mins to London.
5 mins, 50.8220, 0.3820 🚉🏕

4 FALLING SANDS, BEACHY HEAD

LT sands and rocks beneath famous cliffs.

→ From Beachy Head Hotel car park (BN20
7YA, 01323 728060), cross road and descend
hill to beach at Cow Gap, then S 500m.
25 mins, 50.7375, 0.2556 🏊🚗🎎

RIVERS, MOATS & MEANDERS

5 MICHELHAM PRIORY MOAT

Fantastic old priory with gatehouse, watermill and huge moat — actually R Cuckmere.
Michelham Priory Rd, Upper Dicker, Hailsham,
East Sussex BN27 3QS
2 mins, 50.8619, 0.2117 🏊❓

6 LITLINGTON, R CUCKMERE

Wide grassland vale beneath white horse.
Fun at high tide.

→ Approaching from A259 E of Seaford,
footpath to river is on L as you enter Litlington

village, 200m before the excellent Plough and
Harrow (BN26 5RE, 01323 870 632). Head
downstream to footbridge.
10 mins, 50.7920, 0.1505 🏊🍴🚶

7 CUCKMERE MEANDERS

Wide, shallow, warm oxbow lakes cut off
from the main river. Stunning setting with
option of sea swimming too.

→ On A259 W of Seaford. Park at the visitor
centre at Exceat. Follow the path down on the
L side of the valley ½ mile.
10 mins, 50.7707, 0.1544 🏊🏊

8 WALLERS HAVEN, WARTLING

Very remote, wide river, around 15 feet deep
in places with the reed-lined banks. Amazing
wild swim experience.

→ From Wartling (3 miles N of Pevensey
roundabout) head past church to Horsebirdge.
Footpath heads upstream. Or explore
anywhere on the river.
3 mins, 50.8569, 0.3697 🏊🏊🎎

9 DARWELL LAKE AND WOOD

Isolated wooded shores on the W banks of
this reservoir. Be discreet if dipping.

→ On Brightling to Netherfield lane, find

bridleway 500m N of Darwell Hole. Follow for a mile down to the shore.

20 mins, 50.9599, 0.4280 🧍🐾🏊

SACRED & ANCIENT

10 WILMINGTON LONG MAN, WILMINGTON

The tallest chalk figure in the UK, this outline in the hillside is thought to date back beyond the 18th century. Exactly why and how he's here remains a mystery. Look out for the huge yew in the churchyard.

→ From Polegate, heading W on A27, turn L after 2 miles (signed Wilmington/Long Man) and find car park after church on R. 100m further along lane on L find bridleway which climbs directly up to the man (500m). The vast yew stands in Wilmington churchyard.

15 mins, 50.8100, 0.1881 🅱🏞🥾

11 LULLINGTON CHURCH, ALFRISTON

Claimed to be the smallest church in England, Lullington Church was created from the chancel of an earlier church destroyed by fire in the 16th century. Stands remote on a hill above the Cuckmere Valley.

→ Head N for 1 mile from the Plough and Harrow in Litlington (BN26 5RE). The church is signposted L by an obscure white sign. Turn L,

follow road for 50m and look for church on R.

1 min, 50.8069, 0.1675 ✝

12 NORTHEYE LOST TOWN AND SEAPORT

Probably destroyed by a sudden inrush of sea caused by the great storm of 1250, all that remains of this submerged town is a sloping field with grassy bumps – perhaps where walls used to be – and evidence of the old road. Although not much is visible, this is a wonderfully remote spot to bivvy down and stargaze under dark skies.

→ 1½ miles W of the roundabout in Little Common (A259, Bexhill to Pevensey), turn L at two national speed limit signs (just past TN39 4QR). After 300m take the second L down a bumpy track, and follow as far as you can (600m). Northeye covers the grassy expanse past the end of the track.

10 mins, 50.8389, 0.3866 🏔🎲🖼🎌

RUINS & FOLLIES

13 MAD JACK FULLER'S TOWER

Brilliant stone tower, hidden in trees, which you can climb inside. Built by John 'Mad Jack' Fuller, prolific folly builder and squire. There are four other follies in the area to discover too.

→ 300m S of Brightling, direction Netherfield, find footpath on L and follow for 100m. You might also like to seek out Mad Jack's pyramid (in the churchyard of Brightling village itself 50.9631, 0.3969), obelisk (1½ mile W at 50.9660, 0.3771) and 'sugar loaf' cone (2 miles SW at 50.9509, 0.3750).
5 mins, 50.9606, 0.4030 ▣

14 LAKE WOOD & GROTTO, UCKFIELD
Lovely lake with rocky crags and amazing carved-out cave and grotto complex. Beautiful for swimming too.
→ From Isfield continue N towards Uckfield 3 miles. Cross the A22 to find West Park Nature Reserve on L.
5 mins, 50.9762, 0.0820, ▣▣

SUNSET HILLTOPS

15 BEACHY HEAD & SEVEN SISTERS
Dramatic cliffs towering above the English Channel, with views down to the famous red-and-white striped lighthouse and the tidal sands (see listings).
→ From Beachy Head Hotel car park (OK food, BN20 7YA, 01323 728060), cross road and follow footpath towards the cliff edge. Very popular so best visited early or late in the day, or try further W along coast road, such as Belle Tout cliff (50.7406, 0.2088).
5 mins, 50.7384, 0.2529 ▣▣⬛⬛⬛

16 FIRLE BEACON
Ancient Bronze Age barrow right on top of the downs. Popular for paragliding, with secluded spots away from the South Downs Way for watching the sunset over the distant sea. The Ram Inn three miles away (BN8 6NS 01273 858222) makes a great Sunday pub walk.
→ There are numerous footpaths here, and a choice of car parks right on the downs. Perhaps the closest is Bopeep car park (BN8 6PA, 50.8258, 0.1193) at the end of Bopeep Bostal. From here, follow the South Downs Way NW for 1 mile to reach the summit.
20 mins, 50.8336, 0.1080 ▣⬛⬛

WILDLIFE & MEADOWS

17 SEVEN SISTERS SHEEP CENTRE
The world's largest private collection of sheep on a working, family-run farm in the South Downs National Park. Meet the animals, help to bottle-feed the lambs, and pop into the Hay Rack Tea Room for some home-made cake. Limited opening hours, so check before visiting.

→ Gilberts Drive, East Dean, BN20 0AA, 01323 423302.
1 min, 50.7519, 0.2066 🚗🚲🍴

18 LULLINGTON HEATH

Glorious meadow flowers and ponies on one of the UK's largest remaining chalk heaths.

→ Choice of bridlepaths onto the heath from several directions. Perhaps best is from Jevington village – follow the South Downs Way signed down Church Lane (dead-end road, at the red postbox) and continue past St Andrew's Church for around a mile to the heath.
20 mins, 50.7947, 0.1904 🚲🚶🏇🏕

SLOW FOOD

19 MIDDLE FARM, FIRLE

Well-stocked farm shop, restaurant/café and specialist cider room, where you can try more than 100 ciders from the barrels. Watch the old-fashioned apple press in operation during the summer months.

→ Right on the A27, 4 miles east of Lewes, between the turnings to Ripe and Selmeston. BN8 6LJ, 01323 811411.
50.8508, 0.1125 🍴

20 THE BLACKBOYS INN, BLACKBOYS

14th-century traditional pub with a good selection of local real ale.

→ Lewes Road, TN22 5LG, 01825 890283.
50.9627, 0.1655 🍴

21 THE RAM INN, WEST FIRLE

Country pub serving local food, including meat from nearby Firle Estate. Great walks around here - pick up the South Downs Way or visit Charleston Farmhouse of Bloomsbury Set fame.

→ The Street, Firle, BN8 6NS, 01273 858222.
50.8474, 0.0852 🍴🍴

22 THE TIGER INN, EAST DEAN

Cosy traditional pub with rooms in the lovely little village of East Dean. Beachy Head cliffs and South Downs Way nearby.

→ The Green, BN20 0DA, 01323 423209.
50.7589, 0.2059 🍴🛏

23 WILDERNESS CAFE, HADLOW DOWN

Wilderness Wood has a Forest School, woodland products and traditional woodland management. The rustic café offers simple food in a beautiful setting.

→ Wilderness Wood, TN22 4HJ, 01825 830509.
50.9944, 0.1863

CAMP & STAY

24 BELLE TOUT LIGHTHOUSE, BEACHY HD

Quirky and fun hotel high on the cliff edge with fantastic 360 degree views. Pricey, two-night minimum, but an experience not to be missed.

→ Beachy Head, Eastbourne, BN20 0AE, 01323 423185.
50.7381, 0.2145 🏠

25 BIG SKY TIPI HOLIDAYS, HAILSHAM

Set in a two-acre meadow, your tipi overlooks a wildlife-filled woodland with deer and barn owls. An area of dark, unpolluted night skies, it's a five-minute walk to the original Greenwich Observatory.

→ Well House, Wartling Road, Wartling, BN27 1RX, 01323 832325.
50.8648, 0.3509 🏕🏠

26 DERNWOOD FARM WILD CAMPING

Rambling, eco-friendly site in 70 acres of coppice woodland. Gorgeous bluebells in spring, with blackberries, mushrooms and chestnuts to forage in autumn.

→ Little Dernwood Farm, Dern Lane, Waldron, Nr Heathfield, TN21 0PN, 01435 812726.
50.9316, 0.2103 🏕⛺

27 EMBERS CAMPING, HALLAND

Spacious, secluded camping surrounded by woodland and meadow. Campfires encouraged. Eco-friendly shepherds' huts if you prefer more luxury.

→ Next to Bentley Wildfowl and Motor Museum, BN8 5AF, 0845 257 2267.
50.9234, 0.1091 🏕🏠

28 GLOTTENHAM FARM, ROBERTSBRIDGE

Glorious glamping in 20 acres of ancient hornbeam woodland and wildflower meadow. Breathtaking display of bluebells in the spring.

→ 0117 204 7830, Canopyandstars.co.uk Bishops Lane, TN32 5EB.
50.9735, 0.4613 🏠

29 HIDDEN SPRING, HORAM

Back-to-nature campsite surrounded by orchards on a family smallholding.

→ Vines Cross Rd, TN21 0HG, 01435 812 640.
50.9368, 0.2543 🏕🚲

30 THE COACH HOUSE, HEATHFIELD

Restored coach house on a 20-acre smallholding in the Sussex High Weald. Pond, BBQ and firepit in your own patch of garden, with rural views across a wild meadow. Sue will leave you a delicious welcome pack, including home-made bread and farm's own eggs.

→ Beech Hill Farm, Cowbeech Rd, Rushlake Gn, TN21 9QB, 01435 830203. Sawdays.co.uk
50.9297, 0.3067

31 LAUGHTON PLACE, LAUGHTON
Landmark Trust property on the flatlands between Ashdown Forest and the South Downs. This tower used to be the outlook post of a larger 16th-century house but now stands alone.

→ Cow Lane, Laughton, BN8 6DA, 01628 825925. Landmarktrust.org.uk
50.8873, 0.1061

32 FIRLE CAMPSITE
Camp in a lovely downland meadow. The South Downs Way passes nearby, so a good option for ramblers.

→ Firle Estate, Heighton Street, BN8 6NZ. info@firlecamp.co.uk
50.8490, 0.1056

33 SAFARI BRITAIN / MOUNT HARRY
Beautiful pop-up glamping now operating from Mount Harry House country estate with spectacular downland views.

→ Mount Harry House, Offham, Lewes, East BN7 3QW, 01273 474456.
50.8191, 0.0876

34 THIMBLES B&B, HEATHFIELD
Enjoy the good life at Thimbles, from the garden's 89 rose varieties to the breakfasts of hand-reared meats and home-made bread.

→ New Pond Hill, Cross in Hand, TN21 0NB, 01435 860745.
50.9639, 0.2298

35 WIMBLES FARM, HEATHFIELD
About as close to wild camping as you can get. Basic facilities, a stream, a wildflower meadow, and nothing else. Perfect.

→ Look for the sign, as Sat Nav will take you to a neighbour's garden. Wimbles, Foords Lane, Vines Cross, TN21 9HA, 01435 810390.
50.9270, 0.2762

36 HAWTHBUSH FARM, GUN HILL
Cosy shepherds' huts on a 140-acre organic farm, surrounded by wildflower meadows. Or luxurious converted piggery with wood burner and wood-fired cedar hot tub.

→ Gun Hill, TN21 0JX, 01825 212020.
50.9034, 0.2171

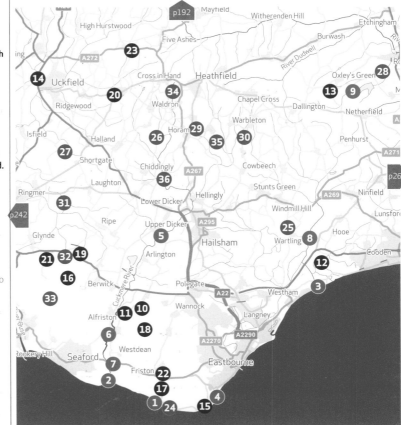

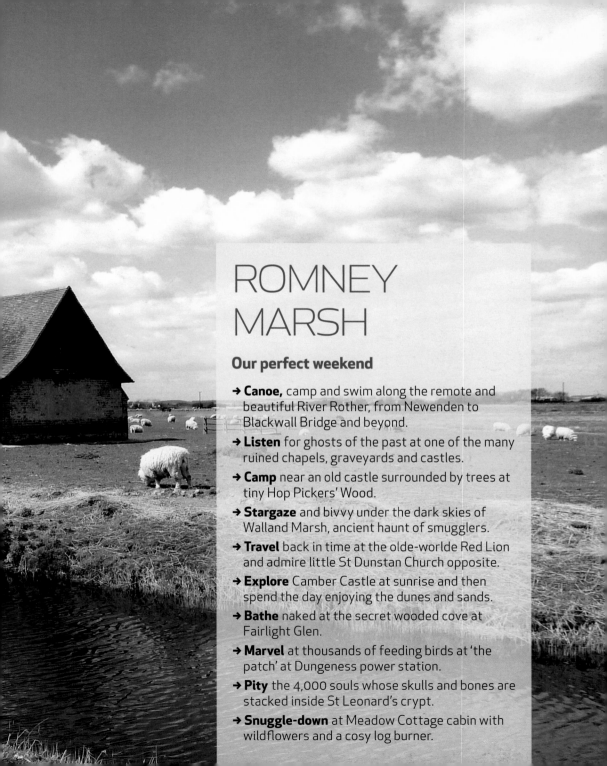

ROMNEY MARSH

Our perfect weekend

→ **Canoe,** camp and swim along the remote and beautiful River Rother, from Newenden to Blackwall Bridge and beyond.

→ **Listen** for ghosts of the past at one of the many ruined chapels, graveyards and castles.

→ **Camp** near an old castle surrounded by trees at tiny Hop Pickers' Wood.

→ **Stargaze** and bivvy under the dark skies of Walland Marsh, ancient haunt of smugglers.

→ **Travel** back in time at the olde-worlde Red Lion and admire little St Dunstan Church opposite.

→ **Explore** Camber Castle at sunrise and then spend the day enjoying the dunes and sands.

→ **Bathe** naked at the secret wooded cove at Fairlight Glen.

→ **Marvel** at thousands of feeding birds at 'the patch' at Dungeness power station.

→ **Pity** the 4,000 souls whose skulls and bones are stacked inside St Leonard's crypt.

→ **Snuggle-down** at Meadow Cottage cabin with wildflowers and a cosy log burner.

The green hills of the North and South Downs give way here to the wild, empty flatness of Romney Marsh, with its remote churches and tales galore of smuggling. To the south are the huge, strange shingle banks of Dungeness and the gentle dunes of Camber Sands.

Once hidden beneath the waves of the English Channel, Romney Marsh was first reclaimed from the sea by the Romans. Drained by ancient dykes, it is still at risk from flooding, and its sea defences are constantly managed to keep homes and farms safe. The ancient sea-cliffs to the north and west are an unsettling reminder of the fact that much of the Marsh exists below sea level.

The Marsh is known as one of the best places in the UK for stargazing because of its huge dark skies, and these were once popular with smugglers too, known locally as 'owlers'. Smuggling – at its peak in the 18th and 19th centuries when wool, spirits and tobacco were heavily taxed – was once so rife here that there are said to be tunnels linking pubs and churches. In fact in 1744 the morning service could not be held in St George's church because the vestry was "full wi' baccy and pulpit full o' brandy" brought in by tunnel from the Bell Inn.

Perhaps the most familiar image of Romney Marsh is that of Fairfield Church standing lonely and remote amid fields and surrounded by watercourses, but there are far more church and chapel ruins waiting to be discovered.

Down south at Dungeness the whole shingle mass is still moving eastwards at two yards per year (or it would be if trucks were not constantly moving the shingle back to where it came from to ensure the nuclear power station does not fall into the sea). There is an 'edge-of-the-world' feeling here, a place frequented by gulls, terns and gadwalls, as well as artists and philosophers who established retreats in the old railway cabins and fishing huts on the bleak shingle spit. This is one of the largest and most important shingle beaches in Europe – a unique and sensitive habitat.

For the best sand in the area, though, head to Camber where there is an uninterrupted stretch of fine sand to the water's edge, with shallow swimming over the warm flats. You can escape among the dunes, bounded in late summer by sea buckthorn with golden berries.

WILD BEACHES

1 CAMBER SANDS WEST DUNES

Great expanse of sand and dunes. Sea is mainly shallow and warm at HT.

→ Approaching from Rye, choose the first car park and park at near end for path through dunes to beach. Don't swim too near the river mouth. The Gallivant, further along on the L, is a trendy place to eat or stay (TN31 7RB, 01797 225057). 3 miles on, heading E out of Camber, is Broomhill beach at Jury's Gap. More desolate with LT sand.

10 mins, 50.9331, 0.7837 ▲

2 CAMBER SANDS EAST KITESURFING

East Camber Sands is perfect for kitesurfing, but can get busy on a warm, windy summer day. The Kitesurf Centre on the sea front provides lessons and kit.

→ Head E out of Camber and 500m after Camber Sands Holiday Park you will see a big gravel car park with a metal shipping container in it R. The Kitesurf Centre is here (TN31 7SB).

1 min, 50.9303, 0.8139 ▼

3 FAIRLIGHT GLEN, COVEHURST

A beautiful LT rock-and-sand cove below woody stream glade, in the unstable greensand cliffs between Hastings and Winchelsea. Path is sometimes blocked by landslips. The rocks have fascinating patterns. Popular with naturists.

→ Follow A259, 2 miles E out of Hastings and turn R at church up Fairlight Rd. After a mile park at the Fairlight Road picnic site on L. Cross road, down track 800m and just before Place Farm (TN35 5DT), by green, bear R then L to find Fairlight Glen footpath sign leading down through woods with stream. Also explore beach to E to Fairlight Cove and W back to Hastings.

20 mins, 50.8652, 0.6317 ▣◈♦⚲▨

4 DUNGENESS EAST, LYDD

Bleak but atmospheric shingle spit. Fishing huts, lighthouse and nuclear power station make for an eerie mix.

→ From Lydd roundabout follow signs to Dungeness and Pilot Inn, built from shipwreck timber (TN29 9NJ, 01797 320314). 200m before pub turn R for 'RH&DR Dungeness' and continue to black-and-yellow-painted Prospect Cottage, R (TN29 9NE). Park beyond and head across the shingle to L (E), through old boats and sheds 300m to reach the sea. Also Romney, Hythe & Dymchurch railway (01797 362353).

5 mins, 50.9225, 0.9816 ▲◈▲

5 WINCHELSEA, PETT LEVEL

Groynes and shingle/sand expanses

→ Continue on road 4 miles E past Fairlight Cove and park near lakes a mile before Winchelsea. Climb shingle banks to beach.

5 mins, 50.9011, 0.7083

RIVER, LAKE & CREEK

6 BLACKWALL BRIDGE, R ROTHER

Very wild and remote fenland swim or canoe. Head off in either direction for several miles without sight of a building.

→ 1½ mile N of Peasmarsh (TN31 6TB) in direction of Wittersham.

5 mins, 51.0010, 0.6854 ▣▲▲▤

7 WALKER OUTLAND, DUNGENESS LAKES

Huge pebble lakes. Nature reserve so be discrete if taking a dip.

→ 1½ miles E of Lydd on Dungeness Rd. Park opp visitor centre (RSPB National Nature Reserve sign – Boulderwell Farm, TN29 9PN), cross road and take footpath gate on L (not main bridleway track) to reach lake shore after 10 mins.

10 mins, 50.9324, 0.9437 ▤♦▲▤

8 NEWENDEN ROTHER CANOE AND SWIM

Lovely river swim and café. Very clean and lined with reeds, purple loosestrife and marsh marigolds. Campsite plus hire kayaks and rowing boats.

→ Park at the boating station (Newenden, TN18 5PP, 01797 253838) and swim either up or downstream of bridge. A canoe journey could be made up to or from Bodiam Castle.

3 mins, 51.0148, 0.6153 🏊🏕️🍴🚣🎣

9 ROYAL MILITARY CANAL, BONNINGTON

This is a lovely open and quiet stretch of this Napoleonic Wars defensive canal, near pretty Saxon church, one of the oldest on the Marshes.

→ Signed St Rumwold church/Newchurch (TN25 7JY) S from Bonnington (B2067) ¼ mile.

5 mins, 51.0707, 0.9435 ✝🏊

RUINS AND SACRED

10 THOMAS À BECKET CHURCH, FAIRFIELD

The image perhaps most associated with Romney Marsh is that of this little church standing alone in the marshes, reflected in the water courses and surrounded by sheep. Built c.1200 with a Georgian interior,

and only the sound of the wind across the marshes outside to disturb the peace.

→ Fairfield (TN29 9RZ) is 2 miles S of Appledore. Obtain the key from Becket Barn Farm, on the opposite side of the road 200m NW of the church.

3 mins, 51.0041, 0.8018 ✝🏊

11 CAMBER CASTLE

Built by Henry VIII to protect the port of Rye, this impressive ruin was abandoned by the mid-17th century and now sits alone in the marshes. Interior only open by guided tour, otherwise access any time.

→ From Rye, take the A259 dir Winchelsea. Just outside Rye, turn L to Rye Harbour Nature Reserve. After 200m is Brede Lock. Take the footpath down by the river, as shown on noticeboard map. Guided tour dates on Wildrye.info. Nearby the popular and beautiful Bodiam Castle (TN32 5UA) is worth a visit too (entrance fee).

20 mins, 50.9335, 0.7336 🏰🚂

12 CHAPEL BANK HILL & GRAVEYARD

Atop a small hill, once surrounded by sea, there are panoramic views across farmland and marshes, and an isolated overgrown graveyard without a church. Open-air

services are still held here once a year. With a peaceful, forgotten feel, it is a glorious place to bivvy out at sunset.

→ From the Ferry Inn (TN30 7JY), follow the footpath that leaves the car park W. Continue for ½ mile, forking left at the bridge and building, until you reach a paved path at right angles to your footpath. Turn R, and follow this up the small hill ahead.

20 mins, 51.0343, 0.7493 ⬛🏕⛪🗑

13 EASTBRIDGE CHURCH

Overgrown remains of once fine medieval church with pinnacled tower.

→ Head N out of Dymchurch on Eastbridge Rd (dir Aldington). After 2½ miles, after Chapel Farm (TN29 0HZ) turn L (signed cycle way 2). Access is via a short footpath through the bushes immediately on your R.

1 min, 51.0511, 0.9580 ⬛⛪

14 MIDLEY CHURCH

This isolated ruined arch is all that is left of a medieval church, probably deserted in the 16th century.

→ From the Rose and Crown Inn, Old Romney (TN29 9SQ), head S towards Lydd on Swamp Road. Stay on road for 2 miles, over level crossing, then take footpath R at first major bend in road (TN29 9PY). Follow path back over train line to ruin (stone archway is visible from a distance).

10 mins, 50.9726, 0.8914 ⛰⬛⛪

15 HOPE CHURCH OF ALL SAINTS

Once a smugglers' meeting place, now ruined. Visit at dusk and imagine the smuggling deeds of yesteryear.

→ Head NW out of New Romney on Ashford Rd towards Ivychurch. After 1 ½ miles look out for kissing gate on R. The ruin is visible across the field.

2 mins, 50.9951, 0.9188 ⬛⛪

16 ST LEONARD'S CRYPT & SKULLS, HYTHE

This vast collection of human remains are stacked and shelved through the chancel of this otherwise ordinary town church. The 2,000 skulls and 8,000 thigh bones are the remains of Saxons who were killed in a battle against the Vikings in around AD500.

→ The Vicarage/Oak Walk, Hythe CT21 5DN, 01303 266217, 10.30 – 4.30pm, Monday to Saturday, except lunchtimes. Admission 50p

1 min, 51.0728, 1.0841 ⬛

30

30

28

38

29

WOODLAND & WILDLIFE

17 WALLAND MARSH DARK SKIES
Romney Marsh is one of the top dark-sky spots in the UK, with wide skies and little light pollution. Perfect for stargazing and wild bivvying.
→ On foot, turn R out of The Woolpack Inn (TN29 9TJ) and take the first footpath L along a muddy track. Head towards wind farm and stop when you find a likely spot, after at least a mile.
15 mins, 50.9746, 0.8224 ▲※

18 THE PATCH, DUNGENESS
A churned-up patch of sea, known to anglers as 'the boil', is created by the nuclear power station's outflow pipes. Attracts seabirds from miles around. Beautiful at sunset.
→ Visible from the beach in front of the power station, from the Old Lighthouse (TN29 9NB). If you don't catch a fish, the Light Railway Café serves fish and chips by the lighthouse (01797 362353).
5 mins, 50.9106, 0.9677 🍴⛟

19 GUESTLING WOOD BLUEBELLS
Ancient woodland with fantastic display of bluebells and wood anemones in spring.
→ Coming along Pett Road from Pett, turn R up Watermill Road, soon after The Two Sawyers pub (TN35 4HB). Keep going for just over ½ mile, until you see the car park to your L, immediately after a wooden gate (L), where the road veers to the R. Find footpaths into the woods from here.
2 mins, 50.8997, 0.6482 🌳

20 FLATROPER'S WOOD WILD BOAR
Wild wood with a growing population of wild boar who originally escaped from a nearby farm in the storms of 1987.
→ From A268 between Four Oaks and Peasmarch, head S on Bixley Lane. After ½ mile, find entrance into woods on L.
2 mins, 50.9761, 0.6502 🌳❓

SLOW FOOD

21 DUNGENESS FISH, LYDD ON SEA
Family-owned fresh fish supplier on Dungeness Point, selling fish caught locally by Dungeness boats. Also keep an eye out for pop-up fish stalls around Dungeness, particularly towards the lighthouse.
→ Sealight, Battery Road, TN29 9NJ, 01797 333012.
50.9291, 0.9732 🍴

22 THE GALLIVANT, CAMBER
Cosy restaurant with rooms, minutes from the beach. 95 per cent of food is from within a 15-mile range.
→ New Lydd Road, TN31 7RB, 01797 225057.
50.9365, 0.7876 🛏🍴

23 THE RED LION, SNARGATE
In the same family for over 100 years. Traditional games, old piano, coal fire, outdoor loos, no food, local cider. St Dunstan Church opposite is famous for its 16th-century wall painting of a ship on the north aisle. Traditionally, such a painting would have let smugglers know that the church was a safe place to hide their goods.
→ TN29 9UQ, 01797 344648. Only open 12–3pm and 7–11pm, Tuesday–Sunday.
51.0218, 0.8365 🍺🍴🍺

24 THE WILD MUSHROOM, WESTFIELD
Elegant restaurant in a converted farm-house, serving fish and foraged local foods.
→ Woodgate House, Westfield Lane, TN35 4SB, 01424 751137.
50.9044, 0.5735 🛏🍴

25 THE WOOLPACK INN, BROOKLAND
600-year-old smuggler's pub in the wilds of rural Romney Marsh. Huge inglenook fireplace, hops hanging from the beams, and a quarry-tiled floor.
→ Romney Marsh, TN29 9TJ, 01797 344321.
50.9856, 0.8174 🍺

26 WEBBE'S ROCK-A-NORE, HASTINGS
Fantastic fish restaurant with fish sourced from the boats on the beach.
→ 1 Rock-A-Nore Road, TN34 3DW, 01424 721650.
50.8562, 0.5955 🍴

27 BADGER BUSHCRAFT
Day-long foraging and wild food course in ancient woodland. Covers practical aspects and theory, including foraging and the law, cooking foraged food, and how to avoid poisonous plants.
→ Tenterden area – exact location given on booking. 01233 756447.
51.0680, 0.6896 🍃

CAMP & STAY

28 CLIFF FARM B&B, RYE
Atmospheric 200-year-old farmhouse with resident sheep and fabulous views over Romney Marsh.

→ Military Road, Playden, TN31 7QD (turn L at the hanging milk churn), 01797 280331.
50.9804, 0.7489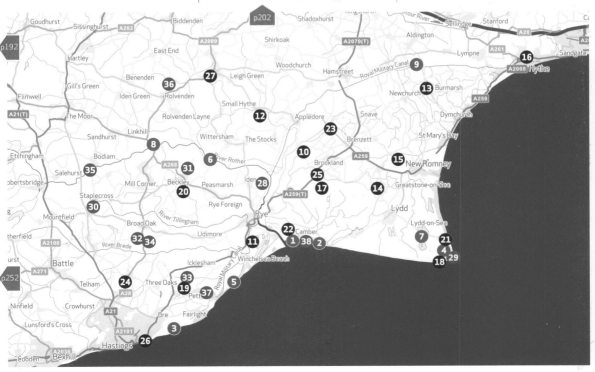

29 COASTGUARD LOOKOUT, DUNGENESS

Former Coastguard lookout tower a few steps from the sea, with the windswept and industrial landscape of Dungeness creating a dramatic and unique atmosphere.

→ Location given on booking. 01227 464958.
50.9119, 0.9722

30 WATTLE HILL OAST, STAPLECROSS

Glorious glamping in tranquil fields, with luxurious facilities. Intimate set-up is especially good for groups.

→ Beacon Lane, TN32 5QP, 01580 830261.
50.9666, 0.5376

31 THE MEADOW KEEPER'S COTTAGE

Hand-built 'gingerbread-style' cottage. Made from local timber and set by a pond with rowing boat and wildflower meadows. Off-grid with cosy log burner.

→ Canopyandstars.co.uk, 0117 204 7830 or Swallowtail Hill Farm, Hobbs Lane, Beckley, TN31 6TT, 01797 260890.
50.9947, 0.6569

32 DOGWOOD CAMPING, RYE

15-pitch secluded campsite set in meadows and woodland. Open all year.

→ The Dogwood Cottage, Cackle Street, Brede, TN31 6DY, 01424 883570.
50.9396, 0.5937

33 FRESH WINDS CAMPING, PETT

Quiet, remote campsite in a corner of a farm. The field and woodland glades are bordered by a stream, and the night sky is truly dark.

→ Pickham Farm, Watermill Lane, TN35 4HX, 07517 488576.
50.9013, 0.6504

34 HARE FARM HIDEAWAYS, BREDE

Luxurious, lantern-lit shepherd's hut in a grassy field, with stunning views across the Brede Valley.

→ Hare Farm, Stubb Lane, TN31 6BT, 07802 979348.
50.9365, 0.6052

35 HOP PICKERS' WOOD, BODIAM

Tiny, secret campsite surrounded by trees and wildlife, near an old castle. Showers and eco-loos in a shepherds hut, with communal fire for sociable evenings.

→ Quarry Farm, TN32 5RA (Exact location revealed upon booking), 01580 831845.
50.9962, 0.5354

36 LITTLE HALDEN FARM, ROLVENDEN

Seasonal camping in a large field surrounded by woodland, with lots of space for kids to run around. Glamping available year-round.

→ Little Halden Farm, TN17 4JL, 07854 523966.
51.0627, 0.6376,

37 LUNSFORD FARM, PETT

Comfortable safari-style tents next to wild woodland, and 10 minutes from the beach. Andrew runs tours of the family farm on Saturday mornings.

→ Pett Road, TN35 4HH, 01420 80804. Featherdown.co.uk
50.8932, 0.6741

38 SEASCAPE SELF-CATERING, CAMBER

Doze off by the wood burner in your large driftwood bed, the sound of the surf in your ears. Wake up in the morning to gaze out at miles of white sandy beach.

→ 19 The Suttons, TN31 7SA, 01797 224754
50.9320, 0.8027

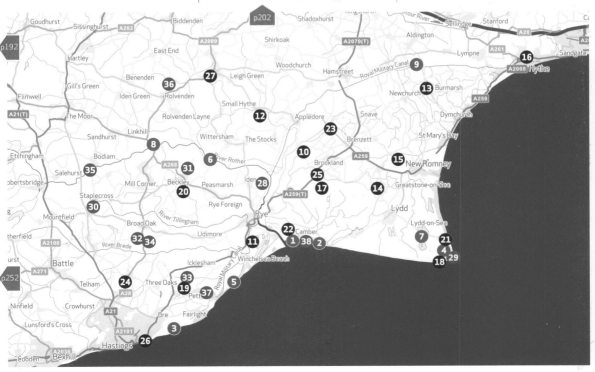

Ordnance Survey National Grid References

Fens & Nene Valley
1 TL 430 839
2 TL 600 975
3 TL 010 833
4 TL 105 974
5 TL 542 947
6 SK 936 080
7 TL 061 929
8 TL 149 878
9 SP 984 853
10 TF 112 054
11 TL 021 832
12 TL 062 985
13 TF 117 016
14 TL 161 819
15 TL 015 912
16 TL 052 989
17 TL 002 987
18 TL 470 859
19 TL 234 848
20 TL 202 892
21 TL 007 802
22 SP 882 836
23 TL 013 834
24 TF 118 029
25 TL 056 882
26 TL 010 833
27 TL 042 880
28 TL 607 918
29 TL 128 942
30 SP 943 831
31 TL 006 818
32 TL 086 941
33 TL 040 848
34 TL 394 971
35 TF 443 083
36 TL 413 933
37 TL 040 863
38 TL 053 817

North Norfolk
1 TF 717 451
2 TF 771 452
3 TF 847 458
4 TF 848 456
5 TF 883 457
6 TF 973 447
7 TF 987 454
8 TG 077 444
9 TF 705 273
10 TF 896 373
11 TG 121 381
12 TF 943 408
13 TF 782 463
14 TF 979 333
15 TF 692 401
16 TG 031 422
17 TF 663 336
18 TG 027 441
19 TF 890 447
20 TG 073 438
21 TF 047 383
22 TF 760 326
23 TF 852 414
24 TG 045 437
25 TF 679 424
26 TF 901 405
27 TG 077 387

Breckland & Mid Norfolk
1 TL 826 872
2 TL 831 950
3 TL 821 946
4 TG 020 185
5 TG 140 136
6 TF 677 194
7 TF 677 859
8 TF 813 148
9 TF 662 207
10 TL 778 891
11 TM 084 903
12 TL 840 876
13 TF 901 219
14 TF 743 057
15 TL 841 841
16 TL 896 884
17 TL 922 995
18 TG 049 229
19 TL 912 886
20 TF 697 228
21 TF 605 012
22 TF 885 036
23 TL 954 870
24 TL 981 876
25 TL 807 946
26 TF 900 117
27 TF 797 228
28 TF 792 042
29 TF 816 151
30 TF 744 014
31 TG 027 238
32 TG 081 143
33 TF 678 027
34 TF 843 171
35 TG 003 105
36 TG 026 165
37 TG 010 022
38 TF 944 066
39 TF 936 123
40 TF 818 090

Norfolk Broads
1 TG 466 242
2 TG 413 289
3 TG 442 264
4 TG 302 180
5 TG 347 248
6 TM 267 824
7 TM 286 847
8 TM 332 908
9 TM 339 899
10 TG 370 191
11 TG 163 304
12 TG 237 228
13 TG 261 201
14 TG 318 156
15 TG 335 049
16 TG 399 161
17 TG 261 204
18 TM 238 986
19 TG 307 067
20 TG 383 156
21 TG 475 045
22 TG 356 147
23 TG 311 306
24 TM 345 991
25 TG 352 058
26 TG 370 251
27 TG 147 305
28 TG 439 261
29 TG 156 410
30 TG 302 181
31 TM 389 909
32 TM 478 971
33 TG 327 150
34 TG 170 322
35 TG 244 341
36 TG 258 078
37 TG 246 410
38 TM 362 931
39 TG 181 243
40 TG 217 336
41 TG 197 420
42 TG 363 107
43 TG 399 072
44 TG 411 265
45 TG 059 310
46 TG 373 190

Bedford & Great Ouse
1 SP 887 640
2 SP 967 723
3 SP 787 396
4 SP 834 428
5 SP 892 508
6 SP 987 552
7 SP 992 581
8 TL 005 529
9 TL 214 669
10 TL 158 685
11 SP 983 398
12 SP 981 357
13 TL 091 388
14 TL 039 395
15 TL 150 454
16 TL 046 400
17 TL 184 697
18 TL 062 666
19 TL 041 352
20 TL 153 563
21 TL 049 574
22 TL 233 534
23 TL 235 510

Cambridge & around
1 TL 542 696
2 TL 220 699
3 TL 284 716
4 TL 367 722
5 TL 475 714
6 TL 535 756
7 TL 439 568
8 TL 461 515
9 TL 677 747
10 TL 335 520
11 TL 294 536
12 TL 224 526
13 TL 704 602
14 TL 546 543
15 TL 430 405
16 TL 366 761
17 TL 302 489
18 TL 339 631
19 TL 487 529
20 TL 409 551
21 TL 655 687
22 TL 571 412
23 TL 342 706
24 TL 465 633
25 TL 434 552
26 TL 542 585
27 TL 445 392
28 TL 400 692
29 TL 488 534
30 TL 679 679
31 TL 339 682
32 TL 325 564
33 TL 428 796
34 TL 329 446
35 TL 253 398
36 TL 451 703
37 TL 531 775
38 TL 627 717
39 TL 644 760
40 TL 516 730

Inland Suffolk
1 TL 856 450
2 TL 868 415
3 TL 958 332
4 TL 974 337
5 TM 067 335
6 TL 955 807
7 TL 823 403
8 TL 977 443
9 TM 248 351
10 TL 764 724
11 TL 976 428
12 TM 081 529
13 TL 918 548
14 TM 171 397
15 TL 930 352
16 TM 226 572
17 TM 188 606
18 TL 914 488
19 TL 844 514
20 TL 950 428
21 TL 833 523
22 TL 740 717
23 TL 963 716
24 TL 825 584
25 TL 940 738
26 TL 854 647
27 TL 821 801
28 TM 118 649
29 TL 982 457
30 TM 051 345
31 TL 813 375
32 TM 040 499
33 TL 974 340
34 TL 935 368
35 TL 782 567
36 TM 206 379
37 TL 992 383
38 TL 979 376
39 TL 972 559
40 TL 950 333
41 TL 834 358
42 TL 782 535
43 TM 177 396
44 TM 086 716
45 TL 986 686
46 TL 979 535
47 TM 205 380
48 TM 225 627
49 TL 970 752

Suffolk Coast
1 TM 478 675
2 TM 488 729
3 TM 467 575
4 TM 368 428
5 TM 283 464
6 TM 402 561
7 TM 392 481
8 TM 283 638
9 TM 357 400
10 TM 307 826
11 TM 522 818
12 TM 477 703
13 TM 307 421
14 TM 435 486
15 TM 479 707
16 TM 261 355
17 TM 360 505
18 TM 456 698
19 TM 331 378
20 TM 500 751
21 TM 275 487
22 TM 421 499
23 TM 260 774
24 TM 356 693
25 TM 478 705
26 TM 297 648
27 TM 296 724
28 TM 294 800
29 TM 497 746
30 TM 389 522
31 TM 344 642
32 TM 367 569
33 TM 338 500
34 TM 425 495
35 TM 357 701
36 TM 452 661
37 TM 299 548
38 TM 265 423
39 TM 402 809
40 TM 275 526
41 TM 456 803
42 TM 452 711
43 TM 355 814
44 TM 428 527
45 TM 321 567
46 TM 306 558
47 TM 344 642
48 TM 395 828
49 TM 394 828
50 TM 249 647
51 TM 247 518
52 TM 462 548

Oxford & Cotswolds
1 SP 188 158
2 SP 264 114
3 SP 291 115
4 SP 325 112
5 SP 393 164
6 SU 205 989
7 SU 224 983
8 SU 230 980
9 SU 256 986
10 SU 353 996
11 SP 442 086
12 SP 492 081
13 SU 531 938
14 SU 547 954
15 SP 521 071
16 SP 505 147
17 SP 668 065
18 SP 484 090
19 SP 273 120
20 SP 295 308
21 SP 378 235
22 SP 486 165
23 SP 255 208
24 SP 631 163
25 SP 609 108
26 SP 335 179
27 SP 466 115
28 SP 313 315
29 SP 204 131
30 SP 586 156
31 SP 334 003
32 SP 226 203
33 SP 282 118
34 SP 501 073
35 SP 687 101
36 SP 228 118
37 SU 577 943
38 SP 259 238
39 SP 320 028
40 SP 532 447
41 SP 440 016
42 SP 352 208
43 SP 270 224
44 SP 647 043
45 SP 334 004
46 SP 440 071
47 SP 487 347

North Chilterns
1 SP 971 002
2 SP 682 251
3 SP 902 133
4 SP 942 141
5 SU 835 943
6 SU 864 952
7 SP 962 071
8 SP 765 115
9 SP 930 072
10 SP 914 091
11 SP 978 220
12 SU 996 948
13 SU 829 947
14 SP 773 007
15 SP 821 040
16 SP 848 067
17 SP 960 168
18 SP 834 062
19 SP 997 186
20 SU 707 935
21 SP 904 088
22 SP 997 101
23 SU 840 970
24 SU 920 963
25 SP 949 131
26 SP 887 108
27 SP 933 138
28 SU 880 994
29 SU 782 972
30 SP 939 168
31 TL 016 098
32 SP 959 014
33 SP 932 136
34 SP 938 036
35 SP 842 084
36 TL 017 099
37 SP 696 089
38 TQ 030 972
39 SP 978 125
40 SU 736 995
41 SP 871 073
42 SU 783 967
43 SP 965 242
44 SU 895 989
45 SP 950 164
46 SP 911 040
47 SP 898 089

Essex Coast
1 TM 176 323
2 TM 189 240
3 TM 221 233
4 TM 264 235
5 TL 967 105
6 TL 905 079
7 TL 930 058
8 TM 051 362
9 TM 074 155
10 TM 247 255
11 TM 085 161
12 TM 009 151
13 TL 801 087
14 TM 081 194
15 TM 065 206
16 TM 030 081
17 TL 876 281
18 TL 815 003
19 TM 119 311
20 TM 190 314
21 TL 775 064
22 TL 880 061
23 TM 047 192
24 TQ 834 991
25 TM 028 203
26 TM 990 323
27 TL 698 173
28 TL 711 042
29 TL 905 317

Herts & Lea Valley
1 TL 315 145
2 TL 332 136
3 TL 394 086
4 TL 387 066
5 SV 000 000
6 TL 278 134
7 SV 000 000
8 TL 368 173
9 TL 111 078
10 TL 538 029
11 TL 222 282
12 TL 347 087
13 TQ 417 975
14 TL 132 300
15 TL 065 295
16 TL 546 201
17 TL 046 312
18 TL 131 006
19 TL 416 106
20 TL 147 317
21 TL 267 155
22 TL 684 328
23 TL 278 023
24 TL 184 212
25 TL 118 107
26 TL 309 271
27 TL 195 168
28 TL 345 122
29 TL 116 052
30 TL 296 069
31 TL 640 018
32 TQ 480 946
33 TL 564 152
34 TL 774 218
35 TL 163 024
36 TL 413 330
37 TL 309 285
38 TL 356 217
39 TL 309 271
40 TL 229 357
41 TQ 439 983

Wild Guide
Southern and
Eastern England
Hidden Places,
Great Adventures and
the Good Life

Words:
Daniel Start
Elsa Hammond
Lucy Grewcock

Photos:
Daniel Start
and those credited

Editing:
Candida Frith-Macdonald
Tania Pascoe

Design and layout:
Oliver Mann
Marcus Freeman
Pavel Jaloševský

Proofreading:
Georgia Laval
Hannah Hargrave

Distribution:
Central Books Ltd
99 Wallis Road
London, E9 5LN
Tel +44 (0)845 458 9911
orders@centralbooks.com

Published by:
Wild Things Publishing Ltd.
Freshford, Bath,
BA2 7WG, United Kingdom

hello@wildthingspublishing.com

Photo credits / copyright: Maps contain data © Crown copyright and database right 2011. All photos © Daniel Start except: pp14-15 Derek Finch, p24-25 ableimages / Alamy, p26-27 Grant Bush, P32-33 Sam Moore /Sussex Scenes, p34-35 Tim Matthews, p40 Alamy/NTPL, p42 (bottom) Adrian S Pye, p44 (top) Andy B Fotherinhay, p44 (top) Kim Fyson, p44 (bottom) John Pilkington, 45 (top) Canopy & Stars, p46 (top) Ferran Pestana, p46 (2nd) Richard Humphrey, p46 (middle bottom) Lucy Grewcock, p46 (bottom) Grant Bush, p50 (middle) Martin Godfrey, p52 (middle) Richard Humphrey, p53 (top) Kim Fyson, p53 (middle) Evelyn Simak, p54 (top) Tim Matthews, p54 (middle) Ian Capper, (bottom) Ian Steel; p55 (middle) Brickyard Camping, (bottom) Canopy & Stars; p56 (3rd) The Real Ale Shop, (bottom right) Cley Windmill; p60 (middle) Steve and Nicky, (bottom) Hugh Venebles; p62 (middle) Adrian S Pye, (bottom) Evelyn Simak; p63 Kim Fyson; p64 (top) The Dabbling Duck, (3rd) English Whisky, (bottom left) Liz West, (bottom right) Canopy & Stars; p65 West Lexham Treehouse; p68 (middle) Graham Horn; p70 (bottom) Fry/ Song of the Paddle; p72 (top) Mira66, (middle) John Salmon; p74 (bottom) Jeffowne, (top) Walpole Arms, (2nd) Barn Café Waxham, (3rd) Deer's Glade; (4th) Burlingham Yurt, (bottom) Gunton Arms; p75 (middle) Lucy Grewcock; p78 (top) Mick Lobb, (bottom) Paul Mills; p80 (top) Grant Bush, (middle) Bjorn Schulz, (bottom) Gothic Bohemia Stock; p82 (1st, 2nd, 5th) Feather Down Farm, (3rd) Ashley Dace, (4th) Christopher Hilton; p86 (top) Hugh Venables; p88 (top) Tim Regan, (middle) Glyn Baker; p89 (bottom left) Adrian S Pye, (bottom right) Philip Halling; p90 (2nd) Canopy & Stars, (3rd) Julian Osley, (4th) Fen End Farm; p94 (bottom) Simon Huguet; p96 (top) David Parker, (middle) Keith Evans, (bottom) Bob Jones, (middle) Adstar, (bottom) Free Photos; p98 Graham Martin; p100 (top) Mike Pendrich, (2nd) Charles Rawding, (3rd) Anchor Inn, (4th) Rushbanks Farm, (bottom) Cobbs Cottage; p101 Twee Gebroeders; p106 (bottom) Evelyn Simak; p107 (top) Mike Baker, (bottom) Evelyn Simak; p108 (middle/bottom) Emmett's of Peasenhall p110 (1st, 2nd) The King's Head, (3rd) Keith Evans, (4th) Gypsy Hollow, (bottom left) Landmark Trust, (bottom right) Bob Jones; p116 (bottom) Brian Robert Marshall; p117 (top) Lydia, (bottom) Chris Gunn; p118 (middle) David Hawgood; p119 Steve Daniels; p120 (top) The Mole & Chicken, (3rd) Glamping Thorpe, (4th) Sandy Lane Farm, (bottom) Helena, p124 (top) Chris Reynolds, p124 (middle) Chris Burke; p126 (middle) Rob Farrow, (bottom) Keith Chapman; p127 (top) Des Blenkinsopp, p127 (bottom) Stuart Logan; p130 (top) Chiltern Ridge Farm, (2nd) Alford Arms, (3rd) Frithsden Vineyard, (4th) Peterley Farm, (bottom) Canopy & Stars; p131 Home Farm Radnage; p136 (all) Lucy Grewcock; p137 (top/bottom) Chris Hamer/Frames of Reference/Rowley Gallery, (middle) Grant Bush; p138 (top) Peter aka anemone project, (2nd) Redbournbury Mill, (3rd) James Lee, (bottom) Springfield Park; p143 Barbara Robinson; p144 (bottom) Roger Haworth; p145 (top) Canopy & Stars, (bottom) Martin Stone; p146 (top) Monika, (3rd) Canopy & Stars, (4th) Layer Marney Tower, (bottom) Alison Rawson; p148 James Petts; p150 (middle) Alan Hunt; p153 (top) Barry Skeates, (middle) Dave S, (bottom) Andrew Smith; p154 (top) Marathon, (middle) Ruth Sharville, (bottom) Fly; p155 (top) Chris Hamer/Frames of Reference/Rowley Gallery, (middle) Mick Lobb, (bottom) Chris Guise; p156 (1st) Royal Standard, (2nd) Paul Matthew, (3rd) Jack Thurston, (4th, 5th) The Crooked Billet; p158 Peter Trimming; p160 (top) Alan Hunt, (bottom) Chris Playll; p163 (top) Peter Trimming, (bottom) Marathon; p164 (top) Malcolm Murdoch, (2nd) Marathon, (3rd) Andy Dolman, (bottom) skiffhire.co; p166 Russ Garrett; p168 (middle) Marathon, (bottom) Simon; p170 (middle) Rob Zweers, (bottom) Liz Henry; p187 Canopy & Stars; p172 (top) Jon Stow, (2nd) The Sportsman, (3rd) Stephen Nunney, (4th) Canopy & Stars; p178 (middle) Andrew Smith, (bottom) Mike Fahert; (middle) Tim Champion, (bottom) Miss Steel, p180 (top) Wellington Arms, (3rd) Adhurst Yurts, (bottom) The Harrow Inn; p182 Helen Dixon/Alamy; p186 (bottom) Len Williams; p187 (middle) Dominic Alves, (bottom) Colin Smith, p188 (middle) Justin Pickard; p189 (top) GES, (bottom) Stefan Czapski, p190 (top) Duke of Cumberland, (2nd) The Green Escape, (3rd) Lockhurst Hatch Farm, (bottom) Long Copse B&B; p192 Peter Trimming, p194 (top) Oast House Archive, p196 (bottom) Marathon, p197 (top) Hugh, p197 (middle David Anstiss, p197 (bottom) Sally, p198 (top) Marathon, p199 Wild Board Wood, p200 (2nd) N Chadwick, (4th and 5th) Hole Cottage, p201 & p199 (bottom) Canopy & Stars, p204 (top) N Chadwick (middle) Paul Plumb (bottom) Brian Fuller, p206 (middle Marathon (bottom) Pam Fray, p207 (middle) Klaus Harenberg, (bottom) Three Chimneys, p208 (top) Happy Fields (middle) Thorpe Farm (bottom) Landmark Trust, p214 (middle) Kent Attraction, (bottom) Oast House Archive; p215 (top) Nick Smith, (bottom) Klaus Harenberg; p216 (top) Amelia Wells, (2nd) Great Broxhall Farm B&B, (3rd) The Goods Shed, (bottom) The Warren (top right) Ye Olde Yew Tree, (bottom right) Fergus the Forager; p217 Paramour Grange; p220 (middle) Chris Gunns; p222 (middle) David Mainwood, (bottom) Jim Champion; p223 Elsa Hammond; p224 (top) New Forest Cider, (2nd) Aldridge Hill, (3rd) Luttrell's Tower; p225 Nina Hale, p228 (bottom) Chris Downer; p230 (top) Stefan Schaitz, (bottom) Peter Boggett; p231 (top) antti nissinen, (middle) Chris Downer, (bottom) Derek Harper; p232 (2nd) Grange Farm, (3rd) Goodleaf, (4th) Compton Farm, (bottom) White Bells; p236 (bottom) ezneily, p238 (top) Richard Paterson, (middle) Pam Fray, (bottom) Peter Scrimshaw; p240 (top) Derek Finch, (2nd) The Horseguards Inn, (3rd) Anthony Brunning, (bottom) Cedar Valley; p242 Pop Up Campsites; p244 (middle) The Anchor Inn, p247 (top) Les Chatfield, (bottom) Leimenide; p248 Vicky WJ; p249 (top) Peter Castelton, (bottom left) Canopy & Stars, (bottom middle) Martin Addison, (bottom right) Billycan Camping; p250 (top) Blackberry Wood, (2nd) The Half Moon, (3rd) Blacklands Farm, (bottom) Pop Up Campsites; p251 Hunter Gatherer Cook; p256 (middle) Marathon, (bottom) Janine Forbes; p257 (top) Safari Britain/Mount Harry; p258 (top) Paul Gillet, (2nd) Hawthbush Farm, (3rd) Whimbles Farm, (4th) Laughton Place, (bottom) Thimbles B&B; p259 Canopy & Stars; p260 Tim Heaton, p262 (middle) Su May, (bottom) Peter; p263 Toby Charlton-Taylor; p264 (bottom) Mark Chambers; p265 (top) Simon Syon, (bottom) Andrew Sales, p266 (top) Wattle Hill Oast, (2nd) Canopy & Stars, (3rd) Cliff Farm, (4th) Seascape, (bottom) Coastguard Lookout.

Author acknowledgements: We would like to thanks all those generously shared their photos with us, and Canopy and Stars, the National Trust, the Wildlife Trusts and Visit Essex for inspiration and information. Dan would like to thank Michael Lee, Ciaran Mundy, Jules Peck, Paul Jess and Myla Rothwell, Yvette Alt-Reus, Jack Thurston, Jonathan Ekstrom, Tom and Tor Currie and especially Tania and Rose. Lucy would like to thank Ella Mynot, Denise Grewcock, Felix Clay, Tom Cox. Elsa would like to thank Steve Bullock, Joanna Hammond, Mark Hammond and Martin Wilson.